THE BATSFORD BOOK OF SEWING

THE BATSFORD BOOK
OF SEWING

Edited by
ANN LADBURY

B. T. BATSFORD LIMITED LONDON

© Coats and Clark Inc, 1967
Revised edition © J. & P. Coats Limited, 1970
Third Impression 1977
First paperback edition

ISBN 0 7134 0199 0

Printed in Great Britain at The Pitman Press, Bath
for the publishers
B. T. Batsford Limited, 4 Fitzhardinge Street, London W1H 0AH

CONTENTS

THE METRIC SYSTEM

1 metre is divided into 100 centimetres (100 cm)
1 centimetre is divided into 10 millimetres (10 mm)
Centimetres and millimetres are used with a decimal point,
eg ten and a half centimetres is written 10·5 cm.

1 metre represents approximately 39 in.

Fabric is sold by the metre instead of by the yard. Therefore
the term meterage is used instead of yardage. In order to
exercise economy in meterage, it should be possible to buy
portions of a metre in multiples of 10 cm, eg 20 cm (0·20 m):
30 cm (0·30 m), etc.

To convert yards to metres, multiply by 0·914. If the answer
does not give a buyable meterage, buy the nearest suitable
quantity above the answer.

Examples
Instead of $2\frac{1}{2}$ yards buy 2·30 metres ($2\frac{1}{2} \times 0·914 = 2·285$ m)

3	2·75	$(3 \times 0·914 = 2·742$ m)
$3\frac{1}{4}$	3·00	$(3\frac{1}{4} \times 0·914 = 2·969$ m)

When dealing with small imperial measurements such as the
width of turnings, etc, it is not always possible to find an
equivalent in metric measure which is both practical and con-
venient in use. In this case it is best to study a reliable
conversion ruler and use the most easily read metric measurement nearest to the original imperial measurement.

Examples

In place of $\frac{1}{8}$ in.	use 3 mm
$\frac{1}{4}$ in.	6 mm
$\frac{3}{8}$ in.	10 mm (1 cm)
$\frac{1}{2}$ in.	13 mm
$\frac{5}{8}$ in.	15 mm
$\frac{3}{4}$ in.	19 mm
1 in.	25 mm

INTRODUCTION

For all who wish to sew, this book has been written in easy-to-follow, simple terms and is illustrated clearly and attractively. It is an addition to a pattern primer, giving the most up-to-date sewing methods which produce the best results. The inexperienced, as well as the experienced, dressmaker will find much information to solve most sewing problems, and which will assist in achieving a professional finish.

The book is arranged according to subject, in alphabetical order. There are references throughout to subjects which are explained in detail under their appropriate headings, and since every subject contains dozens of references to details that do not have headings of their own, there is an exhaustive index. Also, wherever possible, the reason for every operation is given in order that the principle involved may be understood.

All the measurements in this book give metric conversions from imperial units to the nearest millimetre or centimetre, as the case may be. At the time of going to press not all the metric equipment is readily available and it is advisable to make enquiries at your local stockist.

Alterations on Finished Garments

An alteration, not to be confused with a make-over, is an adjustment made in one detail of a garment that is otherwise satisfactory (though more than one alteration may, of course, be needed).

Except in the matter of hemlines, which are dictated by style, alterations are made for fit. They are often necessary in ready-to-wear (which does *not* mean that, if a model you like is not available in your size, you can alter an entirely wrong size to fit!). Alterations may also become necessary in your existing wardrobe, either because you have gained or lost weight, or because of a change in style—meaning usually hemlines.

WHAT CAN AND WHAT CANNOT BE ALTERED

The general principle here is that you can almost always *take in*, i.e., make smaller; *letting out* a garment in order to make it wider or longer may present serious problems.

For instance, you can always
. . . raise a hemline,
. . . raise a waistline,
. . . take in waist and hips,
. . . shorten sleeves,
. . . take in a plain faced neck,
. . . let out seams or hems *if* there is enough fabric *and* it is not marked, clipped or faded.

But you cannot
. . . lower a waistline (there isn't enough seam allowance),
. . . add width to shoulders or sleeve-caps, or to a back in one piece,
. . . let out seams or darts in fabrics that *mark*, because original seamlines will always show (wash-and wear, tricot, taffeta, pile fabrics, etc.),
. . . let out seams where allowance is not wide enough or has been clipped through; or darts that are slashed, or punctured at the point,
. . . let down a hem when outside fabric has faded or hemline fold has left a permanent mark.

Certain alterations, while possible, are inadvisable. You would find it extremely involved to
. . . change an armhole with a sleeve,
. . . change shoulders and neck where there is a collar.

WHEN YOU ARE READY TO ALTER

If you have no one to help you with pinning and marking, you *can* do the job alone by pinning as seems necessary and trying on repeatedly. But it is both easier and safer with a bit of help.

If the zip-fastener is not in a seam you are altering, so much the better. The presence of a zip-fastener, however, should not discourage you. It is easy to take out (see **Ripping Out** at end of chapter on MACHINE-STITCHING); after this, you press the opening allowances smooth. When your new seamline is established, machine-baste opening together and proceed as directed in ZIP-FASTENERS. After a let-out, widen seam allowance with seam binding (p. 171).

The alterations that follow are the ones most often needed. When more than one is necessary (for instance, changing both hemline and side seams), study the steps in the instructions and combine them.

GENERAL ALTERATION IN WIDTH

An armhole-through-hips alteration in the width of a dress is simple, especially if the dress is one-piece, with zip-fastener at centre back (if there is a waistline seam, you remove waistline stay and open waist seam at points of alteration). If you take in or let out a fraction of a centimetre at each side seam and each dart or in-between seam (ignoring centre front and back), it will add up to a sizeable change. For carrying through, see this alteration on a skirt on pp. 11 and 12.

CHANGING A HEMLINE

This is the simplest and most common alteration. It can be made to **straighten**, to **raise**, or to **lower** the hemline. When you buy a garment, an alteration in the hem will often be marked for you at the store. For any change in the hemline:

Take out old hem. In a manufactured garment, this may be chainstitched: Cut through stitching (1), free one loop and pull—in the right direction! Removing seam binding may or may not be necessary. Press hem open. Follow directions in HEMS. When lowering a hemline, it is sometimes necessary to make a **Faced Hem** (p. 97).

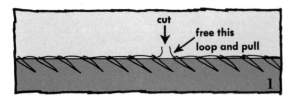

RAISING A WAISTLINE
(all around or in part)

Put on dress. Tie a string around waist. Have someone mark correct waistline with pins along string.

Take off dress. Even out pinned line; replace it with a line of baste-marking. If any points on skirt (centre front and back, side seams, darts, etc.) do not automatically match corresponding points on bodice, be sure to thread-mark position of such points.

Remove zip-fastener, if any, or just bottom half, to clear waistline. Rip out waistline seam or that part of it to be altered. Press open.

With skirt and bodice right sides together, match old waistline on skirt to new waistline on bodice and pin together (2), first at centre front and centre back; then work toward side seams, matching marked points between. Because of the tapering of seams and darts, bodice may now be wider than skirt. Depending on fabric and design, you may be able to ease or gather bodice to skirt, or you may have to take in darts and side seams.

After adjusting bodice to fit, pin again as described, baste and try on. Then stitch new waistline seam and trim away excess bodice fabric even with skirt seam allowance. Replace waistline stay; press. Re-

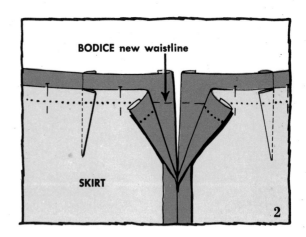

place all construction details (zip-fastener, facing, hooks and eyes, buttons, etc.) as they were before.

DEEPENING BUST DARTS
(to correct underarm bagginess)

This alteration shortens side seams and gives greater fullness in bust.

Try on garment. Tie a string around waist. Have someone check if back needs shortening; if so, mark correct waistline with pins. Pin bust darts deeper to take in excess fullness, tapering to nothing at point (don't worry about open tuck at wide end of darts—this will disappear later). Take off garment.

Open waistline seam across back to about 50 mm. beyond side seams. Open side seams of bodice to within 25 mm. of armhole seam. Take out zip-fastener, if any. Press opened seams.

Transfer pin-markings on darts to wrong side. Mark new stitching line with ruler and chalk. Remove pins.

Re-stitch darts and press. Re-stitch side seams, except any zip-fastener opening (front will now be shorter than back), and press open.

Still wrong side out, fold bodice in half along centre back line and pin side seams and bottom edge together, as shown. Cutting through both thicknesses, trim off excess fabric in back, either tapering as shown, or across back if back needs shortening (3).

Pin and re-stitch waistline seam. Replace waistline stay, zip-fastener, etc. Press.

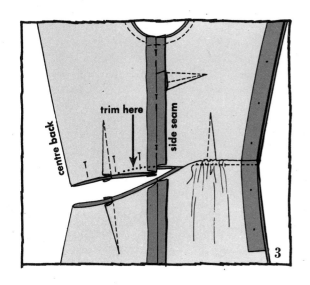

TAKING IN NECKLINE

Unless you are an expert, and know how to re-cut a collar to fit, we do not advise this alteration except for a plain, faced neck. In this case, remove facing and turn to **The Gaping Neckline**, p. 83 in the chapter FITTING A GARMENT.

TAKING IN A SKIRT

This is normally done at side seams alone.

Put on skirt. Have someone pin side seams deeper (taking in zip-fastener, if any) from waist down, so that skirt fits comfortably and smoothly and hangs straight. Then sit down to make sure there is enough ease. Check on fit of waistband.

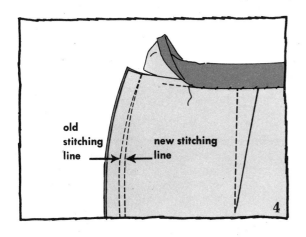

Take off skirt. Transfer pin-markings to one thickness of fabric on wrong side. Remove stitching in hem for a few centimetres at each side seam. Remove zip-fastener if it is in side seam. Waistband does not always need to be removed in its entirety; if it fits, remove stitching as needed to free side seams so that altered seamlines can taper to it. Press seam allowances together. Using chalk and yardstick, mark new seamlines parallel to old ones from hip down through hem.

Stitch new seams (4). Take out old stitching. Trim seams, finish as needed, and press open.

Replace zip-fastener and refinish hem. When replacing waistband, change position of closing as necessary.

WIDENING A SKIRT BY LETTING OUT

If fabric and seam allowances permit (see p. 9), this method is suitable for any skirt, and it is the only possible one for a straight skirt. It is usually done at side seams alone, but if there are more seams, it may be advisable to distribute the amount to be let out equally among them.

Measure your hips (178 mm. below waist); add 50 mm. for ease. Measure your waist, adding nothing.

To measure skirt, fold it lengthwise with side seams together, as shown. Measure from centre front to back at waist and hips (5); double these amounts. The difference between skirt measurements and your own will be total amount of alteration.

If alteration extends to waist, remove waistband. Remove zip-fastener if it is in a seam to be altered. Remove stitching in hem for a few centimetres at seams to be let out.

Do not take out seams. Press seam allowances together (as stitched).

Using chalk and yardstick, mark new seamlines, from hem and either tapering to waistline if waistline is not altered, or carrying the alteration through as necessary. Amount to add at each seam will be: ·
. . . One quarter of total alteration if only side seams are involved.
. . . Otherwise, one half of total alteration divided by number of seams.

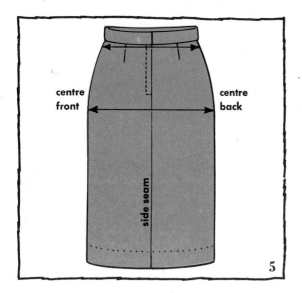

Stitch new seamlines. Remove old stitching. Press seams open.

Replace zip-fastener, adding seam binding to widen seam allowance (see ZIP-FASTENERS, p. 171). Refinish hem. If waistband is included in alteration, lengthen it by adding a piece of fabric at end that will lap under. Replace and press.

WIDENING A SKIRT BY RAISING AT WAIST

A gored, flared, or A-line skirt that is long enough can be widened at waist and hips by raising it at the waistline (6).

Put on skirt. Raise around waistline (opening zip-fastener as necessary) until hips are fitted comfortably. Tie string snugly around waist and adjust skirt evenly. Have someone mark new waistline with pins along string.

Take off skirt. Even out pin-marked line; replace it with line of baste-marking.

Remove waistband and zip-fastener. Press.

Trim away top of skirt 16 mm. above new waistline marking.

Replace zip-fastener, opening seam at bottom to fit. If waistband fits 'as is', it will be necessary either to ease new waistline to it, or to deepen seams and re-fit darts at top to fit. If waistband is too snug, lengthen it with a piece of fabric at end that will lap under. Replace and press.

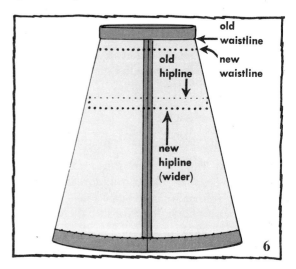

Assembling a Garment

Assembling a garment should be a simple, efficient procedure based on intelligent organization of work. All instruction sheets accompanying patterns follow to some degree a system called *unit construction*, the purpose of which is to eliminate waste motion and unnecessary handling.

You will find that in the two illustrated systems of unit construction that follow, the sequence is slightly different from that given in most pattern instruction sheets. This is, however, the simplest and most streamlined way of assembling a garment, **Unit Construction I** being used on most garments, **Unit Construction II**

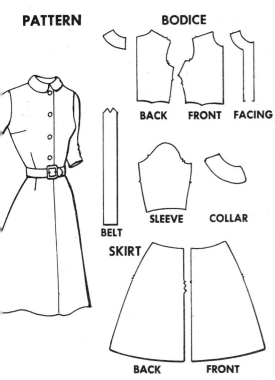

PATTERN

BODICE

BACK   FRONT   FACING

BELT   SLEEVE   COLLAR

SKIRT

BACK   FRONT

UNIT CONSTRUCTION I

1 Complete the skirt front.
2 Complete the skirt back.
3 Join skirt front and back, leaving zip-fastener opening open.
4 Finish belt.
5 Finish sleeves, including hem or cuff.
6 Prepare facing.
7 Finish collar.
8 Complete bodice front. Make button-holes if bound.
9 Complete bodice back.
10 Stitch shoulder seams.
11 Attach collar and facing. Tack facing to shoulder seams.
12 Stitch side seams, leaving zip-fastener opening open.
13 Set in sleeves.
14 Stitch bodice to skirt. Apply zip-fastener. Finish bound buttonholes or make worked buttonholes. Make hem. Make belt carriers (if any). Sew on buttons.

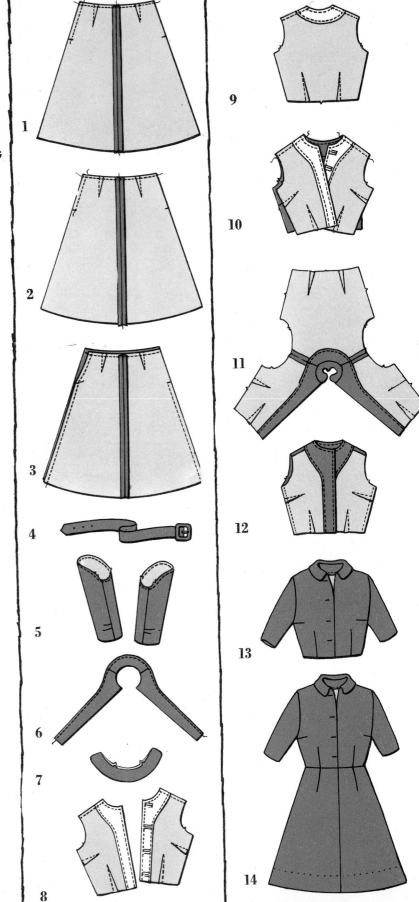

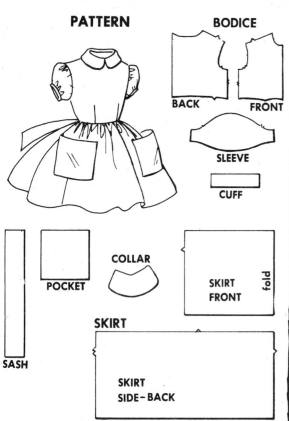

PATTERN

BODICE

BACK   FRONT

SLEEVE

CUFF

SASH

POCKET

COLLAR

SKIRT FRONT

fold

SKIRT

SKIRT SIDE-BACK

UNIT CONSTRUCTION II

1   Finish sash.
2   Make sleeves, leaving cuffs (hems) and underarm seams open.
3   Finish collar.
4   Finish pockets.
5   Complete bodice front.
6   Complete bodice back.
7   Stitch shoulder seams.
8   Attach collar.
9   Sew in sleeves. Attach sash-ends.
10   Stitch underarm seams. Turn up and finish cuffs (or sleeve hems).
11   Complete skirt.
12   Stitch bodice to skirt. Make machine buttonholes, and sew on buttons. Then make hem.

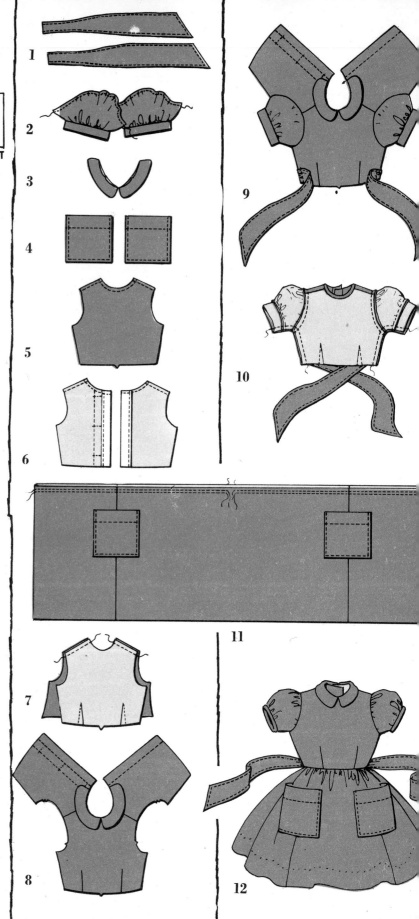

(sleeves sewn in before side seams are stitched) on children's and sports clothes. In both cases, we have applied the principle to a basic dress with bodice, collar, and set-in sleeves. Adapt the idea to your needs, which may be simpler—a one-piece dress, with kimono sleeves or none, will be but a single unit!

And remember that these picture stories just give you the sequence, the 'When to'. For the 'How to' of sewing your garment, continue to consult your pattern instruction sheet, and this book.

UNIT CONSTRUCTION

The principle of unit construction is to do as much work as possible on one garment unit (garment part) before attaching it to another unit—in fact, to complete it when possible; and to complete all the small units (sleeves, collar, belt, patch pockets) first, so that work on the large ones (bodice, jacket, or other) can proceed without interruption.

Before cutting, you have, of course, made any basic alterations necessary, on the pattern. Small alterations after that can be made before attaching the small units to the large ones (see FITTING A GARMENT, p. 82). A skirt and bodice can be pin- or thread-basted together to be tried on, then separated before you proceed.

Practical Procedure

After cutting and marking, sort the cut pieces into a pile, with the pieces to be used first on top (see picture sequence). Put all the small units together. The skirt is usually prepared first, to have it out of the way (when the skirt is separate, it can be finished completely). If, however, small units (such as patch pockets) are to be attached to it, these are completed first, and then are applied to the skirt before it is put together.

Do all you can to one garment part (unit) before attaching it to another. See the picture sequences—in a bodice you not only put in the darts before stitching shoulder seams, but attach interfacing, make bound buttonholes, etc.

Keep garment fresh and unwrinkled by hanging up each unit as it is completed: pin skirt to hanger, hang up top when shoulder seams are stitched. A coat box is handy to store pieces, finished and unfinished, that cannot be hung.

The final steps (zip-fastener insertion, hem, etc.) are done after garment is assembled, as indicated in the picture sequences on pp. 13–14.

Backing or Underlining

Backing, or underlining, which is stitched to the wrong side of an outer section before any seams are joined (the two layers then being handled as one), must not be confused with lining. Lining sections are seamed together separately, then sewed into an otherwise completed garment as an inside finish covering the seams. Backing serves a number of purposes, but is never a finish.

Pattern directions generally do not specify or mention backing. The decision to use it rests more or less with you, and whether the garment fabric you have bought requires it. A garment may be backed in its entirety or in part, the backing serving to reinforce, lend body and/or opacity, and preserve shape.

. . . In certain designs, such as A-line or bell-shaped, or in a bodice shell, backing preserves the silhouette when outside fabric does not have enough body.

. . . With some silks and soft wools, backing will prevent pulling out at the seams.

. . . Lace and sheer fabrics can be made opaque with a backing.

. . . In general, backing gives body where it may be missing. It does not give stiffness or crispness, as interfacing does; and it does not cover raw seams on the inside.

A garment may be both backed and lined, especially if, like a coat or jacket, it must be finished inside.

A WORD OF CAUTION

The whole performance of a backed garment rests on the fact that the two fabrics must react as one. The backing must enhance, not interfere with, the outer fabric. Make sure, therefore, that:

... where the pattern calls for gathers or draping, the backing is soft;

... if the outer fabric is either (a) dry-cleanable, (b) washable, (c) wash-and-wear, the backing has the same properties and calls for the same handling;

... the backing is preshrunk, even if you have to do the shrinking yourself.

If, even after these precautions, a slight discrepancy develops after use, it can be taken care of by a judicious use of the iron.

BACKING FABRICS

There are a number of fabrics, both woven and non-woven, in a variety of weights, that are specially made for backing. You can also use many of the regular fabrics, such as organdie, batiste, lawn, China silk, or taffeta. The important thing is to be sure that the backing is of the right weight—generally lighter than the outer fabric—and that it requires the same handling. A washable backing not guaranteed to be preshrunk must *always* be shrunk before using.

BACKING A GARMENT

After cutting out a garment, remove pattern pieces from sections to be backed *before* transferring any marks. Cut backing from the same pattern pieces, then transfer marks to backing.

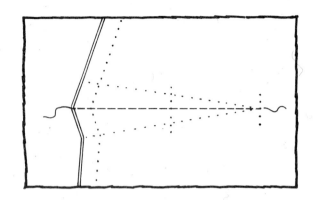

Place unmarked side of backing to wrong side of corresponding outer section; smooth out. Match edges carefully and pin together, leaving seam allowances clear. Place on machine with backing side up. Stitch together on all edges, 13 mm. from edge, but *with the grain* (see **Directional Stitching**, p. 110), which means that you will have to start from the same edge to stitch along two opposite sides, even if on the second trip the bulk of work will have to go to the right.

If there are darts, baste the two layers together along centre of dart before stitching, as shown here.

Construct garment as usual, handling backing and outer fabric as one.

After marking a hemline, hand-baste the two layers together all around, 6 mm. above hemline. Leave this basting in until hem is finished. If backing is of heavy or stiff fabric, cut it off at hemline to reduce bulk. While sewing down hem, catch hem to backing only, but every few centimetres catch outer fabric with a stitch invisible on outside.

Basting (Tacking)

Essentially, basting means temporary sewing, removed after a job is completed. Nowadays it is often done by machine. (It is sometimes used for MARKING —see that chapter). Its usual purpose is to hold two or more layers of fabric together preparatory to stitching. In modern sewing this can sometimes be done with pins only (pin-basting).

When basting is part of the construction process, it is indicated in the directions. Otherwise, depending on the degree of your expertise, you will want to either pin- or thread-baste (to be safe, first pin-, then thread-baste) in the following instances:

... where there are more than two layers of fabric, as in applying collars and cuffs,

... in seams containing fullness, such as ease, gathers, or pleats,

... when setting in sleeves,

... when matching checks and stripes,

... with slippery fabrics, such as satin, velvet, etc.,

... when a garment is to be tried on.

PIN-BASTING

Pin-basting may serve by itself or it may be a preliminary to thread-basting. The position of the pins depends on whether your basting is a preparation for sewing or for fitting.

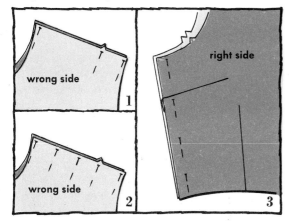

Pinning for thread-basting or for stitching—Place pins at *right angles* to fabric edge (in fabrics that mark, within seam allowance), so they are on top for stitching. Match and pin notches and seam-ends (1), then place pins between, as close as necessary to hold seam securely (2). Remove pins as you stitch. Even a hinged foot will not prevent the needle from striking a pin.

Pinning for fitting—On right side of garment (to allow pins to be moved while trying on), place pins *parallel* to fabric edges (3), on seamline. After fitting, if seamline has been altered, mark new seamline on wrong side; remove pins and baste on wrong side.

THREAD-BASTING BY HAND OR MACHINE

Machine-basting is quicker than hand-basting, of course, but it requires greater expertise. Choose whichever method you prefer; instructions for both follow.

Thread-basting for fitting is done on wrong side. Clip threads as necessary for changes.

Basting of seams is done just outside seamline, to keep clear of final stitching.

To remove basting, clip thread every few stitches before drawing out. This will avoid pulling fabric out of shape.

Hand-basting

Use a good needle, suitable for your fabric. There is special basting thread, but any light-coloured sewing thread will do.

Even basting is done with stitches about 6 mm. long and 6 mm. apart (4). Generally, it is done flat, on the table, as shown (5). When one layer of fabric is to be eased to the other, basting is done over the hand (6), with layer to be eased on top.

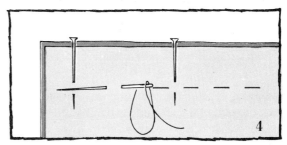

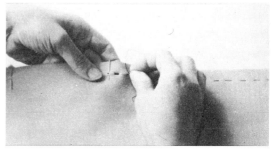

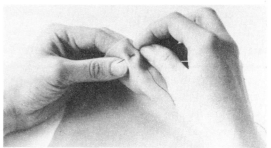

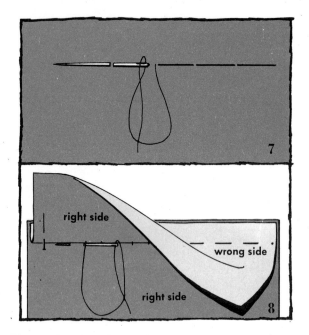

Uneven basting—long stitches on top, short stitches through fabric (7)—is used for marking, and for holding fabric together only where there is no strain, as in a hem.

Slip-basting is done on right side of fabric to match a fabric design at a seam. Use matching thread—you may not be able to remove all of it after stitching because it will be exactly on seamline. Turn seam allowance under on one edge and place fold along seamline on right side of corresponding section. Pin in place, matching design. At right-hand end of seam, bring needle and thread out through fold of upper section. Put needle into seamline of under section, at point precisely opposite where it came out of fold, and bring it out 6 mm. ahead. Take a 6 mm. stitch along fold, again putting needle in exactly opposite where it came out and running needle along inside of fold. Repeat. This actually makes a plain seam with even basting (8).

Diagonal basting is used to hold two or more layers of fabric together; it prevents shifting. It is used in the preparation of pleats. Working on right side of garment, take stitches through all layers, as shown (9), thus forming the diagonal basting.

Machine-basting

This requires some preliminary pin-basting. Then set machine at longest stitch and use matching thread. Where seams are not to be pressed open, machine-basting may be left in.

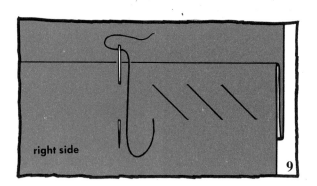

Belt Buckles

The usual fastening for a belt is a buckle. When the belt closure is a simulated tie or a simulated button closure (with sewed-on bow or decorative buttons, etc.), it is fastened with large snaps or strong hooks and eyes.

Belt buckles are available at most stores in a variety of materials—wood, metal, plastic, etc.

The covered buckle is made (covered) with your own fabric. You may:

[a] order it from a store;

[b] make it yourself, with a kit sold for the purpose (directions come with kit);

[c] re-cover an old buckle. If you have a wire-type buckle from an old belt (1), proceed as follows:

Using pliers, carefully remove prong and metal clip. Remove old fabric. Measure around buckle for length

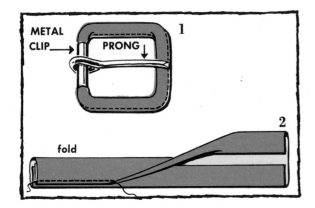

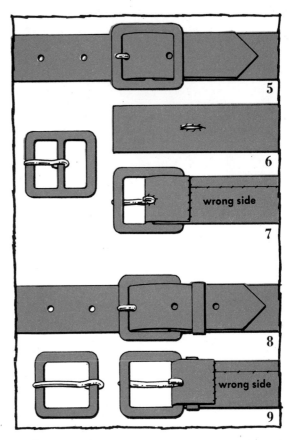

of strip needed. Cut strip on straight grain 28 mm. to 38 mm. wide (depending on thickness of fabric). Fold both long edges in about 6 mm.; fold strip in half lengthwise and topstitch edges together, close to edge (2). Slip cover over buckle. Then replace the prong and metal clip.

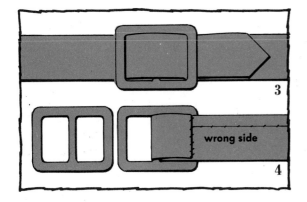

SEWING BUCKLE TO BELT

Buckle without prong (3)—Fold straight belt-end over bar and sew down (4).

Buckle with prong (5)—Cut a 13 mm. slot 38 mm. from straight end of belt. Overcast edges of slot (6).

For a **whole buckle**, fold belt-end over bar with prong through slot; sew down (7).

For a **half-buckle** (8), make a fabric-loop (see next column), long enough to be folded over belt and overlap 6 mm. Sew ends together on wrong side of belt without catching them to belt. Fold belt-end over buckle bar with prong through slot. Slide fabric-

loop close to buckle and sew belt-end down, turning raw edges under (9).

Try on belt. Mark point where prong should come through, and two more points 25 mm. to each side of first. Make three eyelets, using either a metal eyelet kit or by first punching holes, and then finishing them with buttonhole stitch.

Belt Loops

Belt loops, or belt carriers, are necessary for any belt that is not at the natural waistline; or for keeping a narrow belt in place over a wider waistband. They also serve to keep belts from getting separated from garments, particularly coats, bathrobes, etc. The number of loops needed depends on design and function.

For belt loops made of thread, used on most dresses, see THREAD LOOPS.

Fabric Loops

A belt must slide easily through loops. When attaching loops, make sure there is enough slack.

Prepare the number of loops desired in a single strip. The length needed for one loop is equal to width of belt plus 25 mm. (plus a little extra if belt is very thick).

Cut the strip along fabric selvage. Unless your pattern calls for a specific, different width, make strip 19 mm. to 25 mm. wide (the greater width for the heavier fabric or belt) and the total length of loops.

Fold long raw edge one-third to inside; press (1). Fold selvage over it; press. Topstitch along both

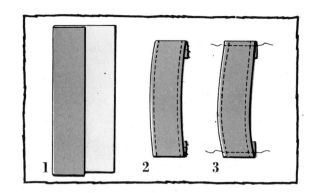

edges. Cut strip into single loop lengths.

Mark position—width of belt centred over belt line, one half above, one half below. Fold under 6 mm. at each end of strip and sew folded ends to garment, by hand (2) or machine (3).

Belts

Belts of leather, suede, plastic, satin, and other materials are bought ready-made. Belts made from the same fabric as the garment, however, are the ones most in demand and are an integral part of the garment. These may be:

[a] ordered from a store;
[b] made yourself with the help of a kit sold for the purpose (directions come with kit);
[c] made yourself without a kit. Following are instructions for making a **Covered Belt**, suitable for any fabric; a **Belt Stiffened with Iron-on Fabric**, suitable for linen, cotton, and other washable garments (but *not* recommended for sheer, napped, or pile fabrics), and a **Corded Belt**.

COVERED BELT

This can be made from any fabric, over a strip of belt backing. Buy it the width of finished belt, or cut it to the required width.

Cut backing to your waist measurement plus 152 mm.

Cut fabric along selvage edge to twice the width

of backing plus 13 mm.; length equal to your waist measurement plus 170 mm.

At one end of backing, carefully measure and cut a point, as shown (1).

Fold one end of fabric strip in half lengthwise, wrong side out. Stitch as shown. Trim seam to 3 mm. (2); press open.

Turn stitched end to right side, opening out strip to form a point. Push point out carefully; place pointed end of backing inside point of fabric; press. Fold long cut edge of fabric over backing, following line of grain; press (3).

Fold and press selvage edge over backing. Pin this edge over the other so fabric is snug over backing (4).

Hem selvage edge down (5). At straight end of belt, trim away fabric 6 mm. beyond end of backing.

If desired, finish by topstitching around belt. Begin at straight end and keep a scant 3 mm. from edge.

To attach buckle, see BELT BUCKLES.

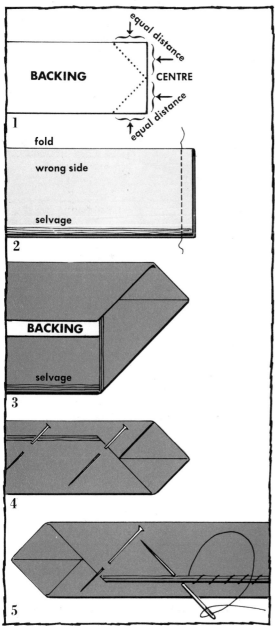

NOTE: If fabric strip for belt cannot be cut along selvage, cut it on lengthwise grain, adding 6 mm. to width. On one long edge, turn 6 mm. under and stitch. Use this edge as 'selvage edge'.

BELT STIFFENED WITH IRON-ON FABRIC

A belt interfaced and backed with iron-on fabric is supple and well suited for washable garments.

Cut a strip of garment fabric twice the width of finished belt plus 25 mm. and as long as your waist measurement plus 152 mm.

Cut a strip of iron-on fabric the desired width by waist measurement plus 140 mm.

Centre one iron-on strip on wrong side of garment-fabric strip, matching edges at one end, as shown (6). Press in place. If iron-on strip consists of more than one piece, have ends just touch, not overlap.

At even end, fold strip in half lengthwise, as shown, wrong side out. Pin together carefully, with iron-on edges exactly even. Stitch across end (7). Trim seam to 3 mm. Press seam open with thumbnail.

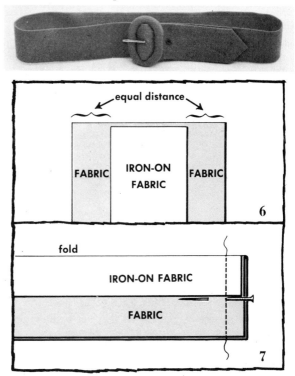

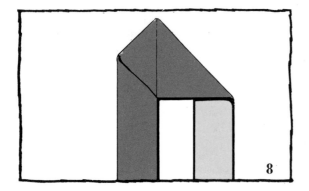

Turn stitched end to right side, opening out strip to form point. Push out point carefully; press with seam in centre. Fold and press fabric toward centre exactly along edge of tape (8). If fabric does not press flat, hold edges together at centre with catchstitch.

Turn in one long edge and hem in position over other long edge.

If desired, finish by topstitching around belt.

To attach buckle, see BELT BUCKLES.

CORDED BELT

You will need covered cord, or corded tubing, of a length equal to twice your waist measurement plus 121 cm. Buy fluffy upholstery cord of desired thickness and follow instructions in BIAS, p. 27.

Fold covered cord in half, with seam facing you. Keep seam on same side (inside) throughout. About

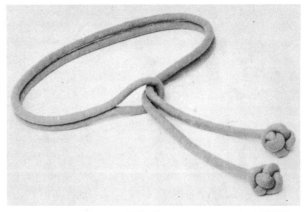

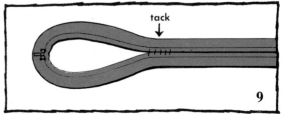

50 mm. from fold, tack together, forming a loop. Sew a hook on end of loop, as shown (9).

Try on belt, pulling both ends through loop. Place a pin (for eye) at point opposite hook. Mark desired length of hanging cord-ends with pins. Take off belt. At pin-mark for eye, tack cords together on inside. On outside, make a thread loop, or attach a straight eye. To finish cord-ends, you can either knot each end into a Chinese ball button (see BUTTONS, p. 40), or attach a tassel, or make a simple knot.

Bias

Bias is any diagonal direction in fabric. *True bias* is the true (45 degree) diagonal across a square of fabric, cutting exactly in half the right angle formed by the lengthwise and the crosswise grains (1). The fabric along this true bias line is the direction in which fabric has the greatest 'give' and flexibility. A close-fitting garment with the centre line on the true bias will mould the body. A narrow strip of bias-cut fabric can be stitched to the edge of a curve without a wrinkle—hence the wide use of bias strips (see next page) in trimming and finishing.

GARMENTS CUT ON THE BIAS

Fabric cut on the bias allows for certain effects—often very elegant—of fitting and draping; and handsome designs can be made with bias-cut stripes and checks. Pattern instructions as to grain must be carefully fol-

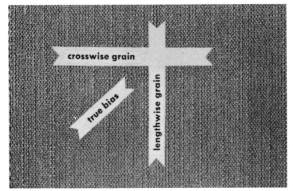

1 lowed: arrows indicating straight grain automatically make the true bias fall where it should.

A bias seam (two bias edges stitched together), whether or not it is on the true bias, may have a tendency to stretch or sag, especially in loose-woven fabrics. To stabilize a seam, use a short stitch or place straight seam-binding over seamline and stitch through all layers.

BIAS STRIPS

Bias strips are used for binding, tubing, piping (see these headings in the present chapter) and facing (see FACINGS, p. 74).

Bias strips may be hand-cut or ready-made. **The Hand-Cut Bias Strip** (see below for preparation) allows you to choose your fabric—matching or contrasting—and your width, and is suitable for any garment. The ready-made or **Packaged Bias Strip** (Coats Bias Binding) provides timesaving finishes for casual clothes.

The **length and width** of a bias strip are determined by the use for which it is intended.

For the **length** required of a bias strip (edge-finish or flat trimming), measure length at place of application with a tape measure; when cutting strips, add 25 mm. for every joining necessary, and at least 102 mm. for a final joining (beginning and end joined after application, as in a neckline). For separate pieces of trimming, such as frogs, make a sample out of tape or cord, then open it out and measure.

For the **width** of a bias strip, see instructions under the heading describing its intended use. 'Cut width' refers to actual width of strip from raw edge to raw edge. 'Finished width' is width that will show on garment (right side or wrong side) being finished or trimmed; it is also the diameter of round tubing. 'Packaged width' is the width of a packaged bias strip (edges folded in), ready for application.

THE PACKAGED BIAS STRIP (COATS BIAS BINDING)

The packaged bias strip, available in a wide range of colours, comes in lengths of 242 cm. and 484 cm. The folded-in edges may be pressed open when necessary.

THE HAND-CUT BIAS STRIP

The length of a single bias strip is limited by the width of the fabric available. The bias cut is about one-third longer than the straight grain, as shown (4). When a long strip is needed, shorter strips may be joined end-to-end, each strip having been cut as long as possible. However, when it is important that joinings should not show, it is best to figure and measure each length so that joinings will fall in inconspicuous places, such as centre back, side seams, under belt, etc.

Locating the True Bias

This may be done in two ways. For either of these methods, lay out a fabric-end and work with a straight edge on the lengthwise grain (a selvage or an edge cut parallel to selvage).

METHOD I . . . Fold the straight edge so that it lies at right angles to itself, along the crosswise grain (2). The fold formed will be on the true bias. Mark fold by pressing; open out.

2

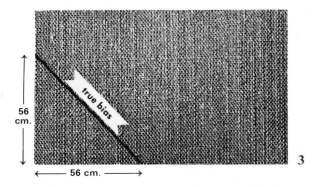

METHOD II . . . Straighten the adjoining crosswise edge. On the two sides of the right angle thus formed, mark off equal distances with yardstick and chalk. The line between the two marks will be on the true bias (3). Mark line with chalk.

Marking and Cutting Bias Strips

Mark a true-bias line on your fabric as shown above. Measuring from the true-bias line, mark the desired width of strip at a few points, then use yardstick to draw a continuous line (4). Repeat for as many strips as you need. Cut along marked lines.

Joining Bias Strips

IMPORTANT: The ends of bias strips to be joined must be on the straight grain and parallel to each other.

If they are not parallel, trim one end to match the other (5).

Place strips right sides together as shown (6): at right angles to each other, with straight-grain edges even but with points extending so that edges cross at *seamline*, forming small angles. Stitch on straight grain, beginning and ending at angle centres. Press seam open and trim to a scant 6 mm. Trim off extending points.

Stretching or Swirling

You will find it helpful to stretch a hand-cut bias strip before using. This is particularly true when making tubing, on which the stitching may break when you turn it. To stretch strip, press firmly while stretching it with the other hand.

Swirling means pressing or steaming strip into a curve, as needed (7).

Final Joining of a Bias Strip (Seam or Lap)

Start application at an inconspicuous spot.

METHOD I (seamed joining) . . . When starting, leave 50 mm. of bias strip free *beyond* point at which you wish joining to be. When, after stitching, you are about to reach that point again, stop just short of it. Cut off strip 50 mm. beyond point. Fold garment (8) so that strips are at right angles as for any joining (when using packaged bias strip, open out folds). Seam ends

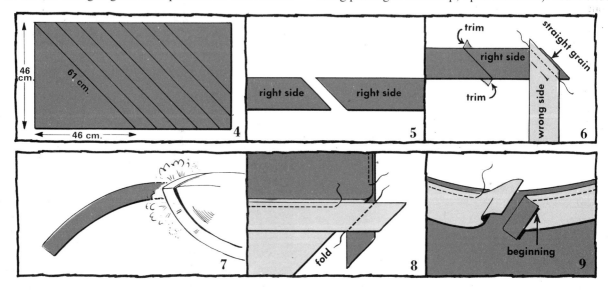

together on the straight grain, close to fold of garment (8). Trim seam; press open. Complete stitching to garment, across joining.

METHOD II (lapped joining) . . . Before beginning to stitch, fold that end of bias strip 13 mm. to wrong side on the straight grain. When completing stitching, cut second end on the straight grain to lap over first for about 13 mm. (9). Stitch across.

Basting

A bias strip should be pinned in place before stitching, especially around curves. On a close curve, basting is definitely necessary.

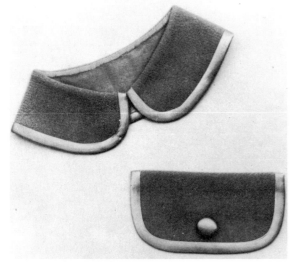

BIAS BINDING

A bias binding is a decorative finish which encases an edge. Its finished width varies, but is seldom less than 6 mm. or more than 13 mm.

Trim away the entire 16 mm. seam allowance (since bias strip covers garment edge, no allowance is needed). *Before* doing this, stay-stitch 19 mm. from raw edge. To bring any binding around a corner see p. 26.

Binding

For either hand-cut or packaged bias strips.

Hand-Cut Bias Strip

Cut strips 3 times as wide as desired finished width

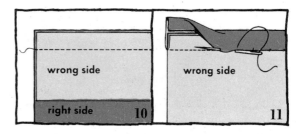

plus 6 mm. Example: For a 13 mm. binding, strips are 38 mm. plus 6 mm., or 44 mm. wide.

Pin or baste right side of strip to right side of garment, with raw edges even; if ends are to be joined, see p. 24 before starting. Stitch at a distance from edge exactly equal to finished width (10). Press strip up; fold to wrong side over cut fabric edges. Turn in raw edge of strip even with stitching line. Slip-stitch to stitching line (11).

Packaged Bias Strip

Applying binding: Mark a line on right side of garment, 6 mm. from raw edge. Open out one fold of bias strip and pin or baste right side of strip to garment, matching raw edge of strip to marked line. Stitch along crease. Fold to wrong side over fabric edges and slipstitch second fold to stitching line.

French Binding

Suitable only for hand-cut bias strips in sheer or lightweight fabrics.

Cut strips 6 times as wide as finished width. Fold strip in half lengthwise, right side out. Press. Pin or baste raw edges of folded strip to right side of garment, all edges even. (If ends of strip are to be joined, see p. 24 before starting, but leave 76 mm. free at beginning and, when joining, open out strip completely.) Stitch at a distance from edge exactly equal to finished width. Press strip up; fold to wrong side over cut fabric edges. Slipstitch to stitching line (12).

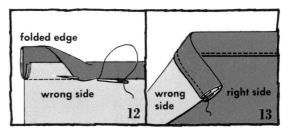

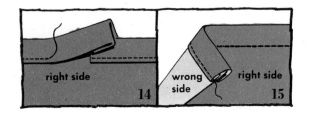

Machine-Finished Binding

Fold binding lengthwise, right sides together, so that one side is a fraction above the other. Insert edge between edges of tape, and topstitch; you will automatically stitch through the wider bottom fold (13). If ends must be joined, lap them (14).

Concealed machine-finish: (If tape-ends are to be joined, see p. 24 before starting.) Fold binding lengthwise so that one side is a fraction above the other. Open out seam allowance on *narrower* fold; place tape along garment-edge right sides together, raw edges even. Stitch along crease. Fold tape up and over garment edge to wrong side. Machine-stitch on right side, on garment fabric but as close as possible to edge of binding, to catch wider fold underneath (15).

Sewing Machine Attachment

A binder can be used for a topstitched application of bias strips. Follow the directions in your sewing machine manual.

Corners in Binding

Outside Corner (as in pointed collars, pockets)

French Binding: When stitching toward corner, stop at width of seam allowance from corner. Cut thread; secure ends. Folding strip as shown, bring it around corner (16). Starting at very edge of corner, stitch as shown across fold and along edge. When finishing binding on wrong side, form mitre at corner.

Machine-finished binding: Stitch to edge of fabric, as shown (17). Cut off thread, form mitre and start stitching again from point of mitre (18). Bring thread-ends to wrong side and fasten.

Inside Corner (as in a square neck)

Regular and French Bindings: Stitch to width of seam allowance beyond corner. Pivot on needle to turn; bring strip around corner, stretching it around needle; continue stitching (19). When finishing binding on wrong side, form mitre at corner.

Machine-stitched binding: Clip carefully about 3 mm. into corner. When applying binding, stitch to width of seam allowance beyond corner. Pivot on needle to turn. Forming mitre, bring tape around corner and continue stitching (20). Fasten mitre in place with a few stitches on wrong side.

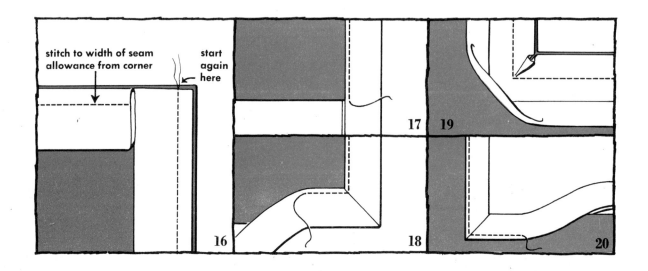

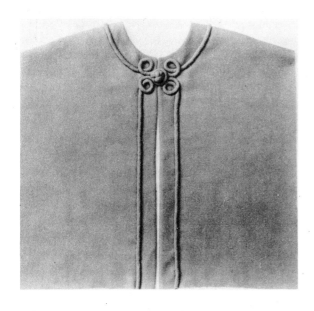

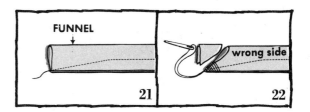

Turning with bodkin or tapestry needle: Thread a bodkin or heavy tapestry needle with about 102 mm. of strong thread, and knot the two ends together. Using a sewing needle, sew this knot of heavy thread securely to point of funnel (22). Insert bodkin or tapestry needle into tube. Push it through, turning tube inside out. Keep seam allowances open. Press tubing flat with seam at centre.

To turn with a safety pin, attach pin to one side of tubing and pull through gently.

BIAS TUBING

Tubing is made by stitching the edges of a bias strip together to form a tube which is then turned inside out. It is used either flat or round; flat tubing is suitable for ties and appliquéd decorations, round tubing (filled with its own seam allowance or with cord) for loops, buttons, ties, belts, frogs, decorations. Tubing is generally made from hand-cut bias strips. Packaged bias tape can also be used if the width from raw edge to raw edge is right. Whenever possible, make tubing without joinings. For turning tubing, use a bodkin, a heavy tapestry needle, or a safety pin.

Flat Tubing

Cut bias strips twice as wide as finished width plus 13 mm.

Fold strip in half lengthwise, wrong side out. For ease in turning later, begin (and end) stitching in a funnel shape, as shown (21); then make a scant 6 mm. seam, stretching strip as you stitch.

Press seam open lightly with tip of iron (if necessary, insert a pencil or rod into tube to avoid creasing). Trim funnel-ends diagonally, as shown, slanting in from the seam (22).

Self-Filled Tubing

The diameter of self-filled tubing depends on the bulk of the fabric used—finished organdie tubing should be no more than 3 mm. wide; satin no more than 6 mm.; other fabrics in proportion to their weight.

Cut bias strips 5 times as wide as finished width.

Fold strip in half lengthwise, wrong side out. Starting (and ending) with funnel shape—see above (21)—stitch midway between fold and cut edges, stretching strip as you stitch.

For turning, see directions for **Flat Tubing**, but do not press.

Corded Tubing

Cord for filling comes in varying thicknesses. Remember that tubing may compress a large, fluffy cord to a smaller size.

To determine width of bias strip, fold a corner of fabric over cord to be used; with a pin, fasten the two layers of fabric together so that cord is tightly enclosed. Cut 6 mm. beyond pin (23). Open out piece—the width between the two parallel edges will be width of strip needed.

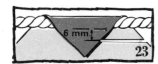

To make a corded tubing, the cord should be twice the finished length of the belt. This length of cord is required to make the turning over of the bias strip easy. Place the cord in the centre of fabric as before, having the extra cord at one end. Baste and stitch

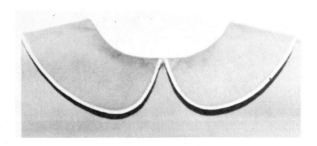

close to the cord and across the end which is in the centre of the cord (24). Trim the seam, then pull the opposite end of the cord so that it turns the tubing on to the extra cord. Trim cord at ends.

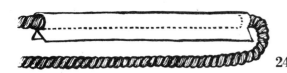

PIPING

Piping is made of a folded bias strip, either plain or corded. Whether piping is placed on an edge or in the body of a garment, it is always caught in a seam.

Corded Piping

To Make Corded Piping

To determine width of bias strip, see **Corded Tubing**, but cut fabric 16 mm. below pin, for seam allowance.

Fold strip in half lengthwise, right side out. Insert piping between edges and baste.

Stitch close to piping using a cording foot in the machine.

Piping is stitched to a single garment section before the two garment sections are seamed together. Pin or baste piping to right side of section, raw edges even. Clip seam allowance of piping if necessary (25).

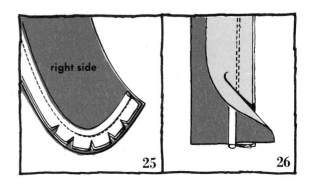

Pin or baste the two garment sections together, wrong sides out and raw edges even. With cording foot, stitch close to piping (26). Finish seam in usual manner.

Plain Piping (uncorded)

Cutting: To determine width, add 16 mm. to desired finished width. Cut strips double the width of that measurement.

Stitching: Fold strip in half lengthwise, right side out. Press. Stitch at finished width from fold.

Applying: Follow directions for corded piping but use ordinary presser foot.

Final Joining of Piping

Start application in an inconspicuous place, leaving 13 mm. of piping free. When stitching piping in place, stop 13 mm. from end. (If piping is corded, pull out 13 mm. of cord at end and cut cord). Rip back a few stitches; fold raw end in and lap over beginning.

Buttonholes

Buttonholes are basically slits cut through the fabric. What interests us is the finish of their edges, which may be bound with fabric, or worked over with thread, either by hand or machine.

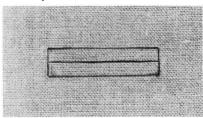

The Bound, or Piped, Buttonhole, almost always finished with self-fabric (the possible exception being trimming fabric), is the one most in vogue today. It is good in all garments except when fabric is unsuitable, i.e....

... sheer, embroidered, or nubbly,
... ravelly (though this can be corrected by backing with iron-on interfacing (see next column),
... untreated cotton, where inside layers may wrinkle when washed.

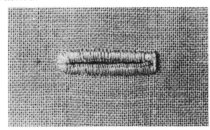

The Hand-Worked Buttonhole is best in lightweight and sheer fabrics, especially on blouses; also in the difficult fabrics mentioned above.

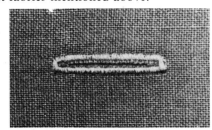

The Machine-Worked Buttonhole is always suitable in casual and children's clothes, which are subject to frequent washings. A carefully-made machine buttonhole, however, can be used in other garments as well.

Buttonholes are most often horizontal; less often vertical; now and then, to carry out a design, diagonal. The making of either bound or hand-worked buttonholes undeniably requires care and precision; it also requires that the grain of your fabric, if it is plain to the eye, be straight. Otherwise, if you do not want machine buttonholes, select a pattern that does not call for buttonholes at all.

FOR SUCCESSFUL BUTTONHOLE-MAKING ...

... Have, first and foremost, a pair of good scissors with *very sharp* blades and points. Also a 152 mm. ruler, a longer ruler or yardstick, and a contrast-coloured pencil, not too hard and very sharp.

... Have on hand, before you even start marking your pattern, the *actual buttons* you are going to use.

... If you are inexpert, try out the directions, *skipping no details*, with a few practice buttonholes on scraps of closely-woven cotton, properly backed (interfaced).

... Never fail to reinforce with *interfacing* any edge that is to have buttonholes, whether the pattern specifies it or not. That edge will always have wear and tear. Avoid loose-woven or ravelly interfacing fabrics, especially for bound buttonholes.

... When garment fabric itself is ravelly, or has 'give' (knit and stretch fabrics), stabilize the buttonhole area by backing it with a piece of *lightweight iron-on interfacing*, 25 mm. wide and 25 mm. longer than buttonhole. Apply these patches to wrong side of fabric before attaching regular interfacing.

... In every case, before making buttonholes in a garment, make a *test buttonhole* to see how this particular fabric handles. Cut a 102 × 102 mm. piece each of fabric and interfacing, on straight grain. Mark interfacing with position line and end-lines duplicating the ones made in **Marking The Garment Section** and baste to fabric as instructed. For a worked buttonhole, baste a second piece of fabric under interfacing. For a bound buttonhole, make test buttonhole after **Preparing the Buttonhole Strip** (p. 31). Follow directions as for actual buttonhole.

MARKING THE PATTERN

Possible Re-spacing—If you have altered the length of your pattern the buttonholes may need re-spacing. As a general principle, top and bottom buttonholes should be placed at same distance from top and bottom edges of garment as they were originally; and the ones between, re-spaced to be at equal distance from each other.

Length of Buttonhole—Buttonhole markings printed on pattern indicate position of buttonhole, not necessarily exact length. To determine the correct length, measure your button, as follows:

DIAMETER + THICKNESS = LENGTH OF BUTTONHOLE

Diameter and thickness added together generally equal necessary length of buttonhole. For instance, a round button, 25 mm. in diameter and 3 mm. thick, requires a 28 mm. buttonhole. Buttons that are fabric-covered, dome-shaped, ball-shaped, or odd-shaped, often need extra length. For such buttons, cut a slit in fabric, measured as above. Try button in slit and lengthen slit until button slides through easily. Length arrived at should be marked on pattern.

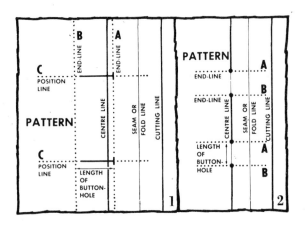

Marking—In diagrams 1 and 2 here, the solid lines represent markings printed on most patterns. Dotted lines represent markings to add for correct and uniform buttonhole length. Use pencil and yardstick.

For **Horizontal Buttonholes** (1) draw in lines A, B, C. At top and bottom of pattern, extend end-lines [A and B] at least 25 mm. beyond existing markings. Extend position lines [C] 25 mm. beyond end-lines.

For **Vertical Buttonholes** (2), draw in lines A and B (end-lines). Extend these lines 25 mm. beyond centre line, which is also position line.

MARKING THE GARMENT SECTION

Here we need accuracy. Lines must not only be correct as to position, but also absolutely on grain if grain is clearly visible. Markings for buttonholes must be on outside of garment, since that is where the greater part of the buttonhole is made. Since dressmaker's carbon paper would leave permanent and visible marks, the marking is done in two steps, the second one by basting through to right side.

Step 1. From pattern to interfacings (3). Place pattern with buttonhole markings over interfacings for both sides of opening; match edges carefully; if interfacing is woven, make sure centre-line is on grain. Pin together through seam allowance along opening edge. Transfer all lines, printed and pencil, to interfacings with dressmaker's carbon paper, using a ruler. Pin interfacings to wrong side of corresponding garment sections, matching edges exactly.

Step 2. From interfacings to garment sections (4). Many fabrics can be marked with machine-basting. Others (taffeta, polished cotton, certain treated fabrics), which show needle-marks, must be hand-basted with a fine needle. On women's clothes, buttonholes are on right-hand side of opening. On left (button) side, baste-mark *centre line only*. On buttonhole side, disregard centre line, unless buttonholes are vertical. If garment fabric has a noticeable grain, put a pin through from interfacing to outside at ends of all marked lines. Machine- or hand-baste on garment side between pin markers, following a thread in grain. If fabric grain is not noticeable, baste-mark by going over lines from interfacing side through to outside.

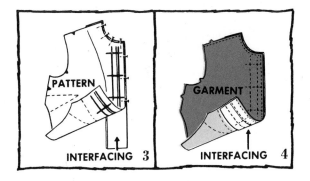

PATTERN   INTERFACING 3   GARMENT   INTERFACING 4

THE BOUND BUTTONHOLE

Bound buttonholes are made first thing after **Marking the Garment Section**, with interfacing attached as described, *before* the section is seamed to any others. The buttonholes can be made in various ways; two most satisfactory types follow—a **One-Piece Folded Buttonhole** and a **Patch Buttonhole** (both begin with **Preparing the Buttonhole Strip**). In both, the finished buttonhole has lips either on the bias or the straight grain, of even width and meeting in the centre; and the outer shape is usually rectangular and must be exactly on grain, especially when fabric grain is noticeable. Width is about 6 mm. overall, a little less if fabric is thin, a little more if fabric is heavy.

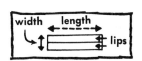

width   length   lips

Either buttonhole can be **corded** to give body to the lips—which in this case *must* be on the bias. At what point and how this is done is indicated in the directions. Soft cord of suitable thickness, soft twine (single or doubled) or doubled knitting worsted (for wool fabrics), can be used for cording.

. . . If you are planning an elegant buttonhole only 5 mm. wide, you will find the half-width measurement for lips hard to locate on a ruler. Instead, mark the 5 mm. on a paper-edge, then fold this in half to mark width of lips (see buttonhole directions).

. . . Do not, unless you are an expert, try to make a bound buttonhole less than 22 mm. long. To fit a smaller button, buttonhole may be shortened after it is finished, by slipstitching lips together invisibly on wrong side, at far end from garment edge.

. . . When buttonhole is finished, press with steam iron or dampened press cloth—lightly, as the added thickness may mark outer fabric.

PREPARING THE BUTTONHOLE STRIP

With this long strip, you prepare the lip-fabric for all your buttonholes at once. The strip may be cut on straight grain, but it is far easier to achieve professional-looking buttonholes when the lips are on the bias; with corded buttonholes this is a *must*.

Measure, mark and cut strips as follows:
WIDTH: 25 mm. for One-Piece Folded Buttonhole.
         Add 3 mm. if fabric is heavy;
         50 mm. for Patch Buttonhole.
LENGTH: Add 25 mm. to length of your buttonhole. Multiply this figure by number of buttonholes, including test buttonhole.

On wrong side of fabric, mark lengthwise centre of strip *accurately* (5). Baste-marking is most exact.

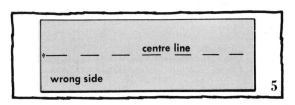

centre line
wrong side   5

. . . To baste-mark, start at one end of strip, with ruler held across it (6). Keep end of ruler (or zero mark) even with edge of strip and your needle pointed to half-width mark on ruler. Take short stitches, moving ruler down the strip about 6 mm. at a time.

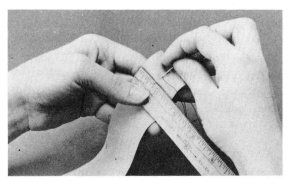

6

... To mark with coloured pencil, place strip on hard, flat surface. Use yardstick, and mark with dashes rather than with a continuous line.

ONE-PIECE FOLDED BUTTONHOLE

Fold both edges of buttonhole strip (5) to centre-line and press (7). Baste-mark 3 mm. from each fold (i.e., halfway between fold and centre), through both thicknesses (8). The two basted lines must be 6 mm. apart. Now cut strip into individual sections (length of buttonhole plus 25 mm.) for each buttonhole. Make test buttonhole, following directions below. When making buttonholes on garment, do not complete each separately. Do one step on all, then the next step on all, etc.

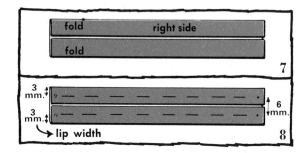

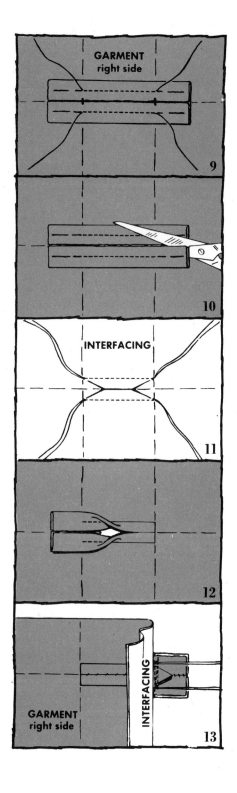

Pin a buttonhole strip over a buttonhole position on outside of garment section, centre line of strip over position line, ends extending 13 mm. beyond end-lines, as shown (9). Baste in place along centre line. Re-connect end-lines, marking across strip.

Starting and finishing at end-lines, stitch over basting lines on either side of centre, as shown (9); leave 76 mm. thread-ends. Check: On both right side and interfacing side, stitching lines must be on grain, 6 mm. apart, extending exactly to end-lines (if necessary, pull out a stitch or two, or put thread-end into a needle and make an extra stitch). If stitching is not perfect, remove carefully and stitch again.

Pull thread-ends to interfacing side. Knot close to fabric, but do not trim off. Remove baste-marking from strip.

Cut strip in two through entire length of centre line (10). Be careful not to cut garment.

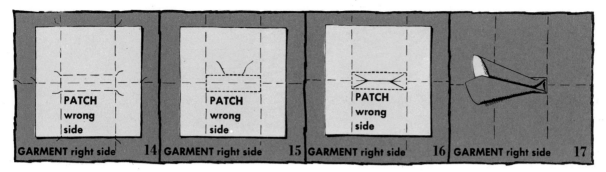

If you want a corded buttonhole, draw short lengths of cord through lips with a tapestry needle. Cut cord-end off even with fabric.

Cut buttonhole opening from interfacing side, through interfacing and garment fabric only: Start cutting at centre and stop 6 mm. from each end-line; then clip into each corner as far as possible without clipping stitches (11). *Be careful* not to cut into strips on other side.

Put strips gently through opening to interfacing side (12). Flatten strips and see that lips meet. Secure lips on wrong side with diagonal basting (remove only after garment is finished). Beyond ends of opening, overcast folds of strips together.

Place garment section on machine right side up. Fold one edge back as far as end of buttonhole, exposing strip-ends with tiny triangle lying on top. Holding thread-ends taut, stitch back and forth across base of triangle at end-line (13). Repeat on other end of buttonhole. Trim off thread-ends.

Remove all baste-markings on garment section. Press buttonholes.

PATCH BUTTONHOLE

Cut buttonhole strip (prepared as directed on p. 31) into individual patches (length of buttonhole plus 25 mm.) for each buttonhole. Make test buttonhole, following directions in next column. When making buttonholes on garment, do not complete each separately. Do one step on all, then next step on all, etc.

Pin patch to outside of garment section, right sides together, centre line over position line, ends extending 13 mm. beyond each end-line. Baste in place along centre line as shown (14).

Draw or baste-mark end-lines across patch, connecting lines on garment. Draw or baste-mark two lines parallel to centre line, 3 mm. above and below, as shown (14). The rectangle formed outlines the buttonhole.

Stitch slowly over outlined rectangle: Start at centre of one long side; at corner, pivot on needle; count stitches across end; pivot and continue, counting off same number of stitches across other end. To finish, stitch over beginning stitches (15). Check stitching on right side of garment. If it is not perfectly on grain, remove carefully and stitch again.

Cut buttonhole through all thicknesses (16): Start cutting at centre and stop 6 mm. from ends. Then clip into each corner as far as possible without clipping stitching. Remove basting on patch.

Put patch gently through opening to interfacing side (17).

Smooth out patch (especially corners); opening should be a perfect rectangle (18). Press lightly to flatten edges.

Working from right side (19), bring a fold of patch even with centre marking, as shown, forming a 3 mm. lip (keep seam allowance out of lip). Secure lip in position with hand-backstitching hidden in seam on long edge. Repeat to form second lip.

If you want a corded buttonhole, draw short lengths of cord through lips of buttonhole with a tapestry needle. Cut cord-ends off even with fabric.

On wrong side (20), secure lips with diagonal basting (remove this basting only when garment is finished). Beyond ends of opening, overcast the folds together.

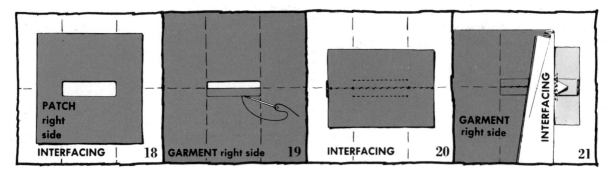

Place garment section on machine right side up. Fold one edge back as far as end of buttonhole, exposing strip-ends with tiny triangle lying on top. Stitch back and forth across base of triangle at end-line (21). Repeat on other end of buttonhole.

Remove all baste-markings on garment section. Press buttonholes.

FACING THE BUTTONHOLES

The wrong side of bound buttonholes is finished after the facing has been applied and pressed. If you have backed garment fabric with iron-on interfacing to keep it from fraying around buttonholes (see p. 29), do the same with facing fabric.

Secure facing in place with pins near sides and ends of buttonholes.

You have a choice of two finishes:

. . . **A two-cornered finish** that is particularly good for springy and ravelly fabrics. From outside of garment, stick a pin through *each end* of buttonhole. On facing side, cut between the pins, following grain. Remove the pins and cut 3 mm. more at each end. Turn both raw edges under as shown, and then hem in place (22).

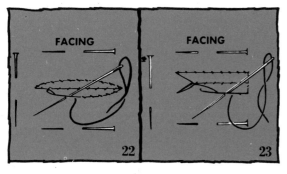

. . . **A finish, shaped exactly like the buttonhole,** good for garments that may be worn open. From outside of garment, stick a pin through *each corner* of buttonhole. On facing, cut through centre of buttonhole and into corners (marked by pins) exactly as you did for the buttonhole itself. Turn raw edges under and hem in place (23).

THE WORKED BUTTONHOLE

Worked buttonholes, whether made by hand or by machine, are worked on the outside of a garment after facing has been applied (for marking pattern and garment, see p. 30). Never fail to make a test buttonhole first (see p. 29).

HAND-WORKED BUTTONHOLE

Depending on fabric, use high quality sewing thread, Coats Drima, Coats Satinised No. 40, Coats Chain Cotton No. 40 or Coats Super Sheen No. 50.

Horizontal hand-worked buttonholes have a rounded fan end near garment opening (where button rests); the other end is finished with a bar tack (24). **Vertical** buttonholes have the same finish at both ends—either bar tacks or fans (25).

Before cutting slit, outline and reinforce buttonhole edges with a row of fine machine-stitching (8 stitches per centimentre) 2 mm. to either side of position line (26). Starting at an end-line, stitch carefully to next end-line; pivot on needle; count stitches across end; pivot and continue around, counting off same number of stitches across other end.

Cut slit between end-lines, starting at centre and cutting toward each end-line (27).

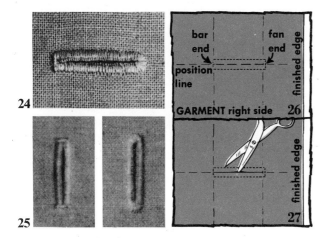

24

25

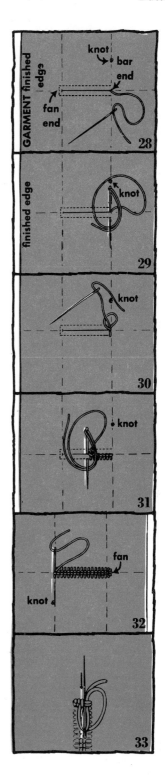

Make a knot in your thread-end. Have garment edge to your left (28). Insert needle into right side of fabric about 13 mm. from bar end, and bring out through slit at that end. Knot will be removed later.

The Buttonhole Stitch is done from right to left, needle pointing toward you. Use machine-stitching as a guide for stitch depth (except at fan end).

Insert needle into slit and bring out just below stitching. Bring thread hanging from eye of needle from right to left under point of needle (29).

Draw up needle away from you (30), so that knot comes at edge of slit.

Repeat this stitch (31), placing stitches close together so that purls cover edge. Work to other end-line.

Where there is a fan, work around fan end as shown (32), keeping stitch depth the same and turning work gradually; make 5 to 7 stitches in fan. Where there is no fan, turn work after reaching end-line.

Cover second edge with buttonhole stitch. When last stitch is completed, put needle through purl of first stitch; bring out just below last stitch (32).

To make bar tack, take one or more stitches across end of buttonhole, spanning width of both rows. Then work over this thread with blanket stitch without catching fabric. Use needle eye-first, as shown (33).

Put needle through to wrong side. On a **horizontal**

buttonhole, run thread under a few stitches and cut. On a **vertical buttonhole**, which has two bar tacks, run thread under stitches to other end of buttonhole and make a second bar tack like the first one.

Cut off extra 13 mm. of thread used for starting, and pull out knot.

To start a new thread while working, run thread under a few finished stitches on wrong side; bring needle and thread through last stitch made..

MACHINE-WORKED BUTTONHOLE

Machine-worked buttonholes are made with a buttonhole attachment or on a machine equipped for zigzag stitching. Follow directions in manuals. Use thread and needle.

. . . For a stronger, better-looking buttonhole, stitch around a second time, making this second row slightly narrower than the first.

Button Loops

Button loops, extending beyond the finished edge of a garment, often take the place of buttonholes.

Any buttons can be used with fabric loops, but the ones most often seen are ball buttons, usually fabric-covered. With braid loops, Chinese ball buttons (p. 40) can, if desired, be made of the same braid. Loops vary greatly in thickness and size, depending on fabric, button, location, etc. They may be part either of decorative or of concealed fastenings.

In decorative fastenings, loops are made of fabric tubing, self-filled or corded, or of round braid. They are used on dressmaker suits, on close-fitting long sleeves or bodices, and on coats and jackets.

In concealed fastenings, a loop, usually single, may be made of thread (as in the neck corner of blouse), or of fabric (for example, in the neck corner of man's sports shirt or underlap of coat).

DECORATIVE FASTENINGS
Row of Loops

Use narrow tubing (3 mm. or narrower), self-filled or corded (see BIAS, p. 27), or round braid.
On an edge to be faced, loops are applied before facing is attached. In this case, the cord should be about three times the length of opening, but it need not be in one piece.

Cut a piece of sturdy paper about 50 mm. wide and as long as opening. On one long edge, mark off seam allowance. Determine size of loop needed for size of button. Measure and mark size of loops on paper as shown (1), without or with intervals (2 or 3).

Place one end of paper and one end of cord under presser foot (always keep *seam of cord*, if any, turned *up*; see 2 and 3), and anchor cord with needle on marked seamline. Form first loop; stitch on seamline.

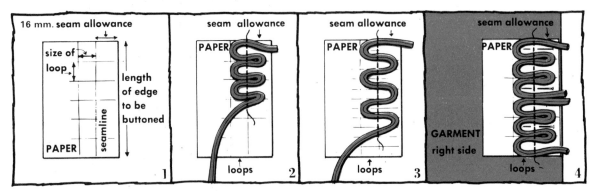

Continue, forming loops as you go, until all loops are attached.

Pin paper to right side of garment, matching edges as shown, loops facing away from edge, as shown (4). Stitch on top of stitching which holds loops. Tear off paper. Apply facing. Trim seam allowances and loop-ends to 6 mm. Finish opening (5).

On a finished edge, loops are applied after edge is finished. Cord should be about twice length of opening and must be in one piece.

Determine size of loop needed for size of button. On garment edge, measure and mark width of loops with pins, as shown (6). On cord, measure and mark size of loops in same manner. Beginning at first mark and matching pins, attach cord to edge with small stitches, sliding needle to next mark through fold of garment. Be careful that seam in cord (if any) is not turned to right side.

Single Loops

Use tubing, either self-filled or corded (see BIAS, p. 27) of a size in keeping with size of button and weight of fabric. Single loops are usually larger than loops in a row. They are always applied to a faced edge, before facing is attached.

With seam of tubing up, pin tubing to right side of garment, forming a loop facing away from edge, large enough to accommodate button (7). Stitch to garment on seamline, as shown. Apply facing and finish.

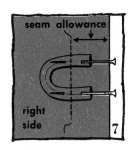

Frogs

Frogs, shown here in two designs, are highly decorative button loops that can be used on any finished front opening. They vary greatly in size, and can be used (I) in pairs (i.e., with the motif repeated on the button side), or singly (II). The button can be a Chinese ball button (p. 40) made with the same cord as the frog, or any shank button.

Use tubing, self-filled or corded (see BIAS, p. 27), or braid. Length needed depends on design. Determine size of loop needed for your button. Draw outline of frog on a piece of sturdy paper (8, 9). Frog will be constructed on this paper right side down, which means that seams on tubing, stitches, and cord-ends will all face up as it is made.

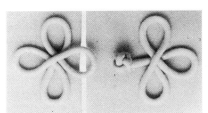

I   II

I. Made from one piece of cord. Starting at centre, baste cord to paper, following outline (8). Sew cord together at crossings. Secure ends.

II. Made from two pieces of cord. Begin by stitching together a small, tight spiral, making sure that visible cord-end and stitches all face you. When spiral is the right size, repeat in contrary direction with other end of cord, to fit design (9). Cut off cord-end in centre of spiral. Baste to paper. Form loops with a separate piece of cord, basting to outline and joining at centre. Sew the two parts together at crossing.

Remove frog from paper; take more stitches if needed. Sew to garment right side up, with garment opening pinned together. Button loop extends beyond edge. If frogs are made in a pair, sew button securely to 'button loop' on left-hand side of garment.

CONCEALED FASTENINGS

Thread Loop—Made after garment is finished (10). See p. 165.

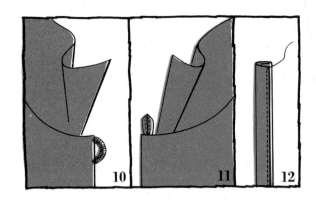

Fabric Loop—Can be bias or straight-grain, and is usually made from garment fabric (11). It is applied before facing is attached—see **Single Loops**, p. 37.
Bias Loop—Made of tubing, either flat or self-filled (p. 27). Size depends on garment.
Straight-grain Loop—Cut a strip on the straight grain, about 13 × 57 mm. Turn in long edges, fold in half lengthwise, and topstitch (12).

Buttons

Buttons, with their companion buttonholes, generally serve as fastenings. They are also, with or without buttonholes, used as decoration—often as counterparts to 'working' buttons (as in most double-breasted garments), or for simulating a button closure.

TYPES OF BUTTONS

Buttons may be made of almost any material—wood, metal, plastic, mother-of-pearl, glass, fabric, crochet cotton, etc.—and in many shapes; they may be plain or fancy. From the standpoint of sewing on the button, however, they fall into just two categories:

. . . the **pierced button**, provided with two or four holes through which it is sewed on;

. . . the **shank button**, which has a solid top and a shank or stem underneath for sewing on. The shank may be in one piece with the button or may consist of a wire or fabric loop.

IMPORTANT: Holes or shank must be free of rough edges, which might cut through the thread.

POSITION OF BUTTONS

Position of **buttons in a closure** is marked after garment is completed. Lap opening of garment as it will be worn, with neck, waistline and/or hem evenly lined up, Through buttonhole, place a pin at exact spot where button is to be sewn, picking up a small amount of fabric: near outer edge with a horizontal buttonhole (1); in centre of buttonhole with a vertical buttonhole.

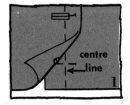

Position of **buttons without buttonholes** (decorative) is marked at the time that all markings are transferred from pattern.

REINFORCING BUTTON POSITION

Buttons need a firm backing. In closures, they usually fall on a faced and interfaced part of garment, but even a decorative button should not be sewn to a single thickness of fabric. When such a button falls in a single-thickness area, or when the existing backing of a 'working' button does not seem strong enough for the strain to which it will be subjected, reinforcing is necessary. This is done in one of the three ways below.

For light and medium-weight fabrics—Cut a circle of iron-on fabric a little smaller than button. Before sewing on button, press circle to wrong side of button position (if possible, between garment and facing).

For any fabric—Place a small square of doubled fabric to wrong side of button location and stitch through it as you sew on button.

On heavy or tailored garments—Hold a small, flat 'stay-button' to wrong (facing) side of garment and stitch through it as you sew on button (2).

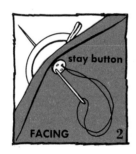

CHOICE OF THREAD

Be sure to choose the right thread for the fabric to which button is to be sewn.

For light to medium-weight fabrics—Coats Drima, Coats Satinised No. 40, Coats Chain Cotton No. 40, or Coats Super Sheen No. 50.

For heavier fabrics—Coats Drima, or Coats Satinised No. 40 (doubled).

For very heavy fabrics—Clark's Anchor Button Thread.

SEWING ON BUTTON

A 'working' button always needs a shank, to allow buttonhole to fit smoothly under it. For a pierced button, a shank is made out of thread (see at right).

Length of shank is determined by thickness of fabric: a sheer fabric will need a barely perceptible one, while with a heavy wool it may be necessary to extend even the stem of a shank button.

When attaching a decorative button, which needs no shank, omit hair grip or other in the instructions below.

Make a small knot at end of thread. On right side of garment (knot will be covered by button), take a small stitch at button position, picking up all thicknesses, but being careful not to let stitch show through facing fabric in a jacket or a coat. Take a second small stitch across the same space.

Pierced Button—Bring thread up through one hole in button. Centring button over stitch, place a hair grip, matchstick, or toothpick (depending on length of shank desired) between button and fabric (3), and take three or four stitches through each pair of holes. Bring needle and thread out between button and fabric, remove hair grip or other, and wind thread a number of times around the attaching thread, to form a shank. Take a small stitch in fabric (4). Finish off thread securely. Buttons become detached quite as often through loosening as through breaking of thread. Take several small stitches under button, looping thread over needle to form knots. **Cut**, do not break thread.

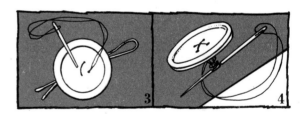

Shank button—If length of shank is sufficient, take 6 to 8 stitches (less if thread is doubled) through shank and finish off as for pierced button. If shank needs lengthening, take a first stitch through shank, then place a hair grip or other underneath and proceed as with pierced button.

MAKING FABRIC BUTTONS

Whether you have fabric buttons made commercially or make them yourself, have them ready before you

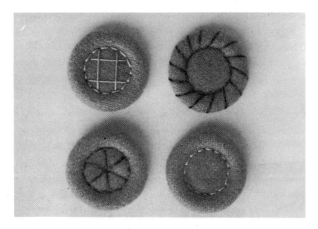

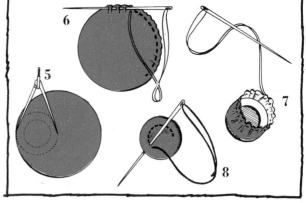

make buttonholes. To attach, catch fabric (or cord) underneath and handle like a shank button.

Covered Buttons are made (covered) with your own fabric. You may:

[a] order them from a store;
[b] make them yourself, using a kit sold for the purpose (directions with package);
[c] make them yourself, using bone or plastic rings as a base, as follows: Cut fabric circles twice the diameter of rings (5). Gather edge (6). Draw up over ring (7), and fasten securely. To trim, use matching or contrasting thread and take stitches inside ring, as shown (8). Optional: Cover back with small circle of fine fabric.

Chinese Ball Buttons are made with a length of round cord, which may be either purchased braid or bias tubing, corded or self-filled (see BIAS, p. 27). Here is estimated amount needed for each:

for 10 mm button:	use 3 mm cord	152 mm length
for 13 mm button:	use 5 mm cord	203 mm length
for 22 mm button:	use 6 mm cord	25 cm length
for 25 mm button:	use 10 mm cord	66 cm length
for 35 mm button:	use 10 mm cord	92 cm length
		(fold in half and work double)

Loop cord as shown in diagrams 9 to 11 (shaded sections indicate part looped in previous steps), keeping loops open while working. Then draw them together, easing and shaping into a ball while keeping the two ends firmly together underneath. Trim off ends and sew flat to underside of button.

Casings

A casing serves to accommodate an elastic or a drawstring. It may be formed by a **hem**, either turned up or bias-faced (top of apron or skirt, bottom of overblouse, neck and sleeves of night-

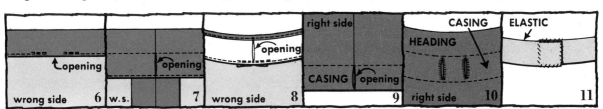

gown, child's dress, etc.), or by a separate bias strip—an **applied casing**—stitched along both edges to the wrong side of a garment (at the waist of a straight dress with no waist seam, below an edge where a single-thickness heading is desired, etc.). A **heading** is a narrow width of fabric that extends beyond an edge-casing and forms a ruffle when casing is drawn up.

MAKING A CASING

Width of casing: Width of elastic or drawstring plus 3 mm. (more if drawstring or elastic has bulk).

Opening in casing: Read instructions that follow under this heading **before** making casing.

A hem used as a casing is machine-stitched.

Casing in Turned-up Hem—For straight edges only.

Turn in 6 mm. at edge; press. Turn hem to desired depth (width of casing; or casing plus heading). Pin. Machine-stitch as shown (1). On a casing without heading, make a second line of stitching close to fold (optional). On a casing with heading, mark width of casing and make a second line of stitching as shown (2).

Casing in Bias-Faced Hem—For curved edges. Also suitable for straight edges to reduce bulk.

Follow directions for **Faced Hem** (see p. 97), using bias strip the width of casing alone or casing plus heading (plus seam allowances). After turning facing to wrong side, machine-stitch edge of facing

in place. On a casing without heading, make a second line of stitching close to fold (3). On a casing with heading, mark width of casing and make a second line of stitching at that distance from fold (4).

Applied Casing—For any place not an actual edge.

Bias strip of nearest suitable width is generally used. For a casing with a single-thickness heading, actual edge of fabric is finished with a narrow hem.

Mark position of upper edge of casing on inside of garment. Pin strip in place; stitch along both edges (5).

OPENING IN CASING FOR INSERTING ELASTIC OR DRAWSTRING

Elastic—Opening is on wrong side of garment.

In a Turned-up Hem—You may either leave a 13 mm. opening when stitching down hem, in which case you backstitch at beginning and end for reinforcement (6); or take out stitches in a seam across casing (7).

In a Bias-Faced Hem of an Applied Casing—Fold bias strip under 13 mm. at beginning and end of application. Make folds meet and overlap stitching at end (5 and 8).

Drawstring—Opening is on right side of garment.

For All Casings—If there is a seam at a suitable location, take out stitches across casing and reinforce end or ends of opening as shown (9). Otherwise, make two worked eyelets or buttonholes in single thickness (outside fabric) of casing, as shown (10).

To insert elastic or drawstring, use a bodkin or a safety pin and push through casing. Be sure not to let elastic twist. To secure elastic, keep the two ends out, overlap and whipstitch together as shown (11), before letting them go into casing.

Collars

Collars vary greatly in shape and size. They may have square or pointed corners or a rounded edge; they may be cut in two pieces (upper collar and undercollar or facing), in one piece (folded), or with undercollar in one with garment body and upper collar in one with garment facing (shawl collar). In all the variations of the collar, however, the basic details in the construction are the same. These details are covered in the following pages, the directions being adaptable to any collar, including one cut as part of the garment body.

Interfacing is generally necessary in a collar, and not only for crispness. The interfacing becomes part of the upper collar and the double thickness prevents the seam allowances from showing through on right side of finished collar. If interfacing is not specified in pattern, see INTERFACING for cutting.

MAKING A PERFECT COLLAR

Directions apply to collars made in one section or in two sections.

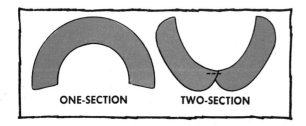

ONE-SECTION   TWO-SECTION

In addition to other markings, make a small clip-mark in seam allowance or cut a notch at centre of neck edge on collar (this will ensure an accurate position on garment later).

For a perfectly even finished edge, mark seamlines on interfacing. Trim away corners of interfacing, if any.

Stay-stitch interfacing, marked side up, to wrong side of upper collar (1). This piece will hereafter be handled and referred to as one piece. (To avoid confusion, stay-stitching is not shown in drawings after this step.)

Stay-stitch undercollar. Pin undercollar to upper collar, right sides together.

With interfacing side up, stitch outer edge on marked seamline (2). On collar with corners, stitch from edge to edge of fabric, as shown, reinforcing corners by shortening stitch at beginning and end; do not stitch ends of collar.

Trim seam allowances to 6 mm. as shown (3).

Grade seam allowances. Clip at 6 mm. intervals (4).

Understitch (5). On rounded-edge collar, understitch entire seam. On collar with corners, start and stop understitching 25 mm. from ends.

Rounded-edge collar is now finished. Turn to right side and press (5-a).

On collar with corners, stitch end-seams, shortening stitch at corners as before (6).

Trim corners (7).

Press end-seams open with point of iron.

Trim, grade, and taper end-seam allowances toward corner (8).

Turn collar to right side, pushing out corners carefully as you do so. Press (9).

One-Piece Collar

This collar, cut in one piece with its facing and folded on its outer edge, is always entirely straight,

TWO-PIECE COLLAR with CORNERS

1

25 mm. **short stitch**   25 mm. **short stitch**

2

6 mm.   **3**   FACING   **4**

COLLAR   FACING

INTER-FACING   **5**

25 mm. **short stitch**   **6**

7   **8**

9

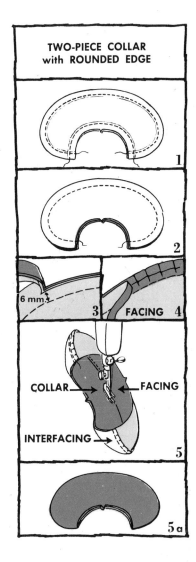

TWO-PIECE COLLAR with ROUNDED EDGE

1

2

6 mm.   **3**   FACING   **4**

COLLAR   FACING

INTERFACING   **5**

5a

with pointed corners. It is best interfaced with very light fabric, cut exactly like outer fabric.

On interfacing, mark seamlines and fold line.

Pin interfacing to wrong side of collar, marked side up. Along fold line, catch interfacing to collar with tiny stitches, about 13 mm. apart and invisible on right side (10). Start and end stitches about 25 mm. in from outer edges.

Stay-stitch 13 mm. from outer edge (11). To avoid confusion, stay-stitching is not shown in drawings after this step.

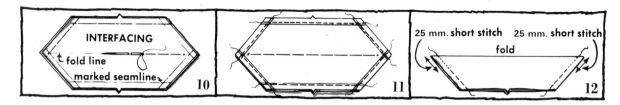

Fold collar in half lengthwise, interfaced side out. Stitch ends, reinforcing corners by shortening stitch (12). Trim corners (13). Press end-seams open with point of iron (see **Underpress**, p. 76).

Trim, grade, and taper seams toward corners (14).

Turn collar to right side. Press (15).

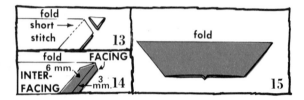

ATTACHING A COLLAR

A collar can be attached to a garment in different ways, depending on the style of the garment. Its neck edge may be caught in a shaped facing all around, or in a shaped facing at front of garment only; or the neck edge may be finished with a bias strip. The pattern primer will tell you what method applies to your garment.

Here, however, are some useful pointers:

IMPORTANT—After a collar is turned, raw edges at neck are no longer even, because upper collar has been brought slightly over outer edge by under-stitching. Do not try to make these raw edges match

—when stitching them to garment, match raw edge of undercollar to neckline. Seam allowance in upper collar will just be a little narrower.

Always stay-stitch garment neckline, so you can safely clip seam allowance before attaching collar.

A two-section collar must be anchored together before attaching, to prevent it from spreading. Overlap ends so that edges meet at neck seamline; baste across by hand or machine (16).

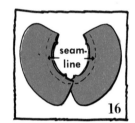

After collar has been stitched to neck edge of garment, trim, grade, clip, and understitch this seam as you would any facing seam (see FACINGS, p. 76).

MAKING A COLLAR DETACHABLE

Any collar can be made detachable by trimming its unfinished neck edge to 6 mm. seam allowance and encasing it in bias binding. This edge can then be attached inside garment neck edge by means of basting or small snap fasteners. On underside of collar, sew ball part of fasteners to bias binding; then —for comfort when garment is worn without collar— sew the socket half of snaps to matching points along the neckline.

Corners

Corners, of various kinds and different angles, occur often in clothing, as these illustrations show. The corners must be neatly made, to avoid bulk and to strengthen seams that are weakened by inside trimming and clipping.

Refer to the following chapters for handling the different corners:

Faced Corners (collars, lapels, cuffs, 1 and 4; neckline, 3). See FACINGS, particularly **Processing the Seam**, p. 76.

Patch Pockets (1), lined and unlined. See POCKETS.

Applied Piece (3)—For outside corners, see **Unlined Patch Pocket,** p. 141. At inside corners, stitch through one thickness on seamline and clip into corners before turning seam allowance under.

Bound Corners—See **Corners in Binding,** p. 26 in BIAS.

Corners at Set-in Piece, such as a gusset (1), or at a specially-designed armhole (2). See GUSSETS.

Slashed Opening at neck (5) or in long sleeves. See PLACKETS.

Cuffs

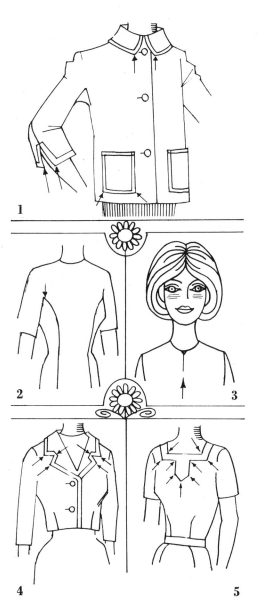

1

2

3

4

5

Cuffs on sleeves vary a great deal in design and construction. A cuff cut in one piece with the sleeve is simply a very deep hem which is partly folded up on outside of sleeve. A cuff cut separately may consist of one piece of fabric folded in half, or of two pieces seamed together. It may be folded back over the sleeve (1, 2), or on itself (French cuff, 3), or consist of a plain doubled band into which the sleeve is gathered (4). Cuff-ends may be closed (1), or open (2), or fastened with buttons or cufflinks (3).

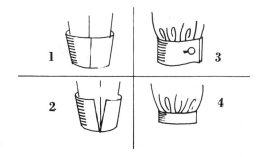

1   3

2   4

Cuffs should almost always have a certain crispness and body, and interfacing is generally specified in conjunction with a cuff pattern. If it is not, and your fabric seems to require the addition of interfacing, cut interfacing from the cuff pattern.

The pattern instruction sheet will tell you how to make and attach your cuffs. However . . .

. . . A cuff with edge-seams is made exactly like a collar. For smooth, sharp edges, follow **Making a Perfect Collar** on pp. 42-44, substituting the word 'cuff' for 'collar' throughout.

. . . If you are attaching a cuff to a gathered sleeve, be sure, when stitching, to have the gathered side (not·the cuff side) up. This allows you to control the gathers more easily.

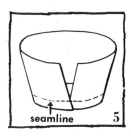

. . . If you are about to attach a cuff with open ends to a closed sleeve, prevent ends from spreading by first overlapping them so that edges meet at seamline; then baste across by hand or by machine (5).

. . . Detachable cuffs are finished like a detachable collar. See COLLARS, last paragraph.

Cutting

Cutting, with its irrevocable aspect—there's no denying that a mistake in cutting cannot be ripped out like a wrong seam—often makes a person nervous, especially if the fabric is expensive. The thing to do is to proceed without haste, and to follow directions. Study your pattern instruction sheet, and take into account all indications on the pattern pieces themselves. What we give you here is the method of procedure.

THE EQUIPMENT

Assemble everything you need:
Cutting surface (large table or cutting board) . . . Shears . . . Tape measure . . . Yardstick and small ruler . . . Pencil . . . Pins and pincushion . . . Fabric (prepared, if necessary—see FABRICS, p. 66) . . . Pattern . . . Iron and ironing board.

PREPARING THE PATTERN

Pick out pattern pieces you will use (depending on what 'View' of garment you have selected on envelope). Smooth out pieces with warm, dry iron. Make pattern alterations, if any (see PATTERNS, p. 121).

Small pieces, if printed together, must be cut apart.

Grain line marks, to serve their purpose properly, must extend the entire length of pattern pieces. Using yardstick and pencil, extend grain line arrows on printed patterns (1); on perforated patterns, draw in entire line.

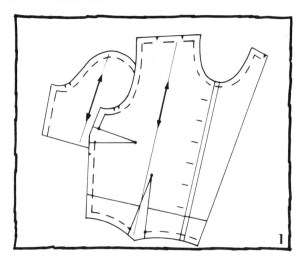

Selecting Your Pattern Layout

On pattern instruction sheet, locate and circle your pattern layout: for the selected *view* of your garment, for your *pattern size*, *fabric width*, and fabric either '*With Nap*' or '*Without Nap*' (2).

. . . See **Buying Fabric** (p. 65) for the fabrics that come under the classification 'With Nap', and why (there are many besides actual napped fabrics).

. . . Fabrics that are 'Without Nap' have no up or down direction in design, weave, or texture, and may be cut with pattern pieces facing in either direction (3) if they are on grain.

. . . Fabrics 'With Nap' must be cut with the tops of all the pattern pieces facing the same way (4, 5).

. . . A true napped fabric (wool broadcloth, flannel, camel's hair, etc.) looks best with nap running toward hem of garment (6).

. . . A pile fabric (velvet, corduroy, etc.) has a richer colour with the pile running toward top of garment (7). Fake fur varies; hold it up both ways and decide.

THE FOLD IN THE FABRIC ·

If your fabric fibre demands it (see FABRICS, p. 66), you will have shrunk the fabric and straightened

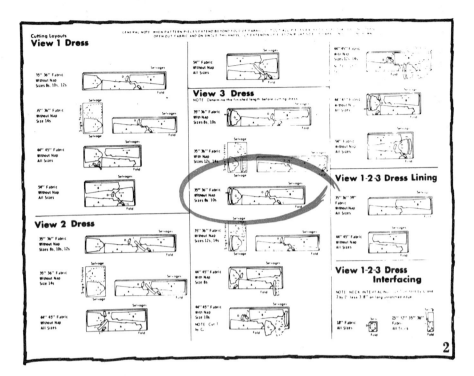

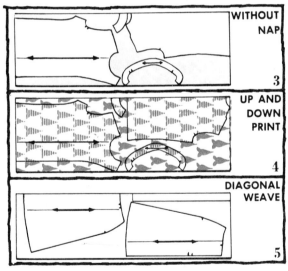

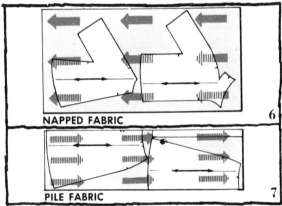

its cut ends. Press out any wrinkles. Cutting layout sometimes calls for disregarding the regular lengthwise fold in fabric. In such a case (see examples below), press out fold. If fold cannot be pressed out, you will have to avoid it as you lay out the pieces. See **A Trial Layout,** p. 50.

Fabric is almost always folded right sides together for cutting. It is cut right side out if it has a design that must be taken into account and that does not show through to wrong side (printed corduroy, bonded fabrics).

Fold fabric as shown in cutting layout on pattern instruction sheet. Never let fabric hang over edge of cutting surface to avoid stretching.

CUTTING LAYOUT A — fold — selvages

FABRIC A-a — fold — selvages

CUTTING LAYOUT B

FABRIC B-a — selvages — crosswise fold — selvages

CUTTING LAYOUT C — selvage — fold — selvage

FABRIC C-a — selvage — right side — double width of fold — selvage

FABRIC C-b — selvage — right side — wrong side — selvage — fold

Layout using regular lengthwise fold (A)

Pin matching selvages together in a few places (A-a).

Layout requiring crosswise fold (B)

Regular fold pressed out. Fold fabric across width, as shown; pin matching selvages together (B-a).

Layout requiring new lengthwise fold (C)

Regular fold pressed out. On cutting layout, identify pattern piece which determines width of fold (in layout C, piece 5). Pick out actual pattern piece and measure width. On fabric, spread out singly, measure double this width from selvage and mark with pins (C-a). Fold fabric, bringing selvage to pin-line; smooth out, and pin selvage along line (C-b).

Layout requiring a combination of folds (D)

In such a case, you position only the pattern pieces requiring a certain fold. Cut these out, then make the new fold.

EXAMPLE: In layout D, two different folds are needed. You would first cut out pieces 2, 3, 4, 5 with regular fold; then press out fold on remaining fabric and fold fabric crosswise. Cut out pieces 1, 6, 7, 8, 9, placed as shown. For piece 9 (belt) open out fold and cut on single thickness.

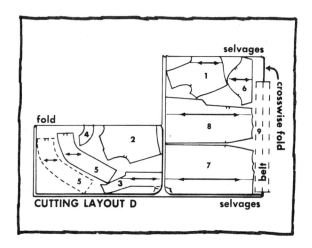

CUTTING LAYOUT D

ARRANGING PATTERN PIECES

If you have bought the correct yardage, as given on pattern envelope, a trial layout will not be necessary (see below for cases requiring a trial layout). Just be guided exactly by the layout you have circled.

... When, on a layout, a pattern piece is shown extending beyond a fold line (piece 9 on layout D), cut out other pieces, then open out remaining fabric to cut this one.

... When a pattern piece is drawn with a broken line (second piece 6 on layout C), it means that *after* other pieces are cut you either:

[a] fold remaining fabric (here, crosswise) and cut piece out through both thicknesses, or

[b] cut piece through single thickness, then reverse pattern (printed side down) and cut piece out a second time.

... When half of a pattern piece is drawn with a broken line (piece 3 in layout B), it means that the piece is a half-pattern, to be cut on a fold. Cut out all other pieces as laid out, then re-fold fabric to cut each of these pattern pieces.

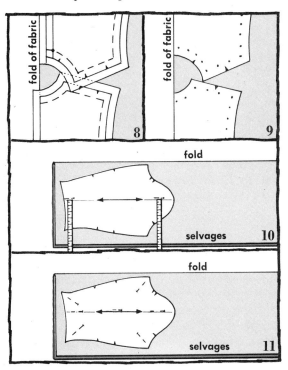

... With a printed pattern, overlap margins to cutting line (8).

... With a perforated pattern, place pieces edge to edge (9).

Place first pattern piece (largest piece located at one end of layout) on fabric. To position grain line, measure distance from one end of extended grain line to selvage (10); pin pattern through grain line. Pin through other end of grain line at same distance (10); then through centre of line.

Smooth pattern out from grain line and pin at opposite corners, then at opposite sides (11). Keep pins inside cutting line of pattern and don't use too many —they can distort the cutting line.

Repeating the same steps for each, pin in place all the pattern pieces that require the same fold in the fabric.

Checks and Stripes

Pattern should have few seams, and preferably be designed for checks or stripes. Because of allowance necessary in matching design, you will need extra yardage.

Checks and stripes may be even (of symmetrical design) or uneven. The uneven design must be cut 'With Nap' so it runs in the same direction on each piece.

EVEN CHECK   **UNEVEN CHECK**

For cutting, these fabrics must be folded very accurately, with edges pinned together so that corresponding lines are matched.

To match checks and large stripes, see that notches that correspond on pattern fall on stripes that correspond on fabric (12).

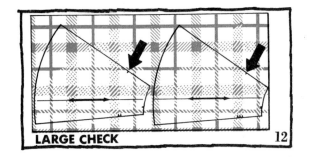

LARGE CHECK   12

Stripes must match at the following places:
... sleeve cap notches and armhole notches at front and back,

... at shoulder notches on kimono sleeves,

... at shoulder seam notches for vertical stripes,

... at centre seams and, when possible, side seams,

... where collars and yokes meet bodice, if they are not on the bias.

Large Printed Designs

Pattern should have few seams. Try to place pieces on fabric so that motifs are arranged for a pleasing effect. Try to match motifs at seams whenever possible.

A Trial Layout

This may be necessary
... if your fabric is of a width not indicated on primer,

... if your fabric is 'With Nap' (see p. 46) and there is no cutting layout 'With Nap',

... if you have been unable to press out the fold in your fabric when necessary,

... if your fabric has a check or other design that must be matched.

To make a trial layout, select cutting layout that seems closest to what you need and place all pattern pieces in proper position, with one or two pins in each. When you have made sure that you have sufficient fabric, *do not cut out* until you have checked each piece for correct grain position, proceeding as directed above and folding fabric as necessary.

CUTTING

Never use pinking shears to cut out pieces—they do not give a reliable cut line.

Cutting lines on patterns are indicated in different ways:

A printed pattern may have either a single or a double line. Cut exactly outside single line; or between two lines.

A perforated pattern is cut out exactly along edge.

Keep fabric and pattern flat on table. Never draw fabric toward you to reach a piece.

Cut with long strokes. When cutting into a corner, open shears only wide enough to have points of blades reach end of cut.

Notches are not really notches any longer, although they have kept that name. A notch is now cut, not into seam allowance, but into adjoining fabric, making a **point** on seam allowance. These are also called balance marks. Two or more 'notches' are cut in a block, as shown (13), rather than singly.

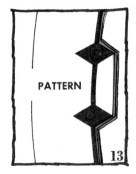

PATTERN   13

In sections that are at centre front or centre back of garment, mark centre points, top and bottom, with a notch or a small clip in seam allowance.

Do not remove pattern pieces from sections cut. You will need them for the next step, MARKING (see p. 112).

CUTTING THROUGH A SINGLE THICKNESS

Some of the new fabrics require that they be cut through a single thickness at a time.

When pattern is to be cut on a fold (usually at centre front or centre back), trim margin from centre ('fold') edge. Pin pattern in place on wrong side of a single thickness of fabric (except for leather, when pattern is placed on right side). With chalk or pins, mark fabric at top and bottom of 'fold' edge of pattern piece. Cut around pattern piece

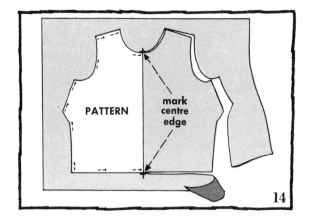

except for 'fold' edge. Unpin pattern and reverse it, matching 'fold' edge to chalk marks. Re-pin and cut out second half (14). When cutting two corresponding sections (sleeves) from a single thickness, reverse pattern for second section.

Darts

Darts are stitched, pointed tucks that shape the fabric to fit the body. They are clearly indicated on patterns. Since their exact length, depth, and position have a great bearing on the fit of a garment, they may need some alteration. This, fortunately, is relatively easy (see **Pattern Alterations**, p. 121).

MARKING

Centre of dart is usually shown by a solid line. If your pattern does not carry this line, carefully measure and mark centre of dart at widest point; then draw a line to point of dart.
Carefully transfer centre line and stitching lines to fabric. Make short crosslines (1) to mark point of dart and matching dots (see MARKING, p. 112).

SEWING

Fold dart on centre line, then pin or baste.

Start stitching from the wide end. To make sure that point will taper to nothing gradually (as it *must*), take two stitches at point, along fold, as close to fold as possible (2). Tie thread-ends.

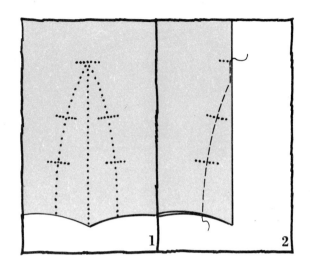

FINISHING

Generally there is no special finish for a dart before pressing; the following cases, however, are the exceptions:

Deep dart—Trim or slash to within 13 mm. of point (3).

Heavy fabric—Slash to within 13 mm. to 25 mm. of point of dart (3).

Lace or sheers, unbacked—Make a second line of stitching 3 mm. from first (4); trim (5).

Double-pointed dart—Clip at widest part; reinforce stitching (6).

Curved dart—Trim to 16 mm.; clip at curve; reinforce stitching.

PRESSING

First press line of stitching as is, but be careful not to put a crease into fabric by pressing beyond point. Then open out garment; to maintain shaping, complete pressing over a pressing ham, or end of ironing board, or sleeve board. Trimmed or slashed darts are pressed open like a seam (3). Vertical uncut darts are pressed toward centre of garment (6). Horizontal and diagonal darts are pressed downward (7). If fabric marks easily, slip a piece of paper between dart and fabric.

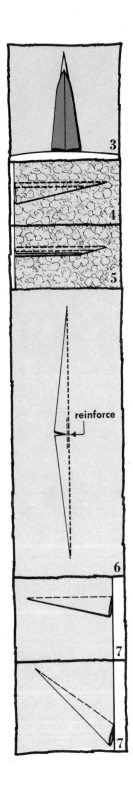

A FEW SPECIAL CASES

Dart in backed garment—In order to keep the two layers of fabric together at fold, machine-baste (on backing side) through centre line before folding and stitching dart. Basting must not show beyond point.

Dart in very sheer fabric—'Bobbin-stitching' will avoid a knot at point, where it might show through. Thread machine as usual, and turn wheel to bring needle and take-up lever to highest point. Then:

Draw out about 51 cm. of bobbin thread through hole in throat plate.

Remove thread from machine needle. Thread bobbin thread through needle, in opposite direction.

Knot bobbin and spool thread together (8). Wind spool, drawing bobbin thread through needle and onto spool (9). Bobbin thread is now continuous from spool to bobbin.

Stitch dart, starting at point. Re-thread machine for each dart.

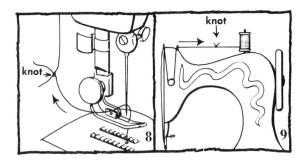

Dart tucks release fullness at one or both ends. Mark and pin or baste as for regular darts. Starting at fold, stitch across to marking; pivot fabric on needle; stitch along marking to edge of garment (10), or pivot again and stitch across to fold (11). Tie the ends. Press toward centre of the garment.

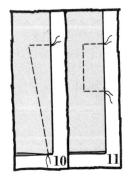

Decoration

Decoration may be something applied to a garment purely as trimming, or it may be a functional detail, done in a decorative manner. Among the latter are a facing turned to the outside (see FACINGS, p. 79), bias binding and piping (see BIAS, p. 25 and p. 28), and self-fringe. The decorations that follow are of both kinds, selected because they are the ones you are most likely to use. They are in alphabetical order.

APPLIQUÉ

Appliqué (1) is a piece of fabric, almost always small and in a contrasting colour, applied as a decoration to a background fabric. Unless the motif is cut out of a print, it is traced on the appliqué fabric with a sharp pencil, on wrong side for hand appliqué, on right side for machine appliqué. It may also consist of bias strips.

For hand appliqué, make a line of machine-stitching, exactly on outline of motif. Cut out 3 mm. outside outline. Pin motif in place. Turning under raw edge along line of machine stitching as you sew, attach edges either with invisible slipstitch (see HEMS, p. 95), or with small blanket stitch (see **Embroidery**, p. 54).

NOTE: Appliqués of felt, which does not ravel, are cut out on outline itself and tacked on invisibly (these are often used on sweaters).

For machine appliqué, cut out motif, leaving about 25 mm. seam allowance all around. Cut an identical piece of a lightweight, heavily sized fabric—the lower the thread count, the better (starched lawn or cheap organdie are very good); place between appliqué and background fabric, and pin. Do not baste, because basting may cause puckering; do not turn edges under. Stitching is done with a close zigzag stitch and with thread matching the appliqué (contrasting thread will show up any imperfection in stitching). Try out stitch length (closeness) and bight (width) on scraps of all layers: background, in-between and appliqué fabric. The narrower the bight, the easier it is to control the stitching. Stitch at slow speed, even with hand on wheel, if necessary, adjusting and manipulating fabric as you stitch, in order to avoid puckers and distortion. If appliqué consists of several pieces do not stitch any part that will be covered by another piece—machine may jam when going over previous stitching and the stitching would show as a ridge when pressed. At end of each stitching line pull threads to wrong side, tie off and clip before continuing. After appliqué is stitched, trim off excess fabric carefully, cutting each layer separately; don't pick up work but cut flat, pulling loose edge of fabric over scissor blade and cutting close to stitching.

Bias strip appliqué can be anything from satin bias tubing pressed flat (see BIAS, p. 27), to ready-made cotton bias tape. The edges are slipstitched in place—in the case of cotton sometimes machine-topstitched. Large, gay initials can be made of bias tape.

Iron-on appliqué is suitable for cotton playclothes, aprons, and children's clothes.

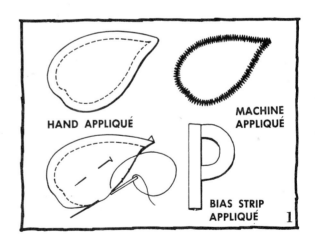

HAND APPLIQUÉ

MACHINE APPLIQUÉ

BIAS STRIP APPLIQUÉ

1

BEADS

Beads are usually attached along an outline lightly marked on outside of fabric. Sometimes they are used to enhance a printed or woven design in the fabric. They can be sewed on singly or in groups,

or they can be strung first on a heavy thread for a continuous line. For illustrations 2 and 3 use a very fine needle; wax the thread with beeswax to prevent twisting. Sew on single beads with a backstitch, working from right to left, as shown (2). For short, straight lines use thread doubled; take 5 or 6 beads on the needle and sew on as shown (3). A string of beads is attached by taking a stitch over the thread between each bead (4). Always fasten thread-ends securely.

BOW, TAILORED

A tailored bow (5), suitable for a dress or a hat, is made from ribbon or flat tubing (see BIAS, p. 27).

Cut a length three times the desired size of bow. Trim ends diagonally—in the case of tubing, turn in end-edges, sew together and press. Fold and tack through centre as shown. Fold another piece over centre, as shown; sew ends together underneath.

EMBROIDERY

Embroidery (6) can be mentioned here only sketchily. **Machine embroidery**, made with zigzag stitch, is described in your sewing machine manual.

Hand embroidery includes smocking, faggoting, cutwork, appliqué, and every kind of decorative stitch made on fabric. We give you here the stitches you may find most useful. Clark's Anchor Stranded Cotton, in which the strands can be divided for finer work, is the thread generally used. Other popular threads are Clark's Anchor Soft Embroidery, Coats Anchor Tapisserie Wool, Clark's Anchor Pearl Cotton Nos. 5 and 8 and Clark's Anchor Coton à Broder.

FRINGE

Fringe comes and goes as a fashion finish; the three main types are discussed below.

Ready-made fringe, in various widths, is usually made of rayon. Sold by the centimetre, it is simply stitched

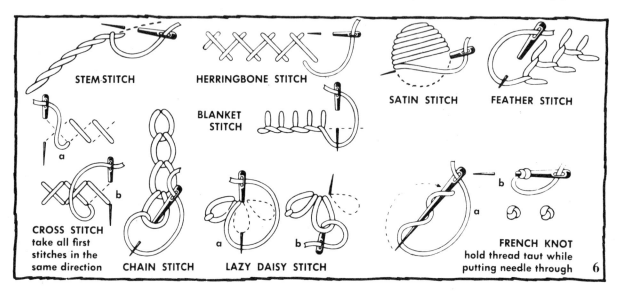

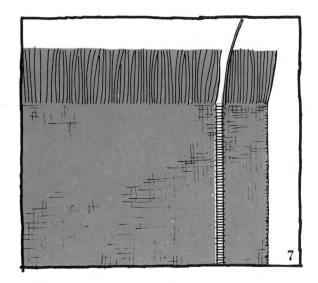

on through the heading, which as a rule is decorative and placed on the outside.

Self-fringe (7) can be very chic, especially in woollens. The fabric edge must be absolutely straight-grain. Draw out a thread along edge and trim edge evenly. Using a pin, draw out a thread at desired depth of fringe. Unless fabric is very firmly woven, make a line of machine-stitching, zigzag or straight, along that line. Beginning at stitched line, draw out threads (be sure to trim away first any selvage left at seams).

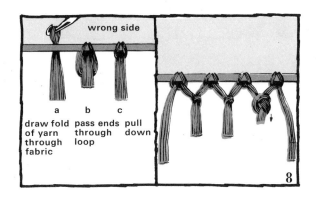

Knotted fringe (8) is made with a crochet hook, generally using yarn. It requires a finished edge. How thick your yarn should be and how many strands you want in each tassel will depend on fabric weight. To determine depth, cut a few strands of yarn, fold and draw through fabric edge with hook, looping as

shown. Trim ends. Using this as a guide, cut a piece of cardboard a little deeper than one strand folded in half. Wind yarn around cardboard; cut along one edge. Put the same number of strands in each tassel, place each at the same depth, and space evenly. If you wish, you can make a much deeper fringe and shorten it by knotting together the halves of two adjacent tassels. You can even make several rows of such knots, as is done for Mexican scarves.

LACE

Lace edging or insertion can be applied by hand or by machine. Fabric edge should be finished. If lace is to be gathered to fabric, draw up the heavy thread along straight edge. To sew on by hand, place lace along edge of fabric, right sides together, straight edges matching. Attach with whipstitch, as shown (9). To sew on by machine, lap straight edge of lace very slightly over edge of fabric, right sides up (10). Attach with narrow, not too close zigzag stitch or straight stitch.

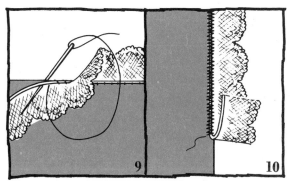

MACHINE-QUILTING

Machine-quilting (11), a very handsome form of decoration, is done before garment sections are assembled if quilting—as is usually the case—is limited to a certain section. Place thin wadding between fabric and lining and baste diagonally all over. A beautiful and very easy design consists of squares on the diagonal. If you get a quilting guide, as shown, you will need to mark only one line in each direction. The others will proceed out from there. Lighten pressure on presser foot. Use Coats Drima, Coats Satinised No. 40, Coats Chain Cotton No. 40 or Coats Super Sheen No. 50.

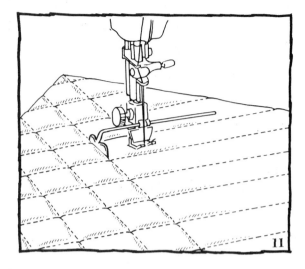

MACHINE-STITCHING

Machine-stitching, i.e., topstitching, can be featured as a decoration by having a thicker thread in the bobbin (underthread) such as Clark's Anchor Pearl Cotton No. 8, Clark's Anchor Stranded Cotton, Clark's Anchor Soft Embroidery or Clark's Anchor Coton à Broder. Machine stitch from the wrong side using a long stitch.

POMPONS AND TASSELS

Pompons (12) are made from yarn. Cut a rectangle of cardboard, a little wider than desired diameter of pompon. Along one longer edge, hold a 152 mm. piece of yarn (doubled, unless yarn is very strong). Then

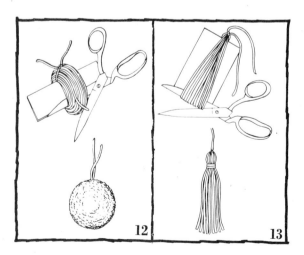

wind a considerable amount of yarn around cardboard, as shown. Tie very tightly with the short piece; cut through on other edge of cardboard, as shown. Fluff out yarn and trim evenly to form a ball. **Tassels** (13) are started like pompons, but are much less full. After cutting yarn off cardboard, wind another short piece just below fold, as shown, tie and trim. Trim ends evenly.

RICK RACK

Rick rack (14) makes a charming trimming on children's and casual clothes. A single strip of rick rack can be sewn on by hand as shown, or by machine by stitching through centre. Two strips of rick rack, in the same or in two different colours, can be interlocked, as shown, for a special effect. Apply in the same manner as the single strip.

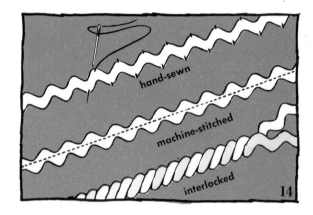

SEQUINS

Sequins (15) are another dressy decoration. They can be bought in ready-assembled strips or 'loose'.

For a continuous line of sequins, mark design lightly on right side of fabric. To attach a ready-

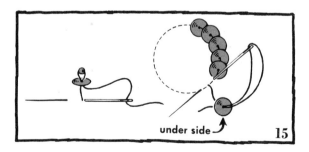

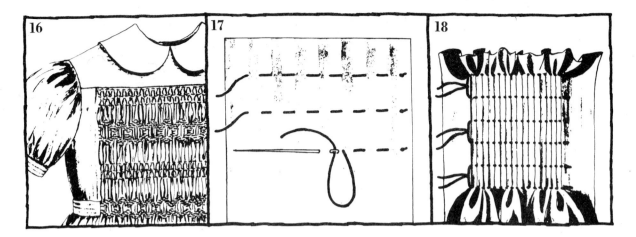

made strip, cut it a little longer than needed. Remove a few sequins at ends and tie thread-ends.

Attach with invisible stitches under sequins. To make a line of single sequins, work from right to left with a backstitch, as shown. Attach single, scattered sequins, with a bead at top, as shown.

SMOCKING

Smocking is most often done on children's clothes. However, where it suits the style, it can add a great deal to an adult garment.

Where a pattern calls for smocking, there will be a transfer sheet with guide-dots, and all necessary instructions. If you wish to add smocking on your own, there are certain things to be remembered:

. . . if possible, keep smocking clear of shaped edges, such as armholes (16). For a beginner, it is easiest to have the smocked section hang from a yoke.

. . . before smocking, fabric must measure three times the finished (smocked) width.

. . . smocking is done before garment is assembled.

In smocking the fabric is first evenly gathered on the wrong side, and gathers (pleats) are held together by embroidery on the right side. Evenness in gathering is essential. Striped (3 mm.) or checked (3 mm. or 6 mm.) fabric provides a built-in guide, and is highly recommended, especially for beginners. With striped

fabric, horizontal guidelines must be added on wrong side with pencil and yardstick, placed to correspond more or less with the embroidery pattern.

Gathering—Use a strong thread of contrasting colour, with a large knot. On wrong side of fabric, lift each stripe as shown (17). Leave thread hanging at end of each row. When all rows are threaded, pull up threads, forming even pleats (18), to a trifle over desired finished width. Secure threads by knotting two rows together as shown. Holding fabric firmly, stroke pleats in position.

General Rules for Embroidering—Depending on effect required use Clark's Anchor Stranded Cotton, Clark's Anchor Coton à Broder or Clark's Anchor Pearl Cotton No. 5 or 8. Work on right side of fabric, from left to right. To start, bring needle out in first pleat; take two tiny backstitches over fold or pleat to secure thread. After finishing a row, bring needle to wrong side through fold of last pleat. Take two small backstitches over pleat; cut thread. If a new length of thread is needed within row, finish old length as just described. Make a knot in new length and bring to right side on the same pleat on which old length stopped. When all embroidery is completed, snip gathering threads on wrong side and draw out.

A great variety of embroidery stitches are used in smocking, often modified by the pattern they form with the pleats. We give you here the Surface Honeycomb Stitch and the Trellis Stitch.

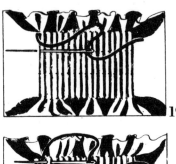

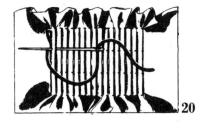

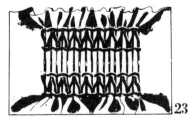

Surface Honeycomb Stitch
To start, see general rules.

With thread *above* needle, put needle through first pleat as shown (19), about 6 mm. below first stitch, With thread *below* needle, put needle through second pleat at same level (20). Draw thread tightly together.

Put needle through same pleat at same level as first stitch (21). With thread *above* needle, put needle through third pleat at same level (22). Draw tightly together. Repeat to end of row. Repeat row as desired (23).

Trellis Stitch
To start, see general rules.

With thread *above* needle, put needle through second pleat (24), slanting needle slightly downward. Put needle through third pleat in same way (25).

With thread *below* needle, put needle through fourth pleat *horizontally* (26).

Put needle through fifth and sixth pleats, slanting needle slightly *up*. With thread *above* needle, make seventh stitch horizontal. Repeat this pattern to the end of the row (27). Repeat the row as often as desired (28).

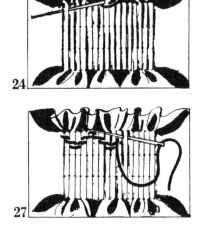

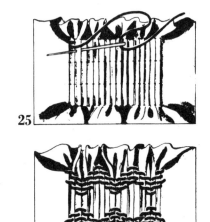

Easing

Easing disposes of small amounts of fullness caused by a fabric edge being longer than the edge to which it is joined (in a seam), or the area to which it is attached (in a hem). For easing a hem edge see HEMS, p. 93.

Easing in seams usually takes place between notches and is indicated on the pattern. A sleeve cap may be eased to the armhole, the back edge of a shoulder seam to the front (1), the back edge of an underarm sleeve seam to the front edge. Ideally, easing should be invisible after pressing. However, fabrics treated for 'easy-care' and such can never be pressed entirely smooth, since they resist easing.

THE HOW-TO OF EASING IN A SEAM

Always ease the longer edge to the shorter; *never stretch* the shorter edge.

The first thing after cutting out (when stay-stitching, if piece is staystitched), make a row of stitching on seamline, using a slightly long stitch (2).

When ready to join sections, pin at notches and other marks. Draw up one end of easing thread(s) until edges match. Holding edge as shown (3), work fabric along easing thread with thumb and fore-finger until fullness is distributed smoothly and evenly, with no suggestion of pleats. In a sleeve cap, draw up first one half of edge, then the other half.

Stitch seam with eased edge on top, for better control.

With edge of iron, press stitched line as is, seam closed, then press seam open.

In *wool*—and wool only—the ease can be shrunk out while pressing the seam open. Work over pressing ham or sleeve board. With a steam iron, hold iron over eased area, and allow steam to penetrate fabric, then lower iron and apply light pressure until ease has disappeared. Use dampened press cloth and touch lightly with hot, dry iron. Other fabrics are handled in the same way, but will not really shrink, although untreated natural fibres may do so to a slight extent. The important thing here is to press seam only, using point of iron, as putting the iron down flat may make creases out of the slight indication of gathers.

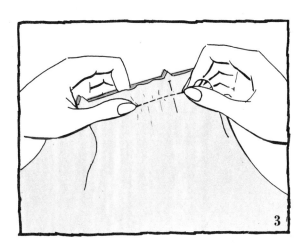

Equipment

A craftsman is no better than his tools. Try not to stint on the quality of your equipment. Invest in the best and give it your best care. You don't need to buy it all at once. In the listing that follows, we have marked with an asterisk the articles you can't reasonably do without (most are quite inexpensive). You can acquire the rest as you go along.

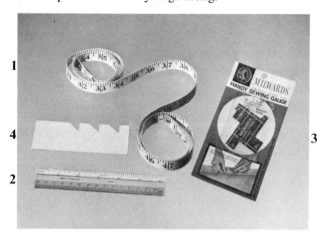

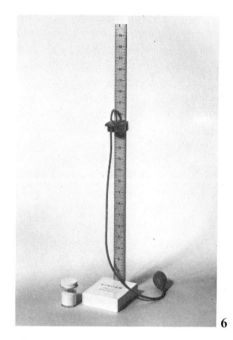

FOR MEASURING

*Tape Measure (1)—Usually 152 cm. long, with metal ends. A good tape measure will not stretch, and has measurements clearly marked on both sides, starting at opposite ends.

*152 mm. Ruler (2)—For marking hem-depth, buttonholes, pockets, etc.

Hem Gauge—A Milward hem gauge for hems of up to 50 mm. (3) or a self-made gauge (4) is handy for marking hems, etc.

*Yardstick (5)—Indispensable for marking straight long lines; often used for marking hemlines from the floor. Should be firm and straight, with smooth edges and clear markings. Metric stick in preparation.

Skirt Marker (6)—This model, worked with a bulb and powdered chalk, allows you to do the job alone.

FOR CUTTING

Scissors—Good scissors make all the difference, and with care last a lifetime. Buy the best you can afford, and treat them with respect: keep sharp, do not drop or use on heavy paper or cardboard, and use another pair for household chores.

*Dressmaker Shears (7)—For cutting out fabric. Bent handles make for accuracy, because they allow fabric to remain flat on table. A 178 mm. or 203 mm. overall length is good. Left-hand models are available.

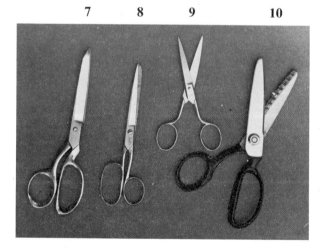

Small Scissors (8)—For general sewing use, trimming seams, clipping threads, etc. A 152 mm. or 178 mm. overall length is recommended.

Sewing and Embroidery Scissors (9)—Equipped with two sharp points, for cutting buttonholes, clipping, and other fine work. You will find these most useful in a 102 mm. or 127 mm. overall length.

Pinking Shears (10)—For finishing seams (never to be used for cutting out). A 190 mm. overall length is good. Left-hand models are available.

***Cutting Surface*—Should be at least 76 cm. wide and 112 cm. long.

FOR MARKING

Milward Dressmaker's Carbon Tracing Paper and Tracing Wheel (11)—For transferring pattern markings to fabric. Paper comes in several colours. See MARKING.

***Tailor's Chalk** (12)—Also used for transferring pattern markings to fabric.

FOR SEWING

***Sewing Machine**—Your major investment. It may be quite small—good second-hand machines are often available—or quite large. Let your budget—and your sewing ambitions!—be your guide. In addition, you will have to decide whether you want to buy [a] a Cabinet or a Portable model; [b] a Straight Stitch or a Zigzag machine.

[a] ...A cabinet model needs room-space of its own. However, it has the advantage not only of being always at hand and ready for work, but also of providing a wide surface, flush with the machine itself, on which to spread your work. Some cabinets also have drawers for keeping gadgets handy.

...A Portable model is useful where space is limited. The machine is usually set up on a table. When buying a portable, check on its weight, to make sure you can lift it easily.

[b] ...Whether you buy a Straight Stitch or Zigzag model depends on the kind of sewing you expect to do. The Zigzag model does straight stitch ordinarily,

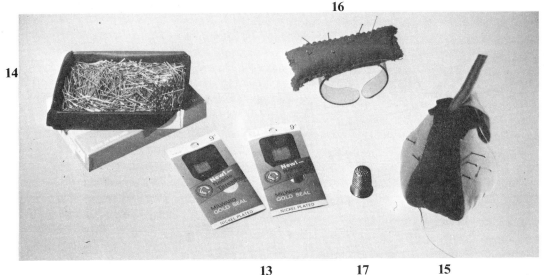

but can swing into zigzag without a separate attachment. If you intend to do decorative stitching (machine embroidery), you will enjoy this feature. Otherwise, zigzag stitch is used mainly for finishing seam allowances and making buttonholes. On a straight stitch machine, a separate attachment makes very good buttonholes.

Whatever type of machine you buy, you will do well to add, right at the outset: (1) a supply of extra bobbins, and (2) a zipper foot.

*Needles (13)—For hand- and machine-sewing. Be sure to have a variety of sizes on hand. See THREAD AND NEEDLES.

*Pins (14)—Use dressmaker steel pins.

*Pincushion (15)—To avoid scattering pins. A wrist pincushion (16) is handiest. You can buy one; or make one by sewing a pincushion to elastic.

*Thimble (17)—For faster, easier hand-sewing, train yourself to use a thimble. Whether it is of metal or of plastic, make sure that it fits the middle finger of your sewing hand.

FOR PRESSING

(here you draw on your household equipment)

*A Good Iron (18) must be on hand, set up, and ready for use throughout any dressmaking (see PRESSING). A combination steam/dry iron is the most satisfactory.

*Press Cloth—Recommended because most fabrics tend to shine if they come in direct contact with iron, and cloth can be dampened to provide the moisture needed for proper pressing of most fabrics. You can buy a piece of unbleached muslin, about 36 cm. × 76 cm., washed to remove sizing, or you can use a piece of old sheeting.

*Ironing Board (19) should be firm and well-padded, its cover clean at all times.

Sleeve-Board (20) is useful for pressing seams in sleeves and other narrow spaces; the ends are good for darts and curved edges. It should be well-padded (add padding as necessary, using old blanket).

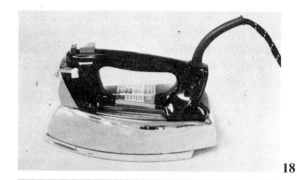

18

19

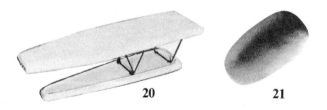

20   21

*Pressing Ham (21)—A firmly-packed, rounded pressing cushion, excellent for pressing curved seams, darts, and especially sleeve caps.

Dress Form—A form to your specific measurements is helpful, especially if you are hard to fit. A number of kinds are available, varying greatly in price.

Fabrics

In the past two decades fabrics have been going through a revolution coupled with an explosion. In the face of all the new man-made fibres, and the new finishes applied to the old ones—a field far too wide to cover here—all we can do is give you such information as will be of use to you in buying and handling fabric.

THE NATURAL FIBRES TODAY

In general, the following improvements may be looked for in the natural fibres:

Woollens, especially the better domestic ones, are now almost always preshrunk, and sometimes washable.

Linens have been made crease-resistant.

Cottons are usually shrink-resistant and, where absorbency (as in terry cloth) is not a factor, have been treated for drip-dry performance—for handling, see **Wash-and-Wear Fabrics**, p. 72.

Silk is much what it used to be, its performance varying with its quality.

THE NEW FABRICS

It would be impossible to enumerate all the new fabrics, let alone describe them. They may consist of 100 per cent synthetics (often a blend of several), or of a blend of man-made and natural fibres. Taken all together, they represent an enormous advance in convenience, wearing properties, variety, and cost-for-performance. They are almost always crease- and shrink-resistant. If they are not always washable, this is due to special texturing rather than to the fibre. To avoid scorching, a cool iron should be used for pressing all synthetic fabrics.

There is, of course, a reverse side to the picture. The new fabrics, and the old ones treated with the new finishes, are not as pliant or absorbent, and are resistant to shaping, often even to pins and needles—see **Buying Fabric**, p. 65, and **Wash-and-Wear Fabrics**, p. 72. Almost all the new fabrics should be handled like **Wash-and-Wear**.

FABRIC CONSTRUCTION

Woven and knitted fabrics—also lace and net—are made from yarn, or thread, spun from one or several of the fibres. Other fabrics, classified as 'non-woven', are made from unspun fibres which are felted or bonded together.

Woven Fabrics

Every woven fabric, no matter what its surface is like, consists of lengthwise threads (warp) through which crosswise threads (called woof, weft, or filling) are woven over and under, back and forth. The basic principle is illustrated here (1). Edges (selvages) are reinforced by doubling the number of warp threads at the sides.

Examine the three basic weaves, shown here (2) greatly enlarged. Note how the diagonal effect of twill weave and the smooth surface of satin weave are achieved, with the direction of threads remaining invariably lengthwise-crosswise.

The same is true of **nap** and **pile** fabrics. A nap is

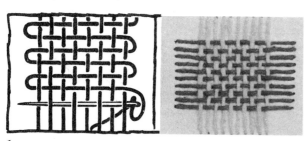
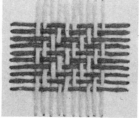

1   PLAIN WEAVE   TWILL WEAVE   SATIN WEAVE   2

created by simply brushing up the natural fuzziness of certain fibres. In pile fabrics, the 'stand-up' threads are added to the basic weave.

Woven fabric, therefore, always has a lengthwise and a crosswise direction, or 'grain.' As it comes from the loom, before it is processed with a **finish**, the fabric is 'grain-perfect', i.e., the lengthwise and crosswise threads run straight, at true right angles to each other.

Knitted Fabrics

The three basic knits, mostly made on circular knitting machines, are shown here enlarged (3).

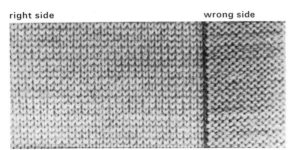

right side   wrong side

JERSEY—single-thread knit, exact reproduction of hand-knitting.

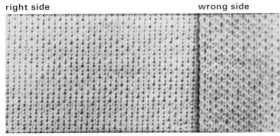

right side   wrong side

DOUBLE-KNIT—two interlacing threads; both sides of fabric very similar.

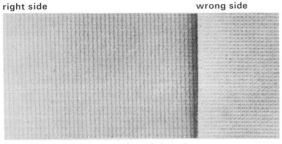

right side   wrong side

TRICOT—knit with a number of threads.

3

Knitted fabrics are not said to have grain. What they have is a *rib*, visible on the right side or on both sides. It is the rib that gives the true lengthwise direction.

Lace (4) and Net

Lace and net are made on special, very intricate machines, from almost any fibre. Since these fabrics have no grain, you follow the design, if any, for lengthwise or crosswise direction.

4

Non-Woven Fabrics

The fabrics described as 'non-woven' are made of fibres either matted together by steam (felt) or bonded by chemicals (synthetics). The synthetics are mainly used for interfacing. Unless these fabrics have a printed design, they can be cut in any direction, and have the advantage of not ravelling or curling at the edges.

FABRIC FINISHES

All commercial fabrics (which do not include hand-weaves, imported or other), are processed with a *finish* when they come from the loom. These finishes in the course of application frequently pull the crosswise threads out of line.

Surface finishes such as the application of a print or a glaze, or the raising of a nap, need not concern us here.

Of the other finishes, the only ones of importance to us are the **permanent finishes**, and their presence or absence in a fabric. These are the new finishes that have made such a difference in fabric performance. New ones are being invented every day. They are responsible for wash-and-wear properties, shrink-resistance, stain- and mildew-resistance, 'permanent press', etc. With the exception of shrink-resistance, however, these finishes have a drastic effect on the fabric grain, which they lock into position, whether distorted or not.

BUYING A FABRIC

Your pattern envelope will tell you what **type of fabric** is suitable and what **amount** you will need.

You will note that yardages indicated are always specified 'without nap' or 'with nap'. 'With nap' takes a little more fabric because, nap running in one lengthwise direction, the pattern pieces will all have to be laid out with their top edges facing the same way. 'Nap', however, does not cover the situation. Any fabric that looks different when held up or down has the same requirement. This means that the *design* (print, weave, check) may go in one direction; or the *weave* (gabardine, twill, whipcord, flannel, satin and sateen) reflects light differently in the two directions; or the *texture* (nap and pile fabrics) looks different.

Still more yardage is needed when a design (check or other) is to be matched at the seams—the larger the design the greater the yardage allowance necessary.

See CUTTING for further details.

Irregular designs, such as florals, need not be matched.

The Fabric Properties

Making sure of fabric properties when buying has become a complex problem.

A man-made fibre, simply by the process of becoming cloth, usually imitates one of the natural ones, often so successfully that we cannot tell them apart. Besides, the old fabrics now imitate each other, and all are blended in countless combinations. As for the finishes that will improve fabric performance—easy-care, crease- and shrink-resistance, stain- and

mildew-resistance—if they are present, they will be indicated on the label.

In short, it is the **label** we go by today (5). If it does not carry the information you want, inquire of the salesperson (or you may find it necessary to go as far as the buyer).

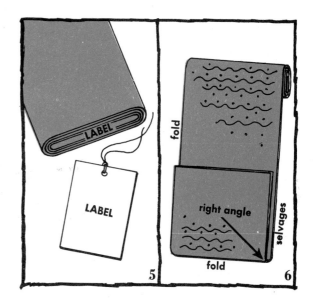

NOTE: In the many small stores where beautiful fabrics are sold, the label may be absent. Here you can only trust your judgment, or go by whatever verbal information you may obtain. Fabric that is 100 per cent synthetic (except rayon) may usually be counted on to have the new permanent finishes. With the other fibres, you should look for specific indication of finish.

Shrink-resistance, indicated by 'Sanforized', 'Preshrunk', or some other descriptive term, is an unqualified *plus* which does not affect response to shaping, grain correction, etc.

The other permanent finishes—crease-resistance, stain-resistance, 'easy-care', 'drip-dry', 'permanent press,' etc., have the effect of locking the grain in position. Where such a finish is present, you are safe with solid colours or overall irregular designs. Where, however, there is a design (checks, or printed motif) that must be at right angles to selvages (in knits, to lengthwise rib), make sure that the design is not out of line, as it will be impossible to straighten it. Before ordering yardage cut, unroll about a yard from the bolt; fold back half a yard, matching selvages (6). If design is not even with fold the fabric will never give satisfaction (on fabric with a lengthwise centre fold, check inside your fold, too).

PREPARING FABRIC FOR USE

A great many fabrics nowadays need no preparation whatsoever (of the fabrics given special notice in the pages that follow, only wool knits, if not pre-shrunk, will need some preparation).

Woven wool, cotton, linen, silk and rayon must be checked for *straightness of grain* and, if necessary, straightened.

Wool, cotton and linen that do not carry one of the non-shrink guarantees (sanforized, etc.), can be *shrunk before using*, whether they are washable or to be dry-cleaned (steam-pressing shrinks fibres).

To test for shrinkage, wash a measured square of fabric, leave it to dry, then press, do not iron. If the fabric has shrunk the measurement will be smaller than the original.

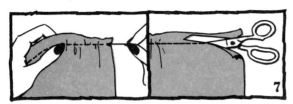

To **straighten fabric**, trim one cut end along a cross-wise thread (if grain is not clearly visible, draw up a thread and cut along pucker, (7)). This should only be done on fabrics which are evenly woven. It is sometimes possible to correct a 'squint' fabric, by grasping the two selvage edges on the bias (two people are needed for wide fabric) and pulling (8). Repeat at various points until ends are even.

To **shrink a washable fabric**:
. . . leave folded and wet thoroughly (9).

To dry, hang smoothly over a straight rod; if grain needs straightening, spread fabric flat, smoothing it so selvages and ends are at right angles to one another (check against table-edges).

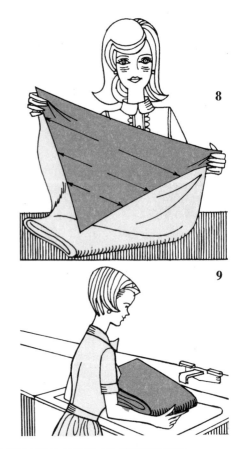

HANDLING THE DIFFERENT FABRICS

We don't have to tell you that chiffon requires a more delicate touch than denim. Any fabric, however, even the sturdiest, is better off for being handled as lightly and as little as possible. This is one reason why sewing techniques are always planned for minimum handling.

The directions throughout this book—which, for happy results, you should look up as you go along and faithfully follow—apply to standard fabrics in standard weights. Certain fabrics, however, require special handling. **Bonded Fabrics, Fake Fur, Knits, Lace, Pile Fabrics, Sheers, Stretch Fabrics, Vinyl,** and **Wash-and-Wear** are each given a section, in alphabetical order, in the pages that follow, with instructions as to the points at which they need special handling. Any detail not mentioned should be handled in the standard manner.

Bonded Fabrics

These consist of a face-fabric fused to a backing fabric. This generally makes a backing unnecessary and ensures that a garment will keep its shape through dry-cleaning or washing (the label will tell you which). Bonded fabrics are gaining so rapidly in popularity and scope that the face-fabric may now be woven or knitted out of practically any fibre or blend; the backing fabric is usually nylon tricot, woven cotton or acetate. Lining may be added or not, as desired.

Cutting—Cut with face-fabric up, so you can use its lengthwise grain for 'straight of goods', or its pattern for matching.

Pressing—Set iron for the fibre on the side which you are pressing. Test first on a scrap of fabric.

Seams—On unlined coats and jackets, make flat-felled seams as follows: After stitching, separate backing fabric from face-fabric on one seam allowance and trim face-fabric to 3 mm. (10). Trim other seam allowance to 6 mm. With full-width seam allowance (backing) on top, fold all seam allowances to one side; fold in raw edge of backing fabric and topstitch or slipstitch fold to garment (11).

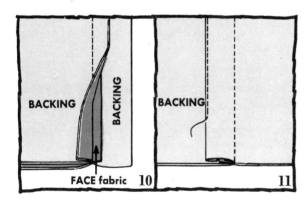

Hem—Sew to backing fabric only.

Buttonholes—Machine-made or bound buttonholes are suitable.

Fake Fur

Technically described as deep-pile fabric, fake fur has a pile of synthetic yarn, and a back, or founda-tion, of woven or knitted fabric, synthetic or cotton. Some fake furs are washable, but most require dry-cleaning.

Pattern—Use simple pattern with few seams, a minimum of detail and darts. Avoid buttonholes—use loops, frogs, or snaps for fastenings.

Backing and Lining—Lining is not strictly necessary except for coats and jackets, but fake fur is more comfortable when lined. If back of fabric is not firmly woven, add backing.

Facings—Facings of self-fabric are recommended only on coats and jackets and when pile is medium-weight. For facing heavy-pile coats and jackets, substitute a suitable lighter-weight fabric (tweed, flannel, etc.).

Preparation of Fabric—Straighten raw edges by cutting along one thread of a woven back; or cut along a line drawn at right angles to rib of a knit-ted fabric. Be sure to check label for shrinking information.

Pattern Alterations—Trim away pattern margins, if any, to make it easier to cut an even edge on bulky fabric. *Do not cut away seam allowances.* Reduce bulk by eliminating seams wherever possible: When a straight edge is to be faced with self-fabric, cut body section and facing in one piece. When a centre seam is on straight grain, cut as if marked to be placed on fold.

Cutting—See **With Nap**, p. 46, and **Cutting Through a Single Thickness**, p. 50. Determine whether you want pile running up or down. Work with fabric spread out wrong side up, and pin pattern to back only.

Marking—Do not cut notches; make marks with chalk on seam allowances, on wrong side. To mark darts, use tailor tacking, pins, or chalk.

Pressing—Pressing with any iron will mat pile. For seams, see below.

Stitching—Never machine-stitch on right side of fabric. Stitch slowly, going in direction of pile, meanwhile pushing pile out of seamline (toward garment, not toward seam allowance) with blunt end of a long needle. After stitching, use long needle or fine comb to pull out (from right side) any pile caught in seam.

Darts—To eliminate bulk, slash through centre fold of dart, stitched as instructed; shear pile from both seam allowances. Sew edges to back of fabric.

Seams—To reinforce shoulder seam, pin pre-shrunk tape over seamline before stitching and include it in seam. To eliminate bulk, shear pile from all seam allowances. Since seams cannot be pressed, open with thumbnail and catch edges of seam allowances to back of fabric.

Facings—Do not understitch or topstitch a facing seam. To keep facing from rolling, pin facing to garment with a line of pins 13 mm. from facing seam. Fold facing back on pin-line and catchstitch to garment (12).

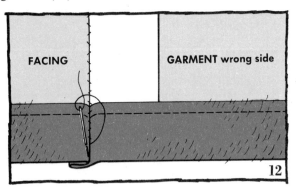

Hems—Catch raw edge of hem to back of fabric.

Zip-fasteners—Use a semi-concealed application. Shear pile off seam allowances. Sew zip-fastener in by hand.

Knits

These may be made from any fibre, natural or synthetic; they are appreciated, among other things, for crease-resistance. Their drawback used to be their tendency to stretch and sag, but this has now largely been overcome with 'no-sag' treatment (see label on fabric). Wool knits not labelled 'pre-shrunk' will need shrinking before use (see p. 66).

Pattern—Circular skirts and bias cuts should be avoided, since knits do not look right on the bias.

Jersey—which comes in both light and medium weights, has a soft look and is well adapted to dresses with draping or design ease. Select simple designs.

Double-knit fabric comes in medium and heavy weight. It combines flexibility with firmness, and is easy to handle and stitch. It is particularly suitable for tailored styles.

When buying a print with a crosswise design, make sure that the *design* is at right angles to the ribs in fabric—not the *fold*.

Preparation—If fabric comes in tubular form, cut it open at one fold, but follow a *rib*, not the fold. Press out other fold—if it refuses to be pressed out, avoid it when laying out pattern (see CUTTING). Make a line of basting along a rib near centre, as a guide for 'Straight of Goods', or 'Straight Grain'.

To control stretch—Stay-stitch all edges of cut-out sections. Pin-baste or thread-baste seams.

Seams—To protect unbacked, very lightweight knits (e.g., nylon jersey) against abrasion by feed dog, place 38 mm. strips of tissue paper under seams while stitching. Then tear away paper.

. . . Zigzag stitch is often found to work well in seams (use smallest bight—see manual).

. . . To stabilize shoulder seams, pin pre-shrunk tape under seam before stitching; include it in seam.

. . . To prevent seam allowances from rolling, make a line of stitching 6 mm. from edge, or finish edges with zigzag stitching.

Bias Binding—The greatest 'give' in knit fabrics is crosswise, not on the bias, as in weaves. For bias binding, cut strip across width of fabric.

Buttonholes—Both bound and machine-worked buttonholes are suitable. For either, first stabilize buttonhole area by pressing oval-shaped patch of very lightweight iron-on interfacing to wrong side of outer garment section.

Lace

May be heavy, fine and filmy, or any stage between. Heavy laces usually contain a considerable proportion of cotton; the others are made of all kinds of fibres and blends.

A decorative lace edge to be used as a finish may be present on the fabric when bought, taking the place of selvage on one or both edges. Otherwise, such an edge can be hand-clipped from the lace when there is a regularly-repeated motif along an edge. Working around the motifs, just clip through the short threads that attach the 'in-between' lace to the motif (13).

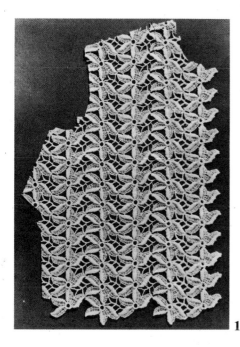

13

Pattern—Choose a simple design with few seams in order to avoid cutting up lace design. Avoid button-holes if possible—button loops of lining or backing fabric can be used instead.

Backing and Lining—Any lace garment not worn over a suitable garment or undergarment must be backed—sometimes both backed and lined. Backing may be transparent, sheer, or opaque; lining is usually opaque. Net is a transparent backing. Sheer backing fabrics, most effective in self- or flesh-colour, include marquisette, organza, and organdie. Opaque fabrics, suitable for both backing and lining, include taffeta, peau de soie, and polished cotton.

Marking—Where there is an opaque backing, mark backing fabric only. Where there is a net backing or none, mark with tailor tacking or basting.

Pressing—For heavy lace, cover ironing board with terry cloth; press on wrong side.

Stitching—To prevent very fine lace from catching in feed dog, place 38 mm. strips of tissue paper under seams when stitching. After stitching, tear away tissue.

Darts—Make dart as usual. Where fabric, whether it includes backing or not, is transparent, make a second line of stitching 3 mm. from first (14); trim close to second line (15).

Seams—For transparent fabric, finish like darts above.

Edge-Finish—A facing, or a hem, made of a tulle (fine net) strip is practically invisible, and is excellent where there is no backing, or one of net. Cut a tulle strip 64 mm. wide on cross grain (tulle has more give on cross grain than on bias). Fold strip in half lengthwise. Stitch raw edges of strip to right side of garment edge, taking a 16 mm. seam allowance. In seam allowance, make second line of stitching 3 mm. from first; trim seam allowance close to second line. Turn tulle strip to wrong side along seamline; slip-stitch fold to garment (16).

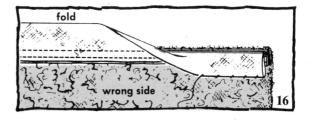

Zip-fastener—Apply as usual, but do last step (outside stitching) by hand.

Buttonholes—Whenever possible, avoid buttonholes. Button loops can be used instead. On backed garments, worked buttonholes are possible.

Pile Fabrics

This usually means cut pile fabrics, such as velvet, velveteen and corduroy (for **Fake Fur**, see that heading). They may be made of any fibre or combination of fibres (pile of one fibre; back, or foundation, of another).

Pattern—Choose a simple design with few seams. For velvet and velveteen do not plan buttonholes unless you have tried one first on a scrap of the fabric.

Cutting—Follow cutting layout 'With Nap' (see CUTTING, p. 46). To ascertain the way the pile 'runs', brush hand lightly over fabric surface: the smoother feel gives pile 'direction', which should go upward in garment for a richer colour.

Marking—Corduroy: any method is good. Velvet and velveteen: use tailor tacking or pins and chalk.

Basting—Hand-basting is necessary throughout, since pile shifts easily.

Pressing—This is a problem with all pile fabrics, velvet being the most difficult, corduroy the least. If fibre content of fabric makes eased seams (such as set-in sleeves) difficult, the fact that there can be no real pressing adds to the difficulty. Here are a few pointers:

. . . Never touch iron to right side of fabric.

. . . Your best help, as good as a 'velvet board', is a piece of your pile fabric, placed with pile to pile of garment. When pressing garment on wrong side, place piece on ironing board, pile side up. When pressing right side, place piece over garment, pile side down.

. . . In any case, always use steam, and press lightly, or you will flatten pile.

Zip-fasteners—Corduroy and velveteen: Proceed as for any fabric. Velvet: Do first step (anchoring zip-fastener) by machine; finish application by hand.

Buttonholes—Corduroy: any type buttonhole is suitable. For bound buttonholes, cut lips on bias.

Velvet and velveteen: avoid machine-worked buttonholes, since attachment marks pile. For bound buttonholes, cut lips on bias.

Sheer Fabrics

No matter what their fibre content, these must be handled carefully. They include dotted Swiss, voile, chiffon, organdie, and batiste, each available in a variety of fibres.

NOTE: A sheer fabric backed with opaque fabric is not handled as a sheer, but as standard fabric. What follows refers to unbacked sheers.

Pattern—Soft, feminine designs with fullness.

Cutting—Where an edge requires a facing, make the entire section double to avoid edges that will show through to right side. A sleeveless bodice, for instance, can be cut double in its entirety. The edges may then be finished with narrow French Binding or a Bias Facing. A shirt-dress type front-facing can be cut in one with the bodice section to eliminate a seam.

Marking—Use Tailor Tacking. Other marks show through on right side and pins slip out.

Basting—Many sheers, especially silks and synthetics, require hand-basting.

Pressing—Use dry iron on all sheers except cottons.

Stitching—To prevent very fine sheers from catching in feed dog, place 38 mm. strips of tissue paper under seams when stitching. After stitching, tear away tissue.

Darts—You can avoid a knot showing at point of dart—see DARTS, p. 52.

Seams and Bindings—Seams are visible from right side, and should be neat and narrow. Make **French Seams** (p. 147) or double-stitched seams (17). If you wish to bind garment edges, do it with a **French Binding** (see p. 25).

Hems—Up to 38 mm. wide on a full straight skirt; very narrow on a circular skirt. See HEMS.

Zip-fasteners—In unbacked sheers, pattern will often suggest snap fasteners instead of a zip-fastener. If a zip-fastener is used, do last step of application (outside stitching) by hand.

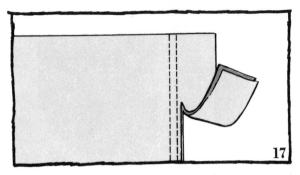

Buttonholes—Where buttonholes are made and buttons sewed on, area must be reinforced with lightweight interfacing. Since the patch of a bound buttonhole would show through, worked buttonholes are best.

Stretch Fabrics

The 'stretch' property, which allows a garment to 'give' while it is being worn and afterwards return to its original shape, is now being added to woven and knitted fabrics of all weights in every kind of fibre—natural, synthetic, or blended. Stretch may be crosswise, lengthwise, or both ways.

Fabrics with *lengthwise stretch* are generally used in slacks and shorts, and *both-ways stretch* in swimsuits and foundation garments.

Pattern—Buy same size as for regular fabric.

Backing, Lining, Interfacing—Stretch fabric is never backed, for obvious reasons. For lining, use tricot, or special lining fabric with 'stretch', and cut it in the same direction as outer fabric. Use interfacing only where stretch is not needed (waistband, lapels, etc.).

Cutting—Allow fabric to relax for 24 hours before cutting, since it is often stretched from being rolled on the bolt. Cut a waistband in direction opposite to stretch (to avoid its stretching).

Pressing—Set iron according to fibre content of fabric. Press lightly to avoid stretching.

Stitching—See heading **Pressure, Tension, Balance**, p. 107 under MACHINE-STITCHING. When stitching in direction of stretch, feed fabric slowly and evenly through machine.

Basting—Hand-baste slippery fabrics, pin-baste others. When stitching, remove pins as you go along.

Seams—Where no stretch is desired (for example, at shoulder seam), lay pre-shrunk seam tape over seamline and include it in stitching. To prevent seam allowances from rolling, make a line of machine-stitching 6 mm. from edge of each. On ravelly fabric, overcast edges by hand or finish with zigzag stitching.

Hems—Pink or overcast edge and make a couture hem.

Zip-fasteners—Apply zip-fasteners in regular manner. When garment has a lengthwise stretch, as in slacks, do outside stitching (last step) by hand.

Buttonholes—May be bound or machine-made. Stabilize buttonhole area by applying an oval patch of very lightweight iron-on interfacing to wrong side.

Vinyl (PVC)

Vinyl or PVC fabrics are increasing in popularity. The types that are available by the yard divide into two groups:

. . . those that are made by spraying clear polyvinylchloride on to fabrics, often printed cotton.

. . . those that are made by bonding a layer of vinyl onto a backing fabric, usually a jersey fabric, but occasionally foam which can have a surface texture to simulate leather.

The second group could of course be classed as bonded or laminated fabrics.

All these fabrics require special handling in making up with consideration for the main characteristics which are:

. . . a certain rigidity and limited draping qualities.

. . . holes made in the fabric are permanent.

. . . the fabrics have no grain and do not fray although the jersey-backed fabrics should be cut with the selvage running down as there is a certain 'give' across the width.

. . . hand-sewing is not easy.

Pattern—Choose a simple style with few seams and with raglan or kimono sleeves as it is difficult to deal with armhole curves and ease. Loose-fitting garments should be chosen with 'A' line skirts.

Pattern Alterations—Fit the pattern carefully before cutting out as any unpicking in the garment will leave holes in the fabric.

Lining—Loose-lining may be used although it is generally unnecessary with the jersey-backed vinyls.

Cutting—Cut out through single fabric, reversing the pattern pieces before cutting again. Spread the fabric wrong side up and attach the pattern with Sellotape instead of pins.

Marking—Mark turnings and darts on the wrong side using a grease pencil, lead pencil or dressmakers' carbon paper, and a knitting needle. A tracing wheel will leave holes.

Backing—Use paper clips or Sellotape for holding seams together while fitting. Any basting must be done in the seam allowance.

Pressing—Do not put an iron directly onto the vinyl side of the fabric. Pressing should be done on the wrong side with a steam iron or using a dry iron over a dry cloth.

Stitching—Use a medium-sized machine needle and set the machine to about 8–10 stitches to 25 mm. The vinyl side of the fabric will tend to stick to the feed dog but it helps to sprinkle talcum powder on the fabric and also to place a sheet of typing paper under the seam, tearing it away after stitching. Always machine slowly oiling the needle occasionally if it sticks in the fabric.

Some of the leather-look jersey-backed vinyls can only be machined with the wrong side of the fabric against foot and against the feed dog and in this case all top-stitching must be avoided.

Avoid hand-sewing where possible.

Darts—Stitch darts to gradual points to avoid bulges at the point.

Seams—Use plain seams or welt seams depending on the type of fabric. Snip all curves well to allow seams to lie flat.

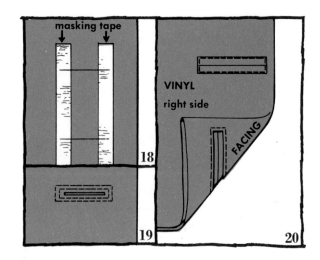

Buttonholes—Make machine-made or bound buttonholes, interfacing the area with an iron-on non-woven interfacing. Mark the position of the buttonholes by accurately scoring the surface with a sharp point, then mark the ends with Sellotape or masking tape (18).

As the fabric does not fray it is possible to machine round twice and cut a slit for the buttonhole (19).

To finish the facing on the back of an ordinary bound buttonhole reinforce with a rectangle of stitching, then cut away a rectangle of fabric (20).

Hems—Keep hems fairly narrow and stick hem with adhesive. A row of large machine stitches can be worked afterwards as decoration if desired.

Wash-and-Wear Fabrics

Also described as drip-dry, easy-care, etc., these are woven or knitted fabrics that are washable, quick-drying, and need little or no ironing. Available in a great variety of weights and textures, they may be made of

. . . 100 per cent synthetic yarns
. . . blended-fibre yarns
. . . treated cotton, wool, or rayon.

The 'wash-and-wear' finish, valuable in itself, also makes the fabric surface smoother and harder, the fabric less pliable and more resistant to handling. It cannot, for instance, be shrunk or shaped by steaming (as for easing a sleeve cap to an armhole) and it may have a springiness that resists a sharp, clean edge-fold or seam. It also tends to pucker at the seams.

Pattern—Choose an uncomplicated design (you may even wish to avoid set-in sleeves), not broken by too many seams. The tendency to pucker is greater on straight-grain seams than on off-grain or bias seams. Therefore, with hard-finish wash-and-wear such as a 'permanent press' fabric, avoid long zip-fasteners on straight grain, and cut facings in one piece with body sections to avoid seams on long, straight edges.

Notions, linings, etc.—A wash-and-wear garment must be wash-and-wear throughout: choose any backing or lining accordingly. Use a strip of your selvage for a waist stay, and avoid seam binding on hems. Make shoulder pads, if any, with self-fabric, and stuff them with Terylene batting; or make them removable.

Cutting—If fabric comes folded through centre, try to press out fold before laying out pattern. If it will not come out, arrange pattern to avoid fold (see CUTTING). If the crosswise threads of fabric are off-grain, you can disregard the fact in the case of solid colours, all-over prints or irregular designs—just place straight-grain marking on pattern parallel to selvage, as usual. Since the finish holds the shape, the garment will still hang right. If, however, you

have made the mistake of acquiring fabric with a design (checks or other) that should be at right angles to selvage but is not (see **Buying Fabric**, p. 65), *follow the design* in placing pattern. The result will not be really satisfactory, but you have no other choice.

Marking—On a smooth fabric of solid colour, the tracing wheel alone (without carbon paper) will often make a sufficiently visible mark (21). Tailor's chalk can also be used. Otherwise, use markings according to type of fabric—sheers, deep pile, etc.

Stitching—Proper **Pressure, Tension** and **Balance** in your sewing machine are of greater importance with these fabrics than with any others. See that heading on p. 107 under MACHINE-STITCHING.

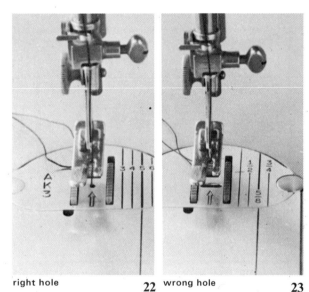

right hole   **22** wrong hole   **23**

Use a throat plate with a round hole (22). The wider oval hole of zigzag machines (23) allows the fabric to be drawn into the hole, and the seam becomes puckered.

Pressing—Three points must be remembered when pressing wash-and-wear:

. . . after setting iron for proper fibre content, *test it* on a scrap of your fabric before using,

. . . creases, once pressed in, stay in. Hence,

. . . be sure of your seamlines (i.e., do your trying on and adjusting) before pressing.

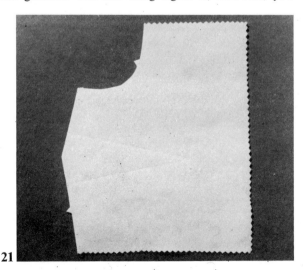

21

Good sewing techniques are particularly important with wash-and-wear; see chapters on SEAMS, HEMS, FACINGS, etc. If your fabric falls under one of the headings that precede this one, there you will find additional pointers on handling.

Facings

A facing is a piece of fabric that doubles and finishes an edge. It is usually a separate piece stitched to the edge (shaped or fitted facing), but may be cut as an extension to the edge (extended facing). A third kind of facing is the bias facing. Complete descriptions follow. A facing is generally on the inside of a garment, but for a decorative purpose may be on the outside (see p. 79). For a lapel, a finished inside facing is partly folded to the outside.

Facings are usually made of the same fabric as the garment. However, a smoother or a lighter-weight fabric may be used to reduce bulk, or for comfort; and a contrasting texture or colour may be part of a design.

A **shaped or fitted facing** (1) is a separate piece of fabric cut to match the outer sections, and on the same grain. Shaped facings (usually with interfacing) are used at front and back openings; at neck and sleeveless armhole edges, and at the underside of shaped collars and cuffs.

An **extended facing** (2) is cut in one piece with the outer garment section, from a single pattern piece. Extended facings (generally with interfacing) are used at front and back openings, and as the underside of straight collars and cuffs.

A **bias facing** (3) is made of a bias strip. It is used on gently-curved edges, such as hems, open necklines, and sleeve edges, and is never interfaced.

OUTER GARMENT SECTION

INTERFACING

FACING wrong side

SHAPED or FITTED FACING

1

fold line

OUTER GARMENT SECTION

FACING

INTERFACING

EXTENDED FACING

2

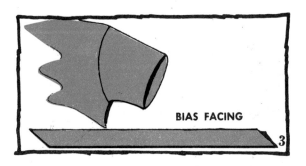

BIAS FACING

3

A well-applied facing has sharp, clean edges and smooth, flat-lying surfaces. These are ensured by attention to the small details in the application, particularly in **Processing the Seam**, pp. 76–77.

NOTE: A special application, which eliminates raw edges of facing and interfacing on washable garments with worked buttonholes (blouses, children's dresses, etc.), will be found under INTERFACING, p. 103.

SHAPED FACING AND EXTENDED FACING

Preparing the Facing

Stay-stitch curved and bias edges to be seamed: join pieces if there are more than one.

If free edge (not to be seamed) is not to be covered by a lining, make a line of stitching 6 mm. from edge.

Finish according to weight of fabric:

. . . on light or medium-weight fabrics, 'clean-finish', i.e., fold raw edge on stitching line and topstitch close to edge (4),

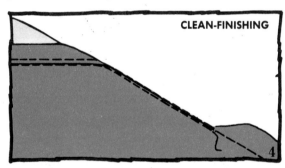

. . . on heavy fabric, pink raw edge outside stitched line (5),

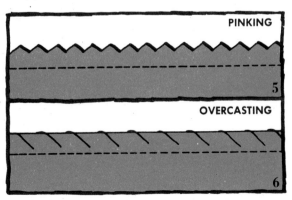

. . . on heavy, ravelly fabrics, overcast raw edge, either by hand (6) or by machine.

Seaming the Facing

Pin or baste facing to corresponding outer section, right sides together, edges and construction marks carefully matched.

. . . if facing is smaller than outer section (a neckline facing, for instance), stitch with facing on top for better control (7).

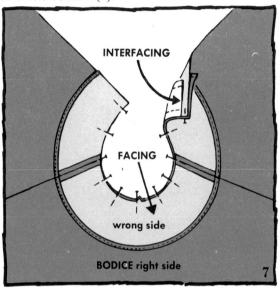

Stitch facing seam as follows:

. . . if seam takes in no outside corners, stitch entire facing to garment in one operation.

. . . if seam takes in outside corners, first stitch the edge between corners and process that seam (i.e., trim, grade, clip, understitch—see p. 76). Then, crossing stitching line at corners as shown, stitch the other edges. In a collar-and-facing assemblage (8), stitch and process the seam in the a-b-c order shown.

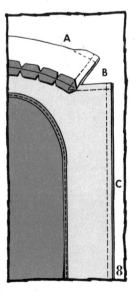

When stitching:

Keep seam even; even a slight irregularity will show on finished edge. Use a seam gauge or mark seamline.

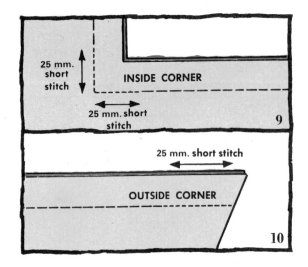

Reinforce corners by shortening stitch (9, 10).

Processing the Seam

Here, in the order in which they are to be dealt with, are the details that make all the difference. Pick out the ones that apply to your seam.

Trim off points close to stitching (11).

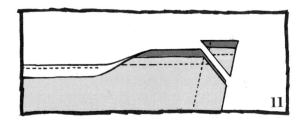

Underpress short seams and lapel seams, neither of which can be understitched (underpressing will flatten seam for a sharp edge in final pressing). Before trimming, open out seam and, on a sleeve board or over a pencil wrapped in cloth (12), press seam open with point of iron only.

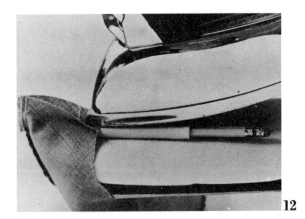

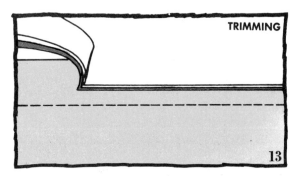

Trim all seam allowances to 6 mm. (13).

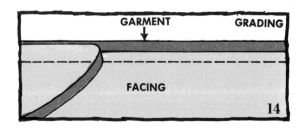

Grade seam allowances, i.e., trim facing seam allowances once more, to 3 mm. (14). If there are more than two thicknesses besides interfacing, trim them to graduated widths between 3 mm. and 6 mm.

Taper outside corners after grading; i.e., trim toward corner as shown (15).

Clip most seam allowances to allow a seam to lie flat after facing is turned. A clip is a straight cut through seam allowance to within a thread of the stitching line. Clip once into a corner (16); clip enough times around a curve to make it lie flat (17,

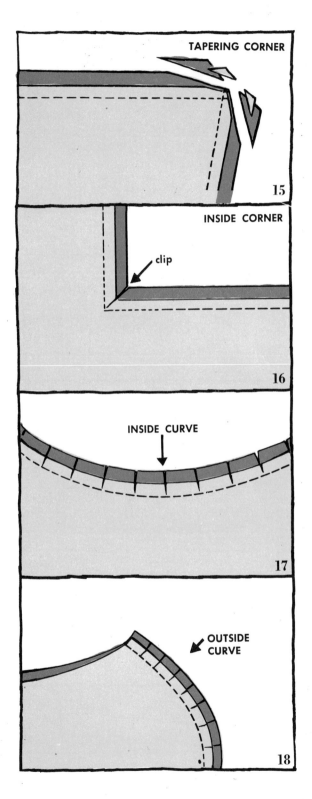

18). The more pronounced the curve and the firmer the fabric, the more clips are needed. They may be as close as 6 mm.

Understitch all facing seams except [a] seams less than 76 mm. long, such as the ends of a straight collar, and [b] seams where understitching would show, as on a lapel. Understitching guarantees that facing will not roll to outside. Place work on machine with facing opened out, right side up. Turn all seam allowances smoothly under facing.

On facing, stitch very close to seam, through all thicknesses (19). On a facing with a lapel, have understitching stop just short of point where lapel is folded to outside. On an outside corner, stop about 25 mm. short of corner.

Press all faced edges carefully after folding facing to inside, on seam. To avoid a shine along edges, use a press cloth with a dry iron. On dark fabrics, use a press cloth even with a steam iron.

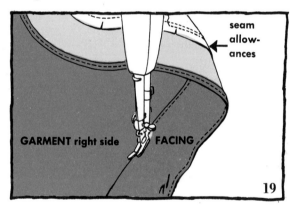

Fastening the Facing

The free edge of a shaped or extended inside facing is never entirely sewn down. However, after garment is otherwise completed, and before lining, if any, is sewn in, the facing and interfacing are fastened in place as follows:

Catch raw edge of interfacing to finished free edge of facing, taking long stitches on interfacing and short stitches on facing.

Tack free edge of facing to inside of garment as

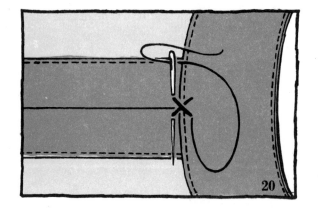

shown (20) wherever there is more than one thickness of fabric (seams and darts).

Anchor facing if fabric is springy or seamed edge will not lie flat. This is done at cross seams (21). Use matching thread. Starting at edge, on outside of garment, machine- or hand-stitch exactly through seam for 25 mm., or more if desired (22). Pull threads to wrong side and tie. This stitching will not show if correctly done.

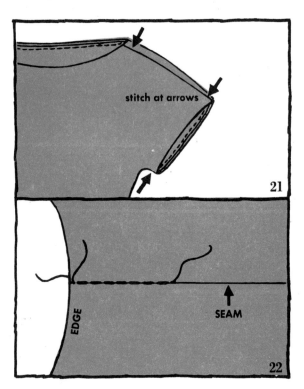

BIAS FACING

A bias facing consists of a bias strip of even width. Join bias strips as necessary (see BIAS, p. 23). If facing is to be applied to a curve, steam-press or 'swirl' entire strip into a curve (23).

Make a line of stitching 6 mm. from outer edge of strip (edge not taken in seam). Stitch strip to edge of garment, right sides together.

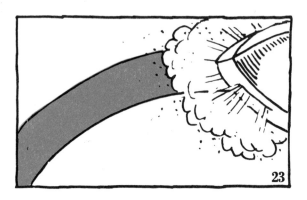

Process seam as described on p. 76 (i.e., trim, grade, clip, understitch). Fold facing on seamline. Turn raw edge under on stitched line.

Slipstitch to garment as shown (24) or baste and topstitch. Press. If bias facing is to be turned to outside as a decoration, follow instructions which follow for **Facing Turned to Right Side**.

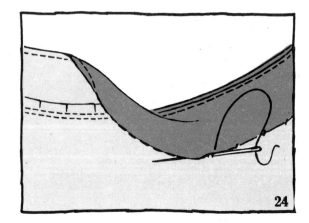

SPECIAL FACING APPLICATIONS

FACING TURNED TO RIGHT SIDE (decoration)

Stay-stitch and join pieces as necessary. Along edge not to be caught in seam, make a line of stitching exactly on seamline. Pin or baste right side of facing to wrong side of garment. Stitch. Trim all seam allowances to 6 mm.; grade by trimming *garment* seam allowance to 3 mm. Clip, if necessary. When understitching, open out facing, turning seam allowances under *garment*; on wrong side of garment stitch very close to seam through all thicknesses (25). Fold

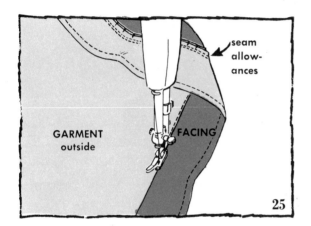

facing to outside, on seam. Trim seam allowance on free edge 6 mm. outside line of stitching. Turn edge under on stitching line; baste. Slipstitch or topstitch to garment. Press.

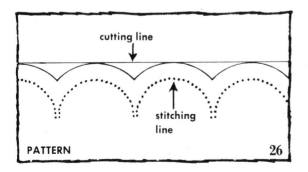

FACING A SCALLOPED EDGE

When cutting out pattern, do not cut out scallops, either on garment or on facing, but cut edge straight along top of scalloped cutting line (26). Trace stitching line to a strip of tissue paper the same length and width as facing.

Pin prepared facing (joined and clean-finished) to garment edge, right sides together. Pin tissue strip over facing, matching edges. Slowly stitch through paper along scallop stitching line, using shortened stitch and taking two very short stitches between scallops (27). Remove tissue paper.

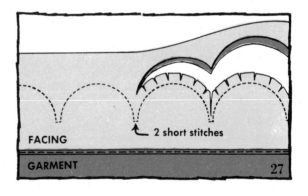

Cut out scallops, leaving a seam allowance of 6 mm. to 3 mm., depending on your fabric. Clip into seam allowance around scallops and into corners between (27). Turn facing to wrong side, carefully bringing seam to edge. Press.

A STEP-BY-STEP DEMONSTRATION

Here, in a shaped neck facing (with or without a collar), is a practical application of some of the procedures described in this chapter.

Stay-stitch neck edge of facing pieces 13 mm. from edge. NOTE: To avoid confusion, stay-stitching is not shown in drawings.

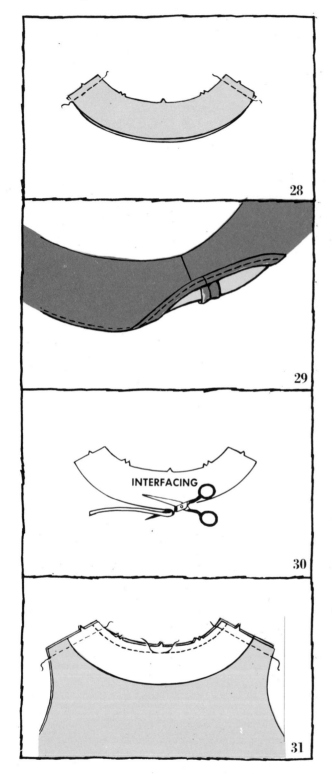

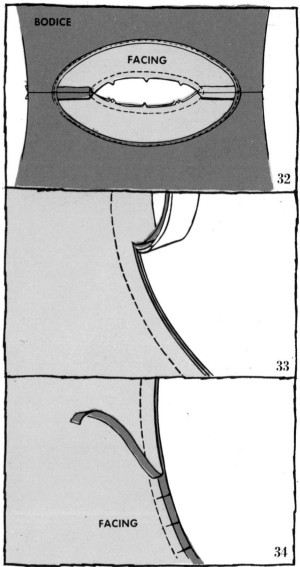

Join back and front facing pieces (28). Press seams open. Trim seam allowances to 6 mm.

Make a line of stitching 6 mm. from outer edge (29).

Trim 10 mm. from outer (free) edge of interfacing (30).

Stay-stitch interfacing pieces to wrong side of garment pieces. Join garment shoulder seams through all thicknesses (31). Trim all interfacing seam allowances to stitching line. Press shoulder seams open.

Pin prepared facing to garment, right sides together, shoulder seams and notches matched. Stitch around neck edge (32).

Trim seam allowances to 6 mm. (33).

Grade and clip seam allowances (34).

`Understitch (35).

Turn facing to inside (36). Catch interfacing to facing. Tack or anchor facing to seams.

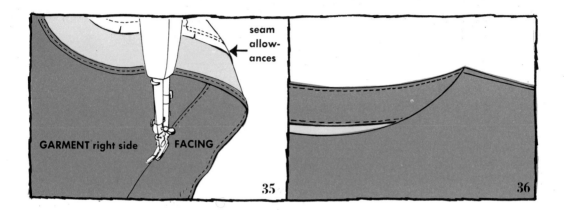

Fasteners

With a few exceptions, such as pullovers, slip-on jumpers, tie-on wraparounds, garments have fasteners at openings. Some, such as buttons and buttonholes, are visible, even decorative; others, like zip-fasteners, snap fasteners, hooks and eyes, are concealed, and purely utilitarian.

For information on BUTTONS, BUTTONHOLES, BUTTON LOOPS, see pp. 29–40. ZIP-FASTENERS, see p. 169.

SNAP FASTENERS
AND HOOKS AND EYES

Snap fasteners are used where there is little strain. Hooks and eyes form a much stronger closure. Both fasteners are attached in much the same way. Depending on weight of fabric, use Coats Drima, Coats Satinised No. 40, Coats Chain Cotton No. 40 or Coats Super Sheen No. 50. Attach fasteners through holes provided for the purpose, taking over-and-over stitches that will not show on outside of garment. For a more professional finish use buttonhole stitch.

Snap Fasteners

The two halves of the fastener—the ball and the socket —are sewed on separately.

Place ball half in position on underside of opening overlap. Conceal knot in thread under fastener. Take 4 or 5 stitches through each hole (1). Fasten thread securely and cut.

To mark place of socket half, pin opening together.

. . . If ball has no hole through centre, rub chalk on it and press firmly against underlay. Some fabrics can be marked like this even without chalk. Centre socket over mark and sew on.

. . . If there is a hole through ball, push threaded needle (no knot) from right side of garment through hole into underlay. Slip ball half off needle and thread. Make knot, centre socket over it and sew on.

Hooks and Eyes

Place hook in position on underside of overlap about

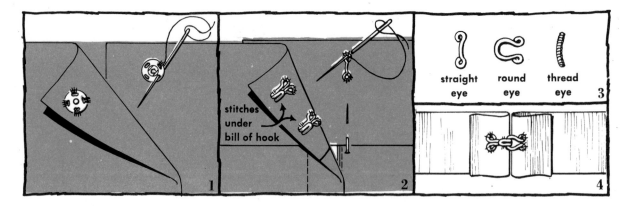

3 mm. from edge. Conceal knot under hook and take a few stitches to secure bill of hook (2). Pass needle through fabric to eyelets of hook and sew in place (2).

With opening pinned together, mark place for eye with a pin on underlay. Sew eye in place (2). There are three kinds of eyes (3):

Straight eye—Used where there is an overlap (2),

as on a skirt waistband.

Round eye—Used where two edges meet (4), as at a waist stay.

Thread eye—The most inconspicuous eye, used in place of the straight eye where there is little strain, as at top of a neck zip-fastener opening. To make, see THREAD LOOPS.

Fitting a Garment

Fitting a garment while sewing it should be a very small operation, involving small changes, the real alterations (if any) having been made in the pattern (see PATTERNS, p. 121).

If you want to check certain points in your garment (neckline, dart position), you can try on the section in question as soon as the requisite darts and seams are stitched (in a bodice or a one-piece dress, these would be darts and shoulder seams). Pin-baste side seams.

The garment should be tried on and fitted at every stage. Fit every process before stitching.

FOR PROPER FITTING

. . . Have someone help you. An adjustment is awfully hard to make on yourself. You can't even pin up a back closure by yourself.
. . . Wear the undergarments you will wear with the finished garment—an undergarment can change the

shape of your body and consequently, the fit of a garment. And wear heels of the same height as those you will wear with the garment.
. . . Try on garment right side out—fit cannot properly be judged wrong side out. If shoulder pads will go into finished garment, pin them in for fitting.
. . . Pin up opening(s). Put on belt, if any.
. . . The hem, of course, is not yet marked, but you can judge fit and hang. Check on the points enumerated as follows, but do not fall into the error so often made by amateur dressmakers: *Do not overfit!* The only place that may be entirely snug is the waistline. At every other point you need ease to look right and move comfortably (just now you're standing still).

CHECKPOINTS

Adjustments are usually made only at basted seams. Remove stitches as necessary and make corrections with pins.

Bustline should be kept easy. A tight or pinched look at this point is particularly sad. Side darts should point to fullest part of bust.

Waistline, while snug, should be so without strain. It may have to be raised or lowered slightly, since all fabrics do not drape in the same manner.

Waist-to-hip area should lie smooth and without strain, with enough ease at hipline so that bending and sitting will not stretch garment. Folds across the back (1) may mean that skirt is too tight, in which case you let out side seams; or that there is too much length between hip and waist, in which case you raise the back at waist (2).

Side Seams, if adjusted (3), should theoretically be altered to the same degree on both sides. In practice, however, the two sides may have to be slightly different for an even hang.

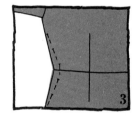

COMPLETING ADJUSTMENTS

After fitting, remove garment, transfer corrected lines (made on outside) to inside with chalk or pins.

Re-pin seams on inside and baste new seamlines.

Try on again to check alterations; then stitch seams, press, etc.

THE GAPING NECKLINE

This is the case mentioned on p. 131 of PATTERNS. It may be caused by a narrow chest or shoulders, or very square shoulders. The alteration needed is not one of the small ones normally done when fitting, but, since it cannot be determined by measurements, you may not have altered your pattern. A word of caution, however: It is safer not to undertake this alteration if neck finish is anything but a plain facing, because the neck finish will have to be altered to fit.

There are three ways of taking in a neckline:

[a] by taking in shoulder seams (this is done for square shoulders).

Try on garment before finishing neckline or armholes. Pin up opening. Have someone pin up shoulder seams, taking up an equal amount front and back. This should be not more than 13 mm. on each side of seam at neck, and should taper to nothing at armhole.

After taking off garment, mark new seamline on inside. Make same alteration on facing. Stitch new shoulder seams on garment and facing. Remove old stitching; trim seams and press.

[b] by taking tucks around neckline. This may be done on front only, back only, or on both.

Try on garment before finishing neckline. Pin up opening. Have someone pin small folds at neck to see how much needs to be taken in. Folds might be either:

. . . Two small soft tucks (4), one on either side of centre (your taste will have to determine best distance; on a square neck, place them at corners). These tucks, being relatively deep, must be measured and shaped on the body. Stitch in place at edge after removing garment.

. . . A number of pin tucks (see TUCKS) all around (5). Five on front and two near centre back will reduce neckline by 22 mm. (each tuck is 2 mm. deep).

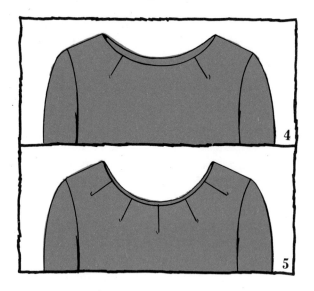

It is best to measure and mark place, direction, and length (38 mm. to 50 mm.) of tucks on inside of garment after taking it off. Place equally, one at centre and two at each side. Stitch tucks on wrong side.

Whether or not facing will still fit as cut after tucks are added will depend on flexibility of fabric. You may want to cut a new facing, using new neckline as pattern. You can also make adjustments at shoulder seams. In any case, facing must be made to fit smoothly.

[c] by taking in neck at centre back (where there is a centre back seam or zip-fastener).

Try on garment before finishing neck. Have someone pin up centre back from neck to waist, taking in an equal amount on both sides of centre. Neckline should lie smooth, but with ease—do not overfit! Then have pins removed one by one and put back through one thickness only.

After taking off garment, mark new line of seam or closure, and continue with construction. When applying facing, trim ends to fit.

Gathers and Shirring

Gathers are formed by drawing up fabric on a line of stitching. They are part of the design of a garment, supplying a soft fullness where needed (1). Shirring, a decorative use of gathers, consists of gathers drawn up on several (three or more) lines of stitching (2).

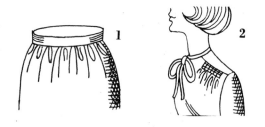

THE GATHERING STITCH

For both gathering and shirring, stitching can be done with hand running stitch (see HAND-SEWING), but is faster and more even when done by machine. Set machine for longest stitch. Stitch on right side of fabric (bobbin thread is easier to draw up, and gathers look best on side that is not drawn up).

GATHERS

Make a row of machine-stitching on seamline and another 6 mm. above (3). If edge to be gathered is long (as in a skirt top), divide it into sections and make separate rows of stitching on each (4). Before drawing up gathers, pin edge to be gathered to shorter corresponding edge to which it is to be attached (waistband, for instance), at notches, ends, centres, etc. (5). Grasping both bobbin threads at one end of rows of stitching, draw up one half of gathers to match flat edge, and fasten threads by winding around a pin (6). Repeat procedure from other end of stitched rows. Distribute and straighten gathers evenly. If necessary put in additional pins (no more than 50 mm. apart), crosswise to stitching. Stitch on seamline, gathered side *up*. Make a second row of stitching within seam allowance. When pressing, avoid flattening gathers; work point of iron into them.

SHIRRING

For first two rows of stitching, follow instructions at left. Stitch additional rows carefully as they will remain visible. Make them even and parallel, an equal distance apart. At *one end* of stitching, bring all thread-ends to wrong side and tie ends of each row separately. Cut off thread-ends. At other end of stitching, hold bobbin threads and draw shirring up to desired width (7). Bring all threads to wrong side and tie each row separately. Cut off thread-ends. For a neat, strong finish at each end of shirring, fold fabric on wrong side and stitch a narrow pin tuck as shown (8). When seaming to a flat piece of fabric, have shirred side *up*. Never press shirred area; work point of iron into gathers below it.

Grain in Fabric

Grain is the direction of the threads in woven fabric.

THE THREE DIRECTIONS IN FABRIC

Every woven fabric, no matter what it looks like, consists of lengthwise threads (warp) through which crosswise threads (called woof, weft, or filling) are woven over and under, back and forth. In the greatly enlarged detail of twill weave shown here (1), you will see how a diagonal effect is achieved while the threads remain at right angles to each other. The same is true of every other weave, including napped and pile fabrics. The *lengthwise* and the *crosswise* grains, therefore, are the direction in which the threads go (2).

The third direction is the diagonal or *bias* (2), which

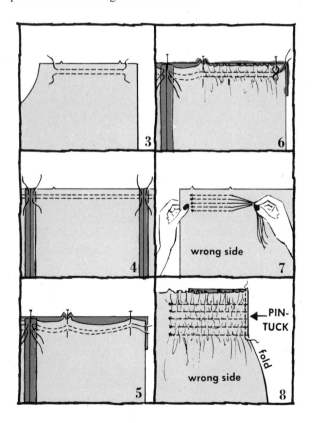

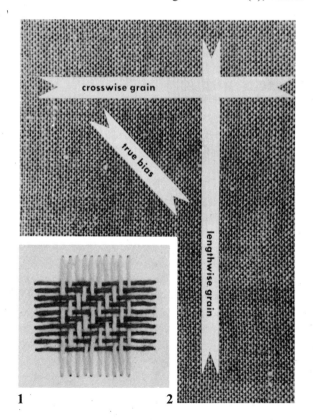

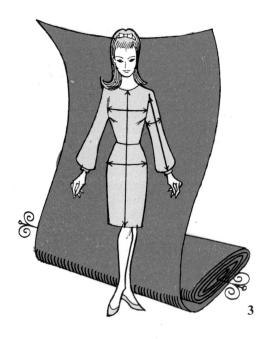

3

slants across the threads at the point where they meet. This is the direction of elasticity and 'give' and rates a chapter of its own—BIAS.

GRAIN AND THE HUMAN FIGURE

The human figure, like the fabric that clothes it, has two directions at right angles to each other: the perpendicular, or 'up-and-down', and the horizontal, or 'across' (3). These correspond with the two grain directions in the fabric, a relationship that has a great deal to do with the fit and hang of a garment. Correctness of grain must be maintained, as the fabric is shaped to fit the third dimension, or bulk, of the body by means of seams, darts and gathers.

As a general rule, a garment is cut with the lengthwise grain—which also happens to be the stronger one—on the perpendicular line of the figure. While this is the most logical and satisfactory cut, there are times when a design, for instance, may demand that the crosswise grain go up-and-down; and in a bias-cut garment the centre line will be on the true bias.

In patterns, arrows marked 'Straight of goods', or 'Straight grain' indicate the lengthwise grain unless

there is some special reason for them to mean the crosswise. This is also true of the 'Lay on Fold' notation along an edge. Correct placing of arrows means correct direction of grain in your cut sections.

GRAIN AND FABRIC FINISHES

Finishes applied to fabrics after they are woven may be either temporary or permanent. In either case, they often cause the crosswise threads—the weaker grain—to be pulled into a crooked or 'off-grain' position.

Permanent finishes (resin treatment, heat setting, and others), except for the shrink-resistance process, lock the grain in position. If the grain is distorted, it will stay that way. These finishes are applied to all synthetics and blends of natural and synthetic fibres; also natural-fibre fabrics labelled 'wash-and-wear', 'crease-resistant', etc.

Temporary finishes, which consist of sizing, are water- and steam-soluble, and will eventually let the threads return to their natural position. These finishes are present only in the natural fibres and in rayon, and only when these fabrics have not been treated with one of the permanent finishes (see FABRICS, p. 65). In other words, their use is diminishing. If one of the fabrics mentioned is not labelled for a permanent finish its finish will be temporary (we must except shrink-resistance, which is permanent, but does not affect grain).

GRAIN IN MAKING A GARMENT

Permanent-finish fabrics—Make sure, as usual, that the 'Straight of Goods' mark on your pattern falls correctly on the lengthwise grain (see CUTTING, p. 49). As we said previously, if it is crooked, it will remain so, and without impairing the hang of the garment.

Temporary-finish fabrics—Any deviation in grain must be corrected before cutting (see **Preparing Fabric for Use**, p. 66) because, the finish being water- and steam-soluble, the threads will eventually return to their natural straight position, and this must not happen *after* garment is finished. When cutting out, pattern indications will place grain correctly. In general, care should be taken not to pull fabric out of shape. See also CUTTING and MACHINE-STITCHING.

Gussets

A gusset is a small, three- or four-cornered piece of fabric inserted into a slash to provide ease.

A gusset appears most often at the underarm curve of a kimono sleeve, in a slash cutting across the seam. If such a gusset is four-cornered, it is inserted after seam is stitched. Since it is far easier to insert a gusset *before* seam is stitched, we recommend converting the gusset into two triangles which, added to each sleeve-half, automatically become a four-cornered insert when they are stitched together at the same time as underarm sleeve seam.

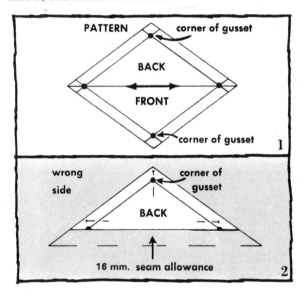

FOUR-CORNERED GUSSET PATTERN INTO TWO TRIANGLES

On pattern pieces for front and back of bodice, compare markings (dots, triangles, etc.) at underarm slash with matching markings on gusset pattern. Mark indicated gusset corners FRONT and BACK, as shown (1). With a ruler, draw a line between the *other* two corners (1). Cut gusset pattern in two on this line.

Pin each triangle to double fabric, allowing for a 6 mm. seam allowance to be added at cut pattern edge (this will be underarm seam). Measure and mark this addition (2).

Cut out pieces. Transfer *all* pattern markings, including seamlines, to *all* gusset pieces.

REINFORCING POINT OF SLASH

The point of an underarm slash is subjected to considerable strain, and since there is no seam allowance there, the gusset is liable to pull out. It is extremely important, therefore, to reinforce point of slash before inserting any gusset. This can be done in one of several ways, always *before* cutting the slash:

[a] **Short-stitch machine-stitching** (3) at point may be sufficient with firmly-woven fabrics. Starting at fabric edge, stitch over marked seamline of slash. At about 25 mm. before reaching point, shorten stitch. Stitch to point; pivot; take one or two stitches across point; pivot again; stitch for 25 mm., change to regular stitch and continue to edge as shown.

[b] **Seam binding** (4). Fold a 76 mm. piece of seam binding into a V, and place over point as shown. Mark point with pin. Machine-stitch as described in [a] above.

[c] **Iron-on interfacing** (5). Before using this, test it by ironing a scrap onto a scrap of your fabric. If results are satisfactory, press a 38 mm.-square piece of iron-on interfacing over point of slash. Mark point and machine-stitch as described in [a] above.

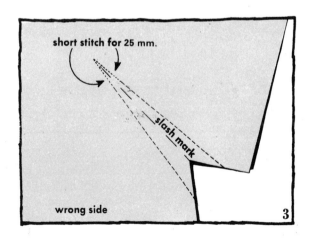

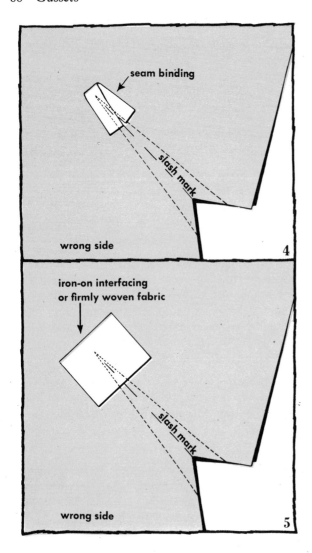

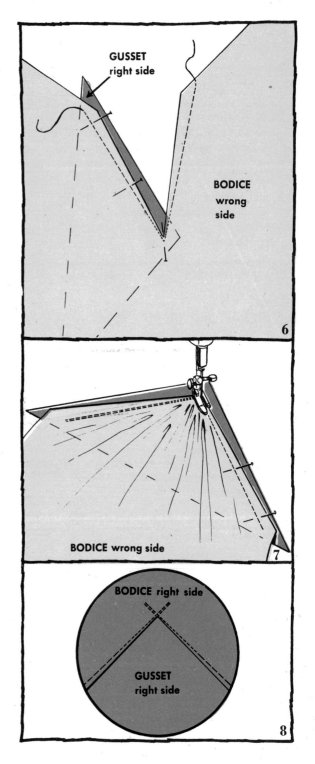

[d] **Thin firmly-woven fabric.** Place a 38 mm.-square of fabric over point of slash. Mark point with pin. Machine-stitch as described in [a] above.

INSERTING A TWO-PIECE GUSSET

Cut slash as far into point as possible without clipping stitching.

To attach first edge of gusset, pin one edge of slash over one edge of gusset, right sides together, matching point of slash to corner of gusset (2) as marked, and stitched line of slash to marked seamline on gusset (6). With garment side up, stitch over stitched line, going toward point; at about 25 mm. before reaching point, shorten stitches. At point, *leave needle down* in fabric.

To attach second edge, pivot free edge of slash and free edge of gusset forward and match and pin as before (7). Stitch with shortened stitch, returning to regular stitch after 25 mm.

Reinforce seam by topstitching through all thicknesses close to seam (8), again shortening stitch before reaching point. At point, continue for 3 stitches beyond, then backstitch to point. Pivot work, backstitch 3 stitches along direction of next seam, then stitch forward, changing to regular stitch after 25 mm.

Repeat with second triangle; stitch underarm seam.

Haberdashery

The items listed as follows, in alphabetical order, consist of all the small articles that, for fit, finish, fastening, etc., may go into the making of one or another kind of garment; thread alone is used for all.

Articles serving as sewing implements are listed under EQUIPMENT. For interfacing, see that chapter.

Belt Buckles are available in metal, plastic, bone, mother-of-pearl, and wood. Fabric-covered buckles can be ordered from a store or made with the help of a kit (see BELT BUCKLES).

Belting comes in two kinds, each with its own purpose:

Washable Belting is used for backing fabric belts. It is available by the metre.

Waistband Stiffening is used in the waistbands of skirts. It is sold by the metre, in black, white, and a few colours (see WAISTBANDS).

Binding is made on the bias and on the straight grain of fabric. Coats Bias Binding is used for binding straight and curved edges and for finishing hems. Coats Seam Binding is used for finishing hems, taping seams, and as a waist stay.

Boning and Stays, the modern, lighter substitutes for whalebone, are used where vertical support is needed, as in strapless tops and cummerbunds. Available by the metre. Stays come in various lengths.

Buttons, for fastenings or decoration, come in a great variety of materials, shapes, and sizes. Buttons covered with your own fabric can be ordered from a store, or made yourself with or without the help of a kit (see BUTTONS).

Cord is used as a filler for corded piping or corded tubing (see BIAS) and for corded buttonholes (see BUTTONHOLES). It comes in many sizes in black and white.

Elastic comes in widths from 6 mm. to several centimetres, in black, white and pink. It is sold by the metre; also in packages.

Hooks and Eyes are the reliable fasteners used at points of strain (see FASTENERS). Regular hooks and eyes are available in sizes from 00 (smallest) to 4 (largest), in black and nickel. Larger hooks can be silk-covered.

Horsehair Braid is used to stiffen hems of flared or full skirts (see HEMS). Available by the centimetre, in various widths, in black and white.

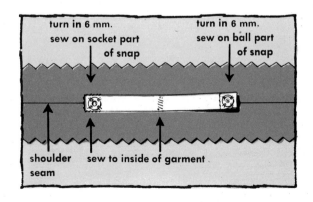
turn in 6 mm.
sew on socket part of snap

turn in 6 mm.
sew on ball part of snap

shoulder seam

sew to inside of garment

Lingerie Strapholders are attached on the inside of a garment shoulder seam to hold lingerie straps in place. They are available in black, white and pink, or can be made as shown, using 76 mm. of narrow tape or ribbon.

Shoulder Pads come and go with fashion, but are always a help to sloping shoulders. They are sold ready-made, in many styles and sizes. They can also be made from a pattern. Use washable pads in washable garments.

Snap Fasteners, are good for closings that have a minimum of strain (see FASTENERS). Available in many sizes, from 000 (smallest) to 10 (largest); in black and nickel.

Thread—See chapter on THREAD AND NEEDLES.

Weights are used to give body to the hang or drape of a garment. They may be placed at hems, or, say, in a cowl neckline. They come in various types:

Round lead weights resemble coins, and are of different sizes (weights). Inquire as to reaction to washing or dry-cleaning. They may be sewn permanently within the layers of a garment or, covered with lining fabric, attached in place with a small safety pin.

Lead weight by the centimetre consists of small flat slugs encased in tape, or small pellets covered with a knitted sleeve. Attach along top edge of hem before sewing down lining.

Gold chain weight is pretty enough to be tacked along the lining, not covered by it.

There is a **Lightning Zip-Fastener** for every kind of opening. They are made in nylon or metal and come in lengths from 102 mm.—65 cm., depending upon the weight and type. Zip-fasteners are available for all dressmaking purposes and also for corsets. A waistband adjuster can be obtained for trousers, slacks, skirts and shorts. Open end fasteners are suitable for cardigans and jackets.

Hand-Sewing

You can be a first-class dressmaker these days, and not know how to 'sew a fine seam' (that's what sewing machines are for!). Still, you must know how to handle needle and thread competently. You will need them for:

Basting, where pin-basting is insufficient and machine-basting impractical—see BASTING and PLEATS. Also for MARKING.

Hemming most garments—see HEMS, Herringbone stitch, Catch-stitch, Hemming and Slipstitch on p. 95.

Tacking—see FACINGS, p. 77; for making **Bar Tacks,** see THREAD LOOPS.

Sewing on Fastenings—see BUTTONS, and FASTENERS.

You also need them for:

Overcasting seams in ravelly fabric if your machine

is not equipped to do it—see SEAMS AND SEAM FINISHES.

Hand-Worked Buttonholes—see BUTTONHOLES, p. 34.

One further consideration: what with becoming ever less of a necessity, hand-sewing is taking on the elegance of a luxury. Careful hand-finishing (such as doing the outside stitching of a zip-fastener application by hand) will give a garment an expensive look.

You will find on the next pages whatever hand stitches are not covered in the chapters named above.

THREAD AND NEEDLE

For any hand-sewing, you generally use the thread you are using in machine-stitching your garment. The needle may be of whatever type you prefer, but pick the size according to your fabric and thread (see FABRIC AND THREAD CHARTS, pp. 151–164).

Thread is generally used single. If, for extra strength (sewing on a button, hand-sewing a zip-fastener), you want to use it doubled, make sure that you draw it out smoothly after every stitch, to avoid forming snags and loops.

The working length of any thread, single or doubled, should never be more than 30 cm. (1).

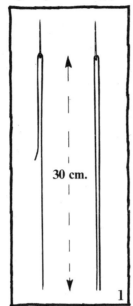

Make a knot at the end of your thread and if you can, tuck knot under a seam allowance, hem, etc. Otherwise, start your sewing with a few tiny backstitches on top of each other. These should be made on the wrong side of your work.

To finish, take a few stitches in same way. Do not cut off thread too close. Take a few inconspicuous running stitches (e.g., through seam allowance) before you clip.

THE MOTIONS OF HAND SEWING

Train yourself to wear a thimble on the middle finger of your sewing hand. You may have been doing without one, but you will find, after an initial feeling of clumsiness, that with this protection you can push the needle forward faster and with much more precision.

Except in a very few cases, hold your needle as shown (2).

How you hold your work will depend on what you are doing. In the chapters which are mentioned on p. 90, you will find illustrations for whatever hand-sewing is indicated.

HAND STITCHES

Running Stitch (3) is mostly used for gathering and shirring by hand. With point of needle, take a number of small forward stitches 2 mm. to 3 mm. long,

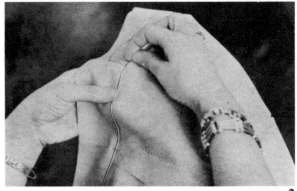

depending on fabric), and slide stitches onto thread as needle fills up. If stitch is used in a seam (this should only be done where there is very little strain—otherwise, it could easily pull out), draw up thread after filling needle, then take a small backstitch before filling needle again.

Half backstitch (4)—Good for any seam, and for hand-finishing a zip-fastener application (see ZIP-FASTENER, p. 173). Bring needle and thread out on stitching line. Take a stitch back about 2 mm.; bring needle out about 3 mm. from where you first came out. Take another 2 mm.-stitch back and continue in the same manner. In a zip-fastener finish, stitches should be tiny and farther apart; it is then called **prick-stitch**.

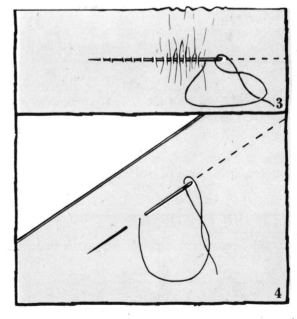

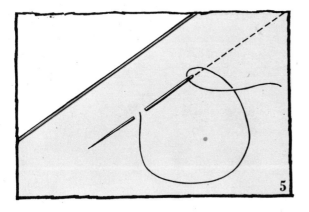

Backstitch (5) makes strong seams. Bring needle and thread out on stitching line. Take a stitch back about 2 mm., bringing needle out 3 mm. forward (i.e., 2 mm. from where you first came out). To continue, keep putting your needle in at end of last stitch and bringing it out one stitch ahead.

Hems

The hem is the last detail, the step that completes a garment. In something ready-made, or that needs bringing up to date, the hem is often the only place requiring an alteration.

A good hem is one that is inconspicuous and even, and that, while giving body to the bottom edge, interferes in no way with the hang of a garment.

Your first consideration should be the proper choice of hem finish for your fabric and garment cut. For general guidance on the type of hem you should use, follow the chart on p. 93.

NOTE: In a case when your fabric is either insufficient or too bulky for an ordinary hem, make a **Faced Hem** (see p. 97).

MARKING THE HEMLINE

The hemline is the line on which a hem is folded up (i.e., the finished edge of garment). It must be at the *right level*, and it must be *even*—that is, at the same distance from floor all around.

A pattern usually indicates depth of hem. If, through measurement and previous experience, or because you have altered the pattern to fit, you know you can use this hemline, proceed as for the **straight skirt**, below.

As a rule, however, you cannot be sure that the length of a garment is right until you have tried it on. And, the human figure seldom being absolutely symmetrical, a skirt with a curved hemline may sag at certain points unless the hemline has been measured up from the floor all around. In other words, for one reason or another, it is usually necessary to put on a garment to mark the hemline. When doing this, wear a proper foundation; put on the belt, if any; wear shoes with heels of the proper height; and stand straight, with arms down and weight on both feet.

A skirt hem is marked all round, preferably with the help of another person. A circular skirt in a non-treated fabric should be allowed to hang for about 48 hours before hem is marked, to let it stretch. If you use a yardstick (1), determine hemline-level and mark it on yardstick with a rubber band.

Helper stands yardstick upright on floor against garment, and marks hemline with a horizontal line of pins, about 76 mm. apart (2). With a skirt marker (see EQUIPMENT) you may or may not need a helper. If you work alone, keep your body straight as you turn, especially when marking the back.

Baste hem on a trial basis after marking, and try on garment again, to check length.

1

Fabric	Style of Garment	Depth of Hem	Choice of Hem Finish
All types and weights except sheers	**Narrow and Medium Full** Straight Gored Flared	50–76 mm.	*Suitable for all fabrics:* Hem with Seam Binding Couture Hem *Lightweight fabrics:* Plain
	Full Gathered, pleated, flared, gored	38 mm.	Any of the above; or Machine-Stitched Hem for light- and medium-weight playclothes and children's clothes
	Circular	6–10 mm.	Narrow Hem
Sheers	**Full*** Circular, gored	6–10 mm.	Hand-Rolled Hem Edge-Stitched Hem

*A narrow skirt in a sheer fabric is usually backed, putting the fabric into the medium-weight category.

TURNING UP AND MARKING DEPTH OF HEM

If fabric is bulky, trim 3 mm. off seam allowances between marked hemline and cut edge, as shown (3). Turn up hem on marked hemline, pinning fold as shown (4) and adjusting fold wherever necessary so line will be even. Then baste close to fold (4), removing pins as you go. Press fold.

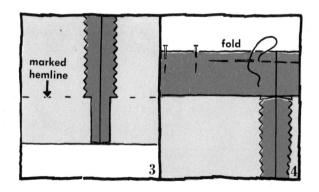

For proper depth of hem, consult chart above, or your pattern. Set or make hem gauge for depth indicated. Measuring from basted fold (5), mark hem all around with sharpened tailor's chalk or with pins *through one thickness of fabric only.* Trim off excess fabric all around on marked line.

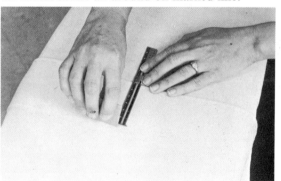

REDUCING FULLNESS IN CURVED HEMS

The excess fullness in curved hems (near seams in gored skirts, all around in circular ones) is eased as follows:

Make a line of stitching (10 stitches to 25 mm.) 6 mm. from cut edge (single thickness), all round. Place garment on ironing board, wrong side out. Wherever

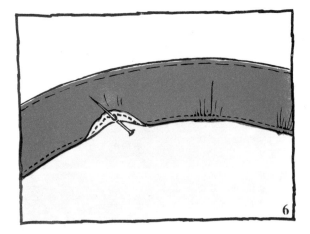

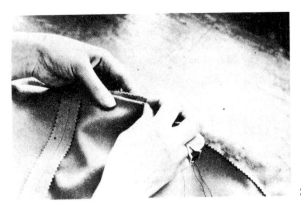

there is a ripple, draw up under-thread with a pin (6), forming a group of small gathers, as shown. Place a piece of heavy paper between hem and garment fabric and press (7), shrinking out gathers in wool and other shrinkable fabrics. On non-shrinkable fabric, press gathers as flat as possible, or make small tucks not more than 3 mm. deep to remove excess fullness.

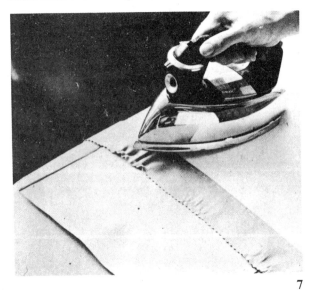

METHODS OF SEWING A HEM

To sew a hem, garment is held with hemline up and wrong side of garment facing you.

Except for Couture Hem (see **Hem Finishes,** p. 95), which is always sewn with inside hemming (8), you have a choice of Inside Hemming or Flat Hemming.

In Inside Hemming, stitches are taken between hem and garment fabric. (Hence, in the finished hem, the thread is protected against friction, the usual cause of a hem's coming undone.) To do this, fold entire hem back against right side of garment, with fold in garment about 6 mm. from hem edge (8). Secure hem with catch stitch.

In Flat Hemming, edge of hem is sewn flat to garment, with stitches taken through hem-edge (10, 11, 12), and close to this edge in garment.

STITCHES USED

For either method, begin hem at a seam, with knot hidden in seam. *Do not pull thread tight,* or outside fabric will show puckers. Take stitches at least 6 mm. apart. In garment fabric, pick up just a thread or two, if possible not going through to right side. Finish a thread-length on hem or in a seam (never in garment fabric), taking a few over-and-over stitches. Cut (do not break) thread. When sewing is finished, remove basting and give a light pressing along bottom edge, keeping iron clear of upper edge of hem.

You have a choice of four stitches:

Catch-stitch is used in Inside Hemming (9). Work from right to left. Take a stitch in hem-edge (or line of stitching). Take next stitch in garment, picking up just one thread in fabric and putting needle through hem-edge (or line of stitching) at least 6 mm. ahead before drawing up thread. Repeat.

Hemming is made by picking up a thread of the fabric then catching the fold of the hem (10).

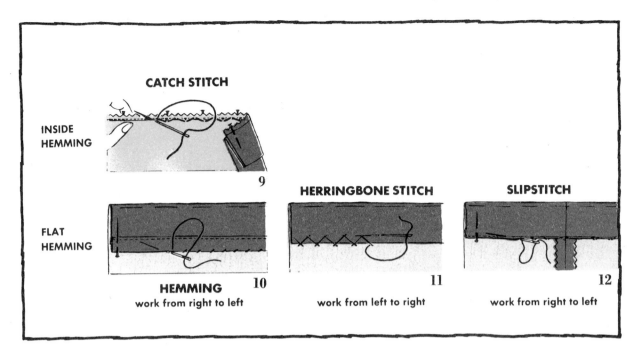

CATCH STITCH

INSIDE HEMMING

9

FLAT HEMMING

HEMMING
work from right to left

10

HERRINGBONE STITCH

11

work from left to right

SLIPSTITCH

12

work from right to left

Herringbone Stitch is very good for knit and stretch fabrics because it has 'give'. Work from left to right, with needle pointing from right to left. Keep thread very loose (11).

Slipstitch (12) is used only in Flat Hemming where there is a turned-in edge. The needle is slipped through folded edge of hem instead of being put through edge of hem.

HEM FINISHES

Your garment is ready for one of these three standard hem finishes after hem has been folded up, basted along hemline, and cut to the correct width.

Couture Hem (13)—An excellent hem, flat and inconspicuous, particularly suitable for most heavy and medium-weight fabrics. It is always sewn with Inside Hemming.

On a straight skirt, make a line of machine-stitching or zigzag stitching 6 mm. below cut edge through single thickness of hem fabric (on a curved-hem skirt you will already have done it while reducing fullness). On firm fabric, pink edge. If fabric is ravelly, overcast edge by hand or machine. Place work on a table, wrong side out. Matching at seams, pin or baste hem in place about 6 mm. below stitching line (14). Sew with Inside Hemming, using catch-stitch.

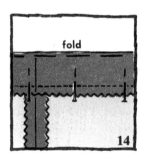

fold

14

Hem with Seam Binding (15)—Suitable for all fabrics, especially for fabrics that ravel easily.

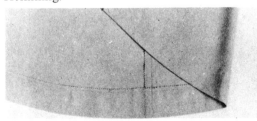

13

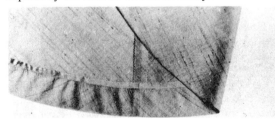

15

Seam Binding may be either straight or bias.

. . . Seam binding is 13 mm.-wide straight tape with a durable woven edge.

. . . Bias binding, particularly good for curved hems, has turned-under edges and is 13 mm. wide.

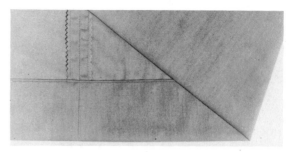

20

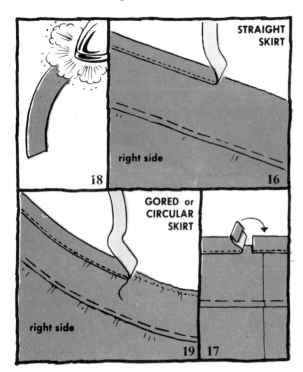

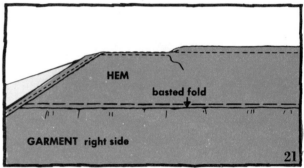

21

On a straight skirt topstitch seam binding to right side of hem about 6 mm. from cut edge, as shown, *easing it to fabric* (16). Overlap end, turned under as shown (17). Place work on ironing board, wrong side out. Matching at seams, pin or baste hem to garment, just below seam binding. Hem in position.

For use on a curved hem, bias binding can be steam-pressed into a slight curve (18). It is then placed to the hem and stitched (19). Finish as above with slip-stitching.

Plain Hem (20)—Used only on light-weight fabrics in straight or narrow gored garments.

On a straight skirt, make a line of machine-stitching 6 mm. from cut edge, through single thickness of hem fabric (on a curved hem, you will already have done this while reducing fullness). Turn edge

to inside on stitching line and topstitch through hem edge only, not garment (21). Place work on ironing board, wrong side out. Matching at seams, pin or baste hem in place about 6 mm. below topstitching. Slipstitch in position.

Machine-Finished Hem (22)—Quick and easy for hems on straight, full skirts of medium-weight cotton (dirndls, aprons, children's clothes, etc.). Eliminates all hand-sewing while looking like a Plain Hem. Edge is stitched and hem is caught in place in one operation. Try it first on a fabric sample.

After **Marking the Hemline** (see p. 92), turn in raw edge of hem 12 mm. and crease. Fold up hem on marked hemline and press a sharp crease. Pin hem in place as shown (23).

22

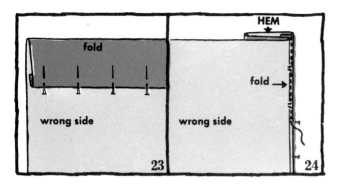

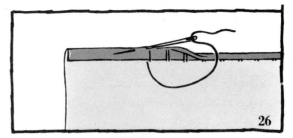

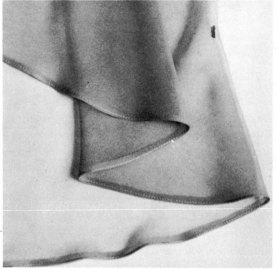

This hem can also be made with a zigzag machine or a Blind-Stitcher attachment (24).

Rolled Hem and Edge-Stitched Hem—These are very narrow hems used on circular skirts of sheer fabric (see chart on p. 93). After **Marking the Hemline** (see p. 92), continue as directed below, following instructions and illustrations exactly.

A Rolled Hem (25)—simplified or other—is an elegant hand-finish for skirts of chiffon, voile, etc.; also for handkerchiefs, scarves, and the like which are made of a sheer fabric.

Simplified Rolled Hem—Trim away excess fabric 6 mm. outside marked hemline. Fold in raw edge 3 mm. Slip needle through fold and anchor thread. Take a tiny stitch in garment below raw edge, then slip needle through fold; repeat as shown (26) with stitches about 6 mm. apart. After every few stitches, draw up thread, forming a roll.

An Edge-Stitched Hem (27) is done by machine and is quick and easy. Place a strip of tissue paper underneath fabric when stitching. Afterwards, tear away paper.

Make a line of stitching on marked hemline. Trim away excess fabric 6 mm. outside stitching. Turn edge to wrong side, folding on stitching line (no pinning or basting necessary) and topstitch on **right side**, a scant 3 mm. from fold. If you want a second line of stitching, make first line a little closer to the edge of fabric.

Faced Hem—A hem is faced with a bias strip (28) if fabric is insufficient; if fabric is too bulky for an ordinary hem; for decorative contrast; or to stiffen an edge (see Horsehair Braid, next page).

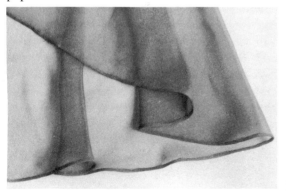

25

28

Ready-Made Hem Facing is of taffeta or cotton, 50 mm. wide, with both edges turned under 6 mm. for easy application.

Hand-Cut Facing—Cut strips at least 64 mm. wide on the true bias; join until strip is a few centimetres longer than edge to be faced (see **The Hand-Cut Bias Strip**, p. 23).

Along one edge, make a line of stitching 6 mm. from edge. With right side up, turn edge under on stitching line and topstitch. This will be the upper edge of the facing.

Ready-made and hand-cut bias facings are applied in the same manner:

After **Marking the Hemline** (see p. 92), trim away

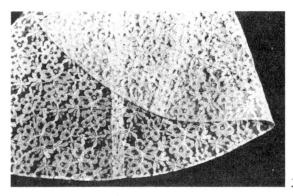

31

excess fabric 3 mm. outside marked line. Beginning at a seam, place right side of facing to right side of skirt, raw edges even (on ready-made facing, open out edge-fold). For a neat finish later, fold back end as shown (29). Stitch 6 mm. from edge, or on crease. Overlap ends. Turn facing to inside on marked hemline. Pin fold (30) and baste close to fold, removing pins as you go. Press fold lightly. With work on ironing board, pin free edge of facing in place. Slipstitch to garment. Slipstitch joining together.

Horsehair Braid is used as a facing to stiffen the hem of a full skirt (31). It comes in several widths.

To apply, trim away excess fabric 6 mm. outside marked hemline.

Wide Braid—Topstitch bottom edge of braid to right side of skirt edge with edge of braid at marked hemline, as shown (32). Overlap ends about 50 mm. With work on ironing board, turn braid to inside of garment and pin, then baste close to fold, removing pins as you go. Hem to garment.

Narrow Braid—Topstitch one edge of braid to garment. Turn braid to inside of garment and topstitch close to edge through braid and fabric, as shown (33). This stitching, so close to edge, is not noticeable on right side. Catch free edge of braid to seams only.

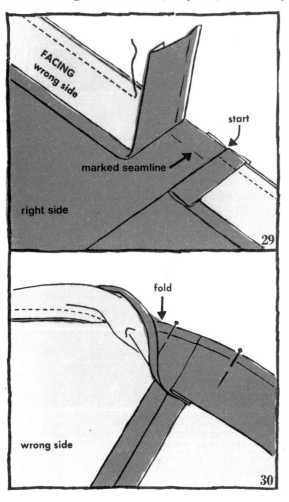

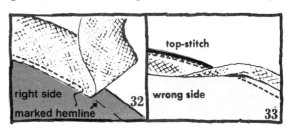

Hem in Pleats—Hem will be as indicated by pattern or by chart on p. 93.

On a skirt pleated all around, complete hem before pressing in pleats.

Pleat with seam in it—Method I (34). Press seam to one side before proceeding with **Marking the Hemline** (see p. 92). Then measure depth of hem on seam above hemline, clip through one seam allowance at that point, and press seam open below it, as shown (35). Within depth of hem, trim seam allowances as shown. Then proceed with turning up and finishing hem.

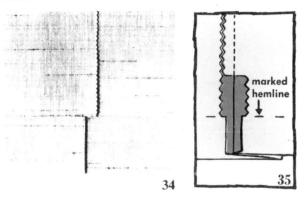

34   35

Pleat with seam in it—Method II (36)—Good for hard-to-press fabrics, such as bulky fabrics, wash-and-wear, etc. When stitching seam in pleat, leave seam open for about 203 mm. from raw bottom edge (37). Complete the garment, *including hem*. Be very careful to have both sides even at open hem (38). Stitch open section of seam *through finished hem*. Turn in corner of

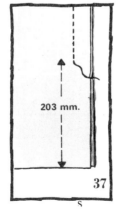

203 mm.

36   37

seam at bottom (39), and whipstitch edges together, as shown. At outside fold of pleat, whipstitch hem edges together for about 3 mm., as shown (39).

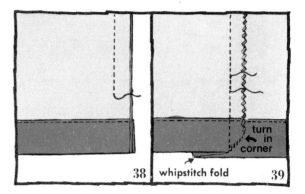

38   whipstitch fold   39
turn in corner

HEM IN A COAT (40)

40

A full-length coat is generally 25 mm. longer than a dress. On any coat, the hem is 50 mm. to 76 mm. deep. It is put in after lining and backing or underlining have been sewn in to within 203 mm. to 30 cm. from bottom edge. At that level, with coat hanging from a hanger, baste lining to coat all around to hold it in place, and let all bottom edges hang free.

Mark length of coat (see **Marking the Hemline**, p. 92). At both front edges, trim off interfacing just above marked hemline. If an interlining is attached to body of coat, trim it at marked hemline.

Turn up hem and mark depth as indicated on p. 93, extending hem through open facing (41). If coat has a curved hem, reduce fullness as indicated under **Reducing Fullness** on p. 93.

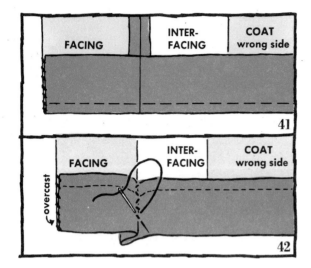

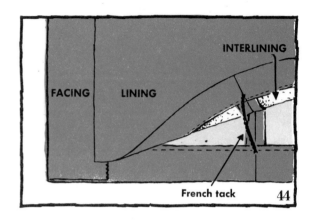

Slipstitch front edges of lining to facings. At each seam, catch lining to coat with a French tack 25 mm. to 38 mm. long (44).

Complete hem, making either a **Couture Hem** or a **Hem with Seam Binding**. Overcast the two side (facing) edges of hem as shown (42).

Press facings to inside. Any topstitching should go in or be restored at this point. If front edges of coat are not topstitched, catch facing hem to garment hem 13 mm. from facing seam (42) to secure facing.

Finishing a Long Coat (bottom of lining left free)

Catch facings to body of garment with 13 mm.-long French tack at hem (43).

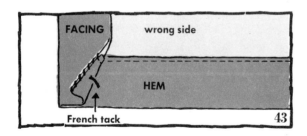

Check length of lining and interlining. Trim lining to 25 mm. below finished coat edge, interlining to 50 mm. shorter than lining.

Finish lining with a 50 mm. **Plain Hem**, turning it up over any interlining (44).

Finishing a Short Coat

Slipstitch bottom edge of facings to coat (45).

Check length of lining and interlining, if any. Trim lining even with finished coat edge, interlining to 50 mm. shorter than lining.

Turn lining under 13 mm. and press. Pin fold of lining to just cover hem-edge (upper edge of hem) and slipstitch (46); fold formed by extra length of lining is for ease. Slipstitch front edges of lining to facings, including fold made by extra length.

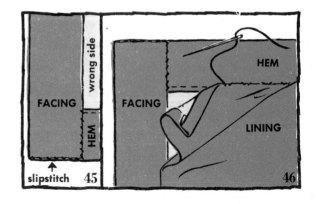

Interfacing

An interfacing is an extra piece of fabric placed between a facing and the outer fabric of a garment. Its purpose is to reinforce and add body and often crispness to the faced area and edge. It improves appearance and preserves shape. It may be of specially-made fabric or not—see next page.

Interfacing is usually specified in patterns. If it is not, you would do well to consider adding it wherever you have a facing, either shaped (1, 2, 3) or extended (4, 5). Interfacing is essential if your garment fabric is soft; less necessary if you are working with, say, treated cotton, where the finish furnishes a certain body. Where there are buttons and buttonholes, interfacing is *always* a good idea.

INTERFACING FABRICS

Fabrics used for interfacings may be either specially made for the purpose, or ordinary fabrics with the suitable properties (see chart on p. 102); besides body, these may be firmness, crispness, or real stiffness. Most fabrics used combine certain of these qualities. If different effects are called for in different parts of a garment, you should use more than one kind of interfacing.

All interfacing fabrics are dry-cleanable, some are washable, and some quick-drying—all these are factors to consider when making your choice. If washable interfacing is not preshrunk, it must be shrunk if you are planning to use it in a washable garment.

Woven interfacing fabrics must be cut on the same grain as facing and outer fabric. Most have a certain 'give' and can be manipulated. Some, containing wool, can be shaped by shrinking, which makes them ideal in tailored woollen garments. Self-fabric does very nicely with smooth (never nubbly

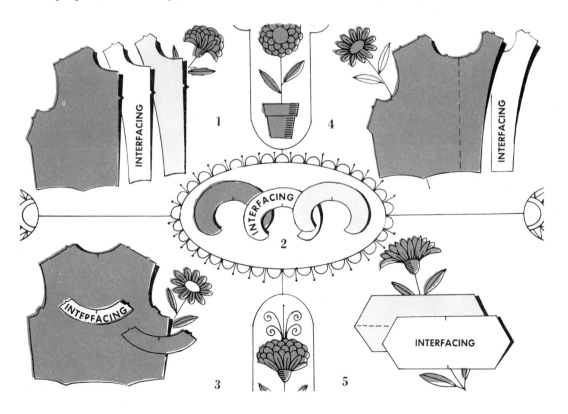

Interfacing	Properties	Typical Uses
Lawn **Cotton Batiste** **and Muslin**	washable—may need shrinking before use—give body but no crispness	**Lawn** or **Cotton Bastiste** with voile, silk, crepe, lightweight linen, broadcloth—**Muslin** with heavier fabrics, generally wool (as in dressmaker suits)
Organdie and Lightweight Crease-Resistant Cottons	washable—preshrunk—give crispness to lightweight fabrics	with organdie, silk, shantung, linen, lightweight wool, cottons, jerseys
Woven Interfacing Fabrics (with grain) various weights	may be washable or dry-cleanable, (see labels)—wrinkle-resistant—give body and firmness—shape retaining some can be steamed to shape	**Lighter Weights** used with wool-type fabrics, shantungs—**Heavier Weights** with heavy fabrics, for tailoring on wool fabrics, for exceptional firmness
Non-Woven Interfacing Fabrics (no grain) various weights	washable—non-shrinking—depending on weight used, provide gentle firmness or real stiffness	**Lighter Weights** used with linen, heavier cottons and wool-type fabrics—**Other Weights** for exceptional stiffness (bags, belts, etc.)
Iron-on Interfacing Fabrics non-woven	washable—depending on weight, provide firmness or real stiffness	used on fine to medium fabrics —on small areas only

or ribbed) wash-and-wear fabrics, smooth cottons, and solid-colour organdie.

Non-woven interfacing fabrics, having no grain, can be cut in any direction. They have less 'give' than the woven ones, but the so-called 'all-bias' varieties can be manipulated to a certain degree.

Iron-on interfacing fabric may be woven (in which case it must be cut on grain), or non-woven. It can be used only where garment fabric is firm enough so outline will not be visible on outside (try it first on a scrap of garment fabric). It is particularly useful for stabilizing ravelly fabric at a buttonhole, or to back a waistband. It is also good for producing a starched effect in a collar. Be sure to obtain directions for use when you buy it, and follow them carefully, especially in regard to amount of heat to apply.

SELECTING AN INTERFACING

It would be impossible to enumerate all the fabrics used for interfacings, and new specially-made ones turn up every day. The chart below will give you the major types, together with what you can expect of them and with what dress fabrics they are suitable. But keep one basic rule in mind: *Interfacing should never be heavier than the garment fabric.*

HANDLING INTERFACING

Cutting (if there is no pattern piece for interfacing) . . . For a shaped facing (1, 2, 3), cut interfacing from facing pattern.

. . . For an extended facing (4), pin facing part of pattern to interfacing fabric, with edge of fabric along pattern fold line (6). Cut out. For collars, cuffs, and waistbands, cut lightweight interfacing from the entire pattern piece, as shown (5).

Marking

Mark centre front and back at neck edge on interfacing.

Mark on interfacing the seamlines that are 'critical',

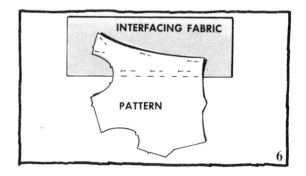

6

i.e., that are curved, or come to points that must match perfectly (collars, cuffs, lapels).

For marking buttonholes, see BUTTONHOLES, p. 30.

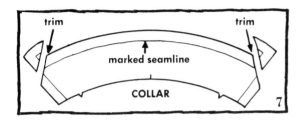

Trimming

Unless interfacing fabric is very lightweight, outer corners (on collars, cuffs, lapels, etc.) should be trimmed away on interfacing (7) before it is attached to a corresponding piece.

Trim 10 mm. from free edges (i.e., those that are not to be caught in a seam) of a neck interfacing, front interfacing, etc. (8). If interfacing fabric is ravelly, make a line of stitching 6 mm. from trimmed edge.

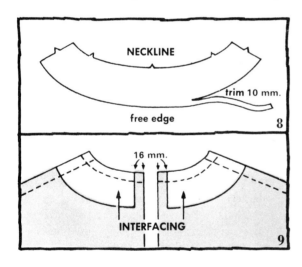

On an interfacing that reaches a zip-fastener opening (as at a neck), trim 16 mm. from the two edges that adjoin the opening (9).

APPLYING INTERFACING

Interfacing is applied to a section before section is either stay- or construction-stitched.

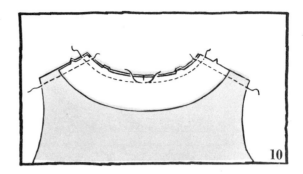

. . . For a shaped facing, pin interfacing to wrong side of outer garment section, carefully matching edges. Stitch 13 mm. from edges (10). When edge is curved or slanted, this serves as stay-stitching.

. . . For an extended facing, place interfacing to wrong side of outer garment section, matching straight edge of interfacing to garment fold-line. Catch edge of interfacing to fold-line with a loose stitch invisible from right side (11). Stay-stitch, taking in interfacing.

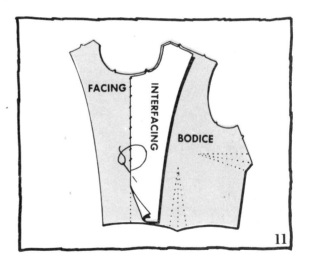

. . . If lightweight interfacing on a collar or cuff has been cut to full outer fabric size, fold interfacing on fold-line, and slipstitch this fold to fold-line of collar with loose slipstitch invisible from right side (12). Open out interfacing and stay-stitch around edges.

. . . On washable garments with worked buttonholes (blouses, children's dresses, etc.), the following finish for an extended facing is very neat and stands up well under washings:

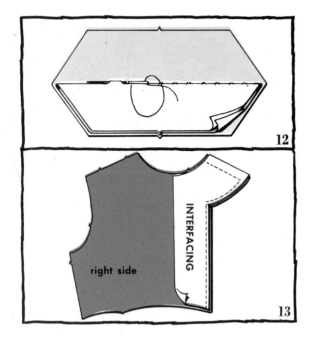

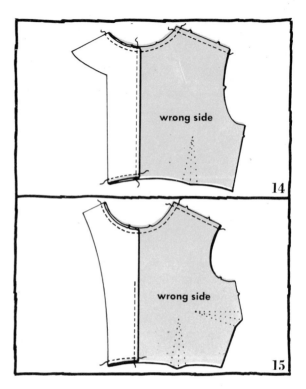

Place interfacing to right side of garment facing, edges matching. Stitch 6 mm. from outer raw edge; if facing reaches to shoulder seam, stitch shoulder 16 mm. from edge (13). Grade seam allowances, clip if necessary, and trim corners. Turn interfacing to wrong side; press. Stay-stitch, taking in interfacing. Stitch down raw straight edge of interfacing, close to edge (14); on an open neckline, stop stitching before point where it would show on outside (15).

Lining

Lining, like backing, doubles a garment. Unlike backing, its purpose is to provide the inside of garment with a finish. It often helps preserve shape (in slacks, straight skirts), but never establishes shape, as backing does. Again unlike backing, which is attached to and stitched with each garment section, a lining is seamed together as though it were a separate garment, and then sewn to garment along the edges.

Since a lining covers all raw seams and edges, it is practically always present in garments that may be worn open, such as coats and jackets—exceptions may be lightweight summer clothes in which seams are carefully finished (see SEAM FINISHES, p. 145), and reversible garments, which are doubled with a true and equal second garment. In dresses, a lining may be added as a luxury touch, but it serves a definite purpose if garment fabric is irritating to the skin or tends to stretch (like some knits, for instance).

LINING FABRICS

The main requisites of a lining fabric are that it be smooth to the touch, soft and pliable, and light enough in weight not to interfere in any way with the hang of a garment. Silk or imitations thereof in rayon and synthetics—China silk, crepe and taffeta, satin and brocade—are most likely to have these qualities, while smooth-surface cotton is often suitable as well. In an ensemble, a coat or jacket may be lined with the same fabric of which the dress or blouse is made. In such a case, the sleeves are often lined with another fabric, especially if the coordinated fabric would not allow them to slip easily on and off.

PUTTING IN A LINING

The instructions that follow are for lining a dress, blouse, or skirt where no such instructions are furnished with the pattern (in general, patterns include lining only for coats, jackets, etc.).

Buy same amount of lining as garment fabric, minus facings, collar, and cuffs.

Cut lining from garment pattern, omitting the details mentioned, or pleat. Transfer all markings.

Complete outer·garment, except for neck edge and hemline. On sleeves, turn up bottom edge and hem. On a sleeveless garment, leave armhole edges unfinished. Leave waistline unfinished on a skirt. Assemble lining in the same way, but leave sleeve bottoms unfinished; leave any zip-fastener opening or location for pleat unstitched. Press seams open;

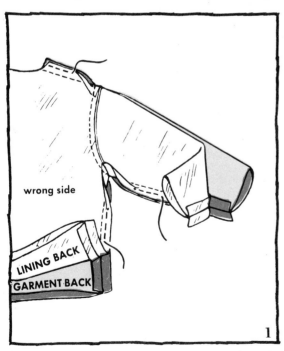

to lessen bulk, press lining darts in opposite direction from garment darts.

Depending on your edge-finishes, attach lining to garment by one of the following two methods:

METHOD I—For use when edges are to be faced, or finished with an edge-finish (braid or bias binding).

With garment and lining wrong sides out, pin back of lining to back of garment, wrong sides together, seams and waistline matching. With loose basting stitch (1), catch one lining seam allowance to one garment seam allowance *exactly* as shown (study the illustration; if you catch the seam allowance along wrong side of seam it won't work). Join seams loosely in this manner at shoulders, along underarms to within 50 mm. of sleeve-ends, and down side seams as far as hipline. Leave zip-fastener area free.

Reaching inside lining and through armholes, put your hands through both lining sleeves at the same time and grasp ends of lining and garment sleeves together. Pull sleeves through, turning body of lining over garment. Entire lining will now be right side out, with garment inside.

Baste lining to garment at neckline, at armholes of a sleeveless garment, or at waistline on a skirt. At zip-fastener opening, fold edges of lining under and slipstitch neatly to zip-fastener tape. At sleeves, trim lining to length of finished edge; turn 13 mm. under and press. Pin and slipstitch this edge over catch-stitched hem at garment-sleeve (2)—the slight extra length in lining is for ease. At a pleat, let lining edge hang free, finished with narrow hems.

Apply edge-finish—facing, bias binding, etc.—to garment, or waistband to a skirt. On a skirt, dress, or coat, hem hangs free; on a blouse or short coat, lining is attached at hem (see HEMS, **Finishing a Coat**, p. 100, for finishing).

METHOD II—For garments that have a front or back opening (coats, jackets, blouses) and where the lining reaches to and finishes all edges.

On both garment and lining, mark hemline and cut away hem allowance 16 mm. from marked line (remember that this makes it impossible to lengthen garment later).

With lining and garment right sides together, baste and stitch around neckline and front (or back) opening; trim and clip seam allowance; understitch.

Stitch bottom edge, leaving an opening as shown (3) through which to turn garment. Press this seam open; trim corners and grade seam allowance.

At shoulder- and side-seams, catch one lining seam allowance to one garment seam allowance with loose

basting stitch as in Method I. Read accompanying instructions (1).

Push garment through opening at bottom and bring it right sides out. Reach inside garment sleeves and through lining sleeves; grasp ends and pull lining through.

Slipstitch opening together. Press garment edge so that lining will not show on right side. To finish sleeves, see Method I (2). On a sleeveless garment, baste lining to armhole and complete with facings of lining fabric.

Machine-Stitching

Before going into the various uses—the *why* and *where* —of machine-stitching, let us consider the *how*, which means the handling of your sewing machine.

The key to success in stitching *any* fabric with *any* kind of thread lies in your sewing machine. Take the time to match the pictures in the sewing machine manual with the machine itself, identifying the different parts and familiarizing yourself with their names. Even if you know how to set in the needle, thread it, wind and insert the bobbin, do these things once by following the manual—you may have over-

looked some extremely helpful detail. And read up on the care of the machine.

PERFECT STITCHING

Your machine will stitch perfectly if you are particular about certain points in its use (for details see the headings that follow this listing):

. . . a clean sewing machine,
. . . thread and needle chosen to suit the fabric,
. . . pressure on presser foot correct; thread tension

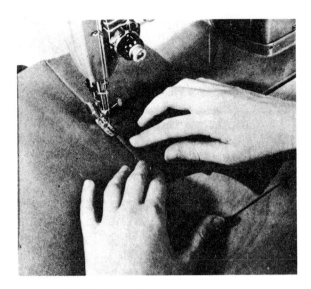

correct; stitch balanced,

. . . stitching started and ended correctly,

. . . pace of stitching steady and even.

A Clean Sewing Machine

Keep your machine covered when not in use.

Be sure to have a 'lint brush' handy; it is inexpensive, and available in most places where sewing machine supplies are sold. Before using machine, whisk brush around each side of feed dog and around bobbin case.

How often you clean your machine more completely depends on how much you use it. You must do so in any case if you have stitched linty or fuzzy fabrics; also before oiling. Remove throat plate and bobbin case (if removable) and go over machine thoroughly with brush.

The manual will tell you how, when, and where to oil. One drop in each place is sufficient. Use machine oil, and never over-oil.

If a scrap of thread is caught in bobbin case, turn balance wheel slightly to release it, then draw thread out (using tweezers if necessary).

Thread and Needle to Suit Fabric

For choice of thread, needle, and stitch length, see FABRIC AND THREAD CHARTS, pp. 150–164.

Pressure—Tension—Balance

Pressure on presser foot is regulated by pressure regulator, which may be a thumbscrew on top of machine (1) or a dial inside. Locate it on your machine. Amount of pressure needed varies with weight, finish, fibre, and bulk of fabric. When pressure is correct, the two pieces of fabric—top and bottom—are held firmly but lightly in place and the two travel under needle at the same rate.

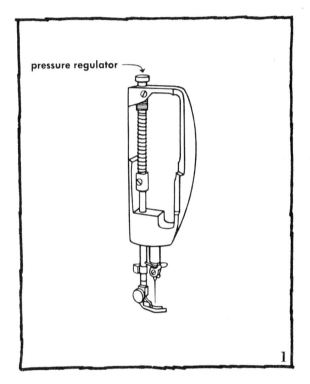

Tension of thread is regulated for needle-thread by tension dial (2), for bobbin-thread by screw on bobbin case (3). Today's fabrics call for a medium thread tension. Too tight tension causes puckered seams (4).

A balanced stitch means that stitching line looks the same on both sides (needle-thread and bobbin-thread), the two threads having equal tension (6).

Pressure, tension, and balance can be checked and adjusted by means of a single test, which should be made for each new fabric to be stitched.

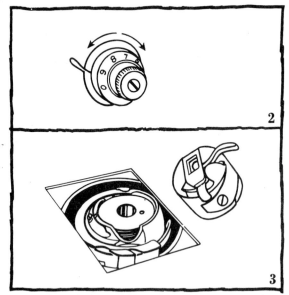

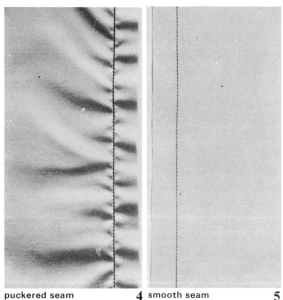

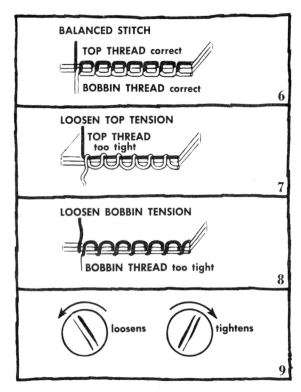

puckered seam **4** smooth seam **5**

Test-Seam

NOTE: On all screws and dials, a counter-clockwise turn loosens, a clockwise turn tightens (9). To adjust a screw, give it only a *slight fraction* of a turn (equivalent of 5 minutes on clock face).

Thread machine for what you are about to sew. From scraps of the fabric you are using, cut two strips, about 203 mm. long, on lengthwise grain (crosswise or on bias for knits, because stitches sink into ribs). Place pieces together, edges even, and pin crosswise at top and bottom. Stitch as shown (10), continuing to bottom pin.

. . . **If a ripple forms** in top layer, as shown (10), pressure is too heavy; loosen pressure regulator. If fabric does not feed through properly, pressure may be too light; tighten pressure regulator.

. . . **If seam is puckered** (4), tension is too tight; loosen top tension and bobbin screw.

. . . **If stitching is tighter on one side** of fabric than on other, stitch is not balanced; loosen tension on that side (either tension dial or bobbin-case screw, 7 and 8).

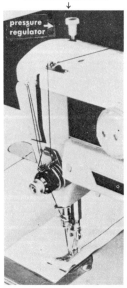

pressure regulator

10

If you have made an adjustment, cut off test-seam and repeat test until seam is smooth (5), the same on both sides, and forming no ripples.

Starting and Ending

The following steps, which are essential to good stitching, will become automatic after you have taken them a few times.

Before starting to stitch:

Be sure that thread-take-up lever is raised to highest point—or thread will come out of needle with first stitch. Turn wheel by hand if necessary.

Bring needle-thread under presser foot and extend both needle and bobbin thread-ends backward—this prevents thread from snarling in bobbin case or catching in seam.

Place fabric under presser foot with bulk of fabric to left and seam edge to right. Never let machine run without any fabric under presser foot.

Before lowering presser foot, lower needle into fabric by turning balance wheel by hand—thus placing needle exactly where you want it.

Lower presser foot. Stitch.

At end of stitching line:

Raise take-up lever to highest point, turning wheel by hand—thread cannot be drawn out otherwise, and may break.

Raise presser foot.

Remove work by drawing it to the back, then cutting threads—you will find that this prevents strain on needle and leaves thread-ends in the proper place for next stitching.

NOTE: If stitching line needs to be secured at beginning and/or end, take a few stitches in reverse, or leave thread-ends long enough to tie.

To tie threads, draw needle-thread end through to other side; tie the two ends; clip.

Stitching Pace

Train yourself to stitch at a steady, even pace, even if you have to go slowly. Stitching done in spurts becomes uneven.

CHECK-LIST FOR TROUBLE SPOTS

Common sewing machine failures usually have a simple explanation. Check the following in the cases indicated:

Thread breakage—Improper threading of either top or bobbin-thread . . . Starting machine with needle in incorrect position . . . Needle improperly set . . . Bent needle . . . Tension too tight . . . Needle too fine for fabric or thread . . . Rough spots on needle eye, throat plate, or bobbin case . . . Lint or thread-ends around bobbin case.

Irregular or skipped stitches—Sewing in spurts . . . Pressure too light . . . Needle wrong size for thread or fabric . . . Pulling fabric.

Machine stuck—Bits of thread caught in bobbin case holder.

Needle breakage—Wrong needle for machine . . . Needle improperly set . . . Presser foot or attachment improperly set . . . Wrong size needle for fabric . . . Stitching over pins . . . Pulling fabric . . . Bobbin inserted incorrectly.

MACHINE-STITCHING APPLIED

There are two kinds of machine-stitching: straight and zigzag (a novelty is chain-stitch). Zigzag, being used mainly for embroidery, seam finishing, and buttonholes, need not concern us here.

Straight stitching, although it has no variations except in stitch-length, is referred to in various ways that describe its application, use, and location. Following are the terms most often used.

Plain stitching, without further definition, is of course the most common. When it is used for joining seams— **construction stitching**—it is good to make it *directional* when possible (see next heading). For selecting correct stitch-length for fabric, see FABRIC AND THREAD CHARTS, pp. 150–164.

In general, remember that well-made, expensive clothes have stitches as short as fabric requirements allow, while bargain-basement clothes invariably have long ones.

Topstitching is stitching that is visible on outside of garment. It is done from outside whenever possible, because [a] most machine-stitching looks much better on top than underneath, and [b] stitching-line can be better controlled from visible side. The stitch length is often shortened for the sake of looks.

Edge-stitching is stitching done close to an edge (finished or turned under), and may be either on inside of garment or on outside (in which case it becomes topstitching). For even stitching, guide fabric edge along some point on sewing machine, or along inside edge of presser foot.

Basting Stitch and **Gathering Stitch** simply mean the longest stitch on your machine. See BASTING and GATHERS.

Ease-stitching is the line of stitching that serves for drawing up a piece of fabric to be eased to another. See EASING, p. 59.

Stay-stitching is a line of directional stitching made inside a seam allowance, before construction-stitching, to keep an edge from being pulled out of shape in handling (see **Directional Stitching,** on this and the following page).

DIRECTIONAL STITCHING

Most of the seams you stitch are neither straight-grain nor true-bias. In other words, most seams are 'off-grain'. In loose-weave fabrics, particularly, such seams are easily pulled out of shape. In order to guard against this, it is good to acquire the habit of stitching directionally, i.e. with the grain and not against it.

Some patterns have printed arrows at seamlines to show correct stitching direction. In the absence of these, remember that, where the shape allows, you stitch from *wide to narrow*. For instance,

. . . from *hem to waist* in a skirt,

. . . from *underarm to waist* in a fitted bodice.

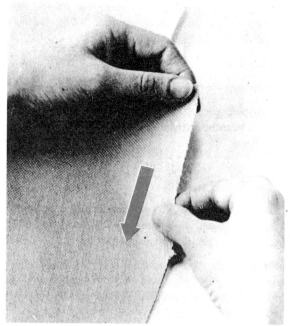

with the grain   11

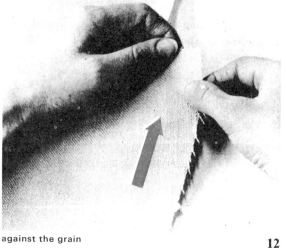

against the grain   12

At less clearly-defined cut edges, determine direction by sliding your thumb and forefinger along the edge (the 'stroke-the-kitty' test):
(. . . if edge stays smooth (11), you are going with the grain (smoothing kitty's fur). Stitch in that direction.

. . . if threads at edge get ruffled (12), you are going against the grain (ruffling kitty's fur). Don't stitch in that direction!

In curved seams, the grain naturally changes direction as an edge turns. You cannot, however, change the direction of your construction-stitching. That is one reason why stay-stitching is important with loose-weave fabrics. As you can see by the diagrams at right (13), at evenly-curved edges, stay-stitching is done in two runs, one in each grain direction; at an uneven curve, stay-stitching is done in direction that stays longest with the grain (see armhole curves in diagram).

To sum-up, try to make your construction-stitching directional as a matter of habit—loose fabric or firm, edges stay-stitched or not. But forget about it at most curved seams—where fabric is loose-woven, these should be stay-stitched.

Stay-stitching, which is strictly directional, stabilizes the grain at off-grain edges. With loose-grain weaves, it should always be done. On fabrics firmly woven or with a firm finish, it can safely be omitted.

Stay-stitching is done on the separate garment pieces the first thing after cutting and marking. Use matching thread and ordinary stitch. Stitch through a single thickness of fabric, 13 mm. from cut edge (so it will be outside construction-stitching); at a zip-fastener placket, place stay-stitching 6 mm. from cut edge.

Diagrams (13) show where and in what direction to stay-stitch. At any other off-grain edges, straight or curved, 'stroke the kitty' to determine direction of stitching.

When garment sections are backed, stay-stitching is omitted, because backing is attached with directional stitching (see BACKING), in this case often referred to as stay-stitching.

RIPPING OUT STITCHING

The term seems to imply tearing apart, which is exactly what must *not* be done. Clip through a stitch about every 50mm. and pick out stitches with a pin or a needle.

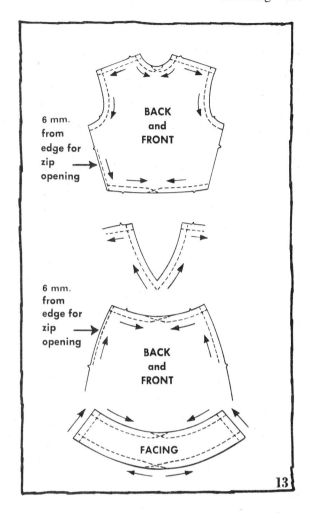

In some cases a stitch unpicker which can be bought specially for ripping out stitching and cutting buttonholes may be used. If you have this tool be careful not to cut the fabric.

Marking

Marking is a step a professional dressmaker never neglects but a home-sewer resists (which explains many a 'home-made look'). It is marking that allows you to sew with precision and safety, without fumbling.

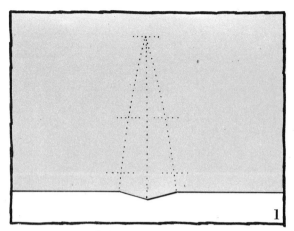

Once you have discovered how quickly it is done, and what a help it is in both your work and its results, you will not want to sew without having every pattern-mark on your fabric.

Marking means transferring pattern markings to fabric sections. It is done the first thing after cutting; *do not separate* pattern pieces from sections until you have transferred marks.

Construction details (darts, tucks, reference points for assembling) are marked on wrong side of fabric, or on backing fabric if backing is used.

Position marks for buttonholes, pockets, pleats, and trimming, which must show on right side, are first marked on wrong side. They are then transferred through fabric by means of baste-marking by hand or machine, unless tailor tacking, which shows on both sides, has been used as marks.

WHAT TO MARK

Matching-points—A circle shows where sleeve crown matches shoulder seam, where collar ends at a lapel, where fabric meets in a dart, where outside details are applied.

Centre-points—If they are on a fold, mark them in seam allowance (not only on main sections, but on collars, yokes, etc.) if you have not already done so while cutting.

Darts—If you are using tracing paper, make a short crossline (1) at point of dart and at alignment marks (circles). If pattern does not give centre line of darts,

measure centre of dart at widest point and draw line to point. You will fold dart on this line.

Seamlines on critical outlines, such as curves and points on collars, cuffs, lapels, etc., where two finished edges will face each other and must match perfectly. Also mark inner corners on a square neck so you will know when to pivot. Mark seamline on the section which will be on top when stitching, i.e.,

. . . on facing, when facing is smaller than garment section (e.g., lapel or square neck facings),
. . . on interfacing, when garment section, facing, and interfacing are the same size (e.g., collar or cuffs).

Do not mark arrow showing grain direction. This arrow serves only for placing pattern correctly on fabric.

HOW TO MARK

Printed or perforated patterns allow for any method of marking. Your choice will depend, not only on your

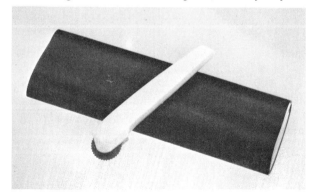

personal preference but also to a great extent on the fabric you are using.

Dressmaker's Tracing Paper and Tracing Wheel

Recommended for most firm, smooth fabrics, except sheers and lace, where marks would show through; or tweeds and spongy fabrics, on which marks are often unreliable and sometimes don't show.

Milward dressmaker's tracing or carbon paper, a specially-prepared waxed paper, comes in a few colours. Select a colour not in too great contrast with fabric, as it will not come out with pressing or washing. Always begin by test-marking a scrap of fabric, doubled as instructed below.

Tracing wheels can be used on most fabrics, and will even mark certain plain-weave, solid-colour wash-and-wear cottons without tracing paper.

Two layers of fabric, with pattern on top, are marked as follows: Fold sheet of tracing paper in half across width, with marking surface inside. Cut off a strip (2) about 50 mm. wide (each strip can be used many times).

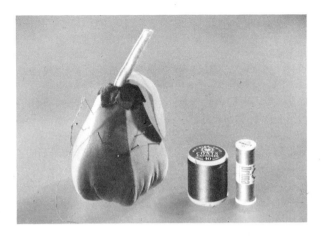

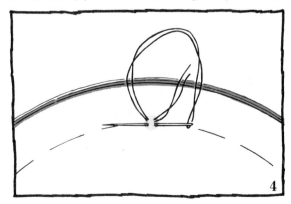

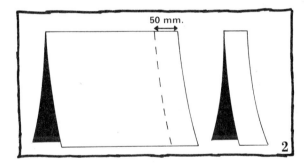

Tailor tacking is made with needle and thread.

Use a long thread, doubled, without a knot. At point to be marked, take a small stitch through pattern and both layers of fabric. Draw up, leaving a 25 mm. end. Take another stitch at same point, leaving a loop of 25 mm. or more (4). Cut thread, leaving a 25 mm. end (5).

Slip bottom half under fabric and insert upper half between fabric and pattern (remove pins only as needed). In this way, the two marking surfaces will be against the wrong side of both garment sections. Place a piece of cardboard or a magazine under work to protect table surface. Follow lines on pattern with wheel (3), using ruler for straight lines.

Tailor Tacking

A slightly slow, but excellent method, suitable for all fabrics, leaving no permanent marks, and visible on both sides of fabric.

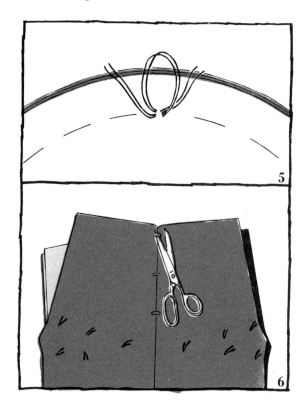

When all points are marked, remove pattern. Gently separate the layers of fabric to the extent of the thread loop and cut through threads, as shown (6). Little tufts of thread remain in each fabric layer as marks. Tailor tacking can also be made in a continuous line. In this case, it is necessary to clip the loops and remove the pattern. Separate as above.

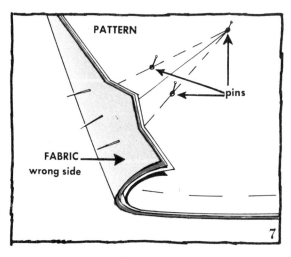

Pins

Quick, and usable on all fabrics. Be careful, however — pins slip out!

At each point to be marked, put a pin straight through pattern and fabric (7), to stick out on other side. Turn section over and put in another pin, in opposite direction, as close as possible to each pin.

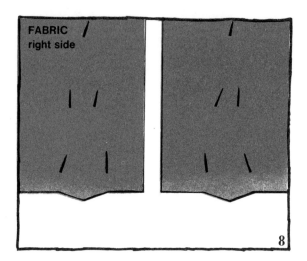

Remove pattern carefully. Separate the two layers of fabric, each one with pins bristling on right side (8).

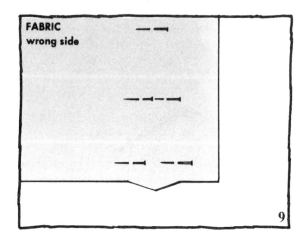

On wrong side, without ever entirely removing a pin from fabric, draw out each pin and pick up a few threads of fabric at the same spot (9). Push pins in far enough so they won't slip out.

Chalk

Chalk-marking is quick and easy, and very useful at times. It does not, however, show on all fabrics, or make reliable marks on nubbly weaves.

At each point to be marked, put a pin straight through pattern and fabric, to stick out on other side (7). Remove pattern carefully. On wrong side of both layers of fabric, use sharpened chalk to mark places where pins are. Remove pins. If desired (in darts, for instance), connect marks with chalk lines.

Patterns

Dress patterns are most carefully designed and accurately drafted. To begin with, they are based on data compiled from surveys made of the body measurements of a representative segment of the female population. Basic body measurements, therefore, are standard, and the same in all makes of patterns.

Patterns, however, are not cut to exact body measurements. This would produce skin-tight garments, entirely unwearable. A considerable allowance (ease), especially in the width, must be added for the wearer's comfort and freedom of movement. How much allowance is needed, and how it is distributed, is left to the pattern companies' quite careful discretion, and varies with each; this is why you, individually, may have 'better luck' (i.e., a better fit) with one brand than with another.

Patterns are offered in a vast variety of **styles,** in different **figure-types,** and in just about as many **sizes** as women and girls come in. Which combination of

these is right for you, or how to alter the nearest fit to your figure, is what concerns us here.

THE RIGHT PATTERN FOR YOU

To dispose of the question of pattern-brand: Here you can only proceed by trial. You may prefer the styles of one make to those of another, but no measurements will give you a clue to the subtle differences in line and cut that exist between them. For a first garment, choose a simple style (or a Basic Pattern—fitted bodice, straight skirt, set-in sleeves) in any brand. Patterns, incidentally, are never returnable to the store.

Style, figure-type, and **size,** the three other things you must decide upon, are very closely interrelated. To get the complete picture, you should read what follows about all three. Remember that correct choice of figure-type and size not only makes for good fit, but keeps alterations to a minimum.

Style is design, and has nothing to do with fit. Select a style that you like, and, until you are expert in dressmaking, steer clear of complicated designs! Every major pattern company has certain models designated as easy to make.

Figure-Type is what is meant by 'Misses,' 'Half-sizes,' 'Juniors,' and the other categories described, with sizes and measurements, on pp. 117–118. These categories, determined by the variations in our shapes, are very important—even the pattern-books are divided and indexed according to figure-types. They do not *necessarily* represent age-groups. What they are based on is proportion: the proportion to each other of the different measurements of the body, particularly length in proportion to width. Since it is undeniable, however, that age does have something to do with a person's shape, styles—both in patterns and in ready-to-wear—are usually designed to be suitable for the age-group implied by the figure-type ('Half-sizes,' for instance, are designed for more mature women; the whole 'Developing Figures' division is for girls in their teens, etc.). This does not make *all* of them unsuitable for other age-groups. This is where your taste and judgment come in.

You have, of course, been buying your ready-made

clothes for a certain figure-type. The chances are that your measurements will place you within the same category. If they do not, and you find that your proportions belong to a figure-type well outside your age-group and taste, be extra-careful in choosing your style. If the styles offered in that category are not at all appropriate for you, it is better to look under another figure-type, where the combination of measurements may not come as close to yours, but your taste is satisfied. Of course it may mean an alteration in the pattern.

Size is established by the four measurements—bust, waist, hips, and 'back waist length'—which appear as 'Standard Body Measurements' on pattern envelopes and are given on our **Chart of Types and Sizes** on pp. 117–118. Correct size ensures a minimum of alterations, if any. Pattern sizing has been changed by all major Pattern companies to correspond more closely to standard ready-to-wear sizing. The new style patterns have the NEW Sizing. However, it will take some time before all the patterns in the catalogues have this NEW Sizing. Meanwhile you will have to be very careful when choosing a pattern to be sure you buy the right size.

As a general rule, you will be buying one size smaller in the NEW Sizing than you did in the former sizing. However, since the NEW Sizing measurements for bust, waist, hip and back waist length and their proportions to each other have been changed, it is most important that you consult the measurement charts very carefully before deciding on the right siz patterns.

The charts in this book represent the NEW Sizing but the method of using them to determine your size is the same for NEW Sizing or former sizing. The former sizing charts will continue to be available in the pattern catalogues until all patterns are made in the NEW Sizing.

On p. 119 you will find instructions for making your **Personal Measurements Chart** in order to check your pattern for fit. Since taking even the first four measurements (the ones just mentioned) requires the help of another person and other preparation, it is a good idea to make this entire chart now, even though you will not need Measurements 5 to 11 until later.

We suggest two ways of determining your pattern size:
. . . If your ready-to-wear clothes fit you well, buy your pattern for the same figure-type and *the same size* for NEW Sizing patterns, but one size larger for former sizing patterns. For example, if you wear a Junior Size 11 in ready-to-wear you may choose a Junior Size 11 in NEW Sizing but Junior Size 13 in former sizing (for safety, compare the first four of your body measurements with the measurements on pattern envelope).

. . . Otherwise, read the description of each figure-type on the **Chart of Types and Sizes** and decide which ones may best be suited to you. On each of these charts, circle the measurements that match yours. If any one of your measurements falls between two on a chart (see example Mary Mythical's chart on p. 121), place the circle between the two; if it is closer to one than the other, circle the closer one.

Now compare the charts marked, and see which one best combines your measurements within one size (again, see Mary Mythical's results on p. 121). The kind of garment you are making, and the comparative ease or difficulty of alterations, make correct measurement more important at certain points than at others. For instance:

. . . In a dress or a blouse, correct **bust** size will ensure against the rather difficult alteration of the armhole-and-neck area. Pattern ease, however, will take care of a bust up to 25 mm. larger than the pattern.

. . . A straight skirt, shorts, or slacks, should have correct fit at the **hips**—the waist is easy to enlarge or take in.

. . . A full skirt usually goes by **waist** measurement, but, again, an alteration at the waist is easy.

. . . A loose-hanging or semi-fitted garment needs correct **bust** size and nothing else.

You may end up choosing a type and size in which no measurement is exactly yours, but all come reasonably close. In the unlikely event that, after buying a pattern and comparing all its actual measurements with your own (as directed on p. 119) you discover that another figure-type or size would require less alteration, we suggest that you buy this other pattern rather than make elaborate alterations on the first one you bought.

CHARTS OF TYPES AND SIZES

Based on Body Measurements

NEW
Sizing

Here are the eight figure-types devised to cover all the variants of the feminine form. All pattern companies make patterns in various types, based on the standard body measurements (proportions) shown in the chart for each, though some companies call the figure-types by slightly different names. We have divided them into two major groups—Developed Figures and Developing Figures—the latter belonging, generally, to young girls. It is between these two groups as a whole that the differences in proportions are the most pronounced. The 'Back Waist Length' is the clue to the wearer's height, though this would not hold true for a heavy person, with a rounded back. Styles offered in each are also described.

DEVELOPED FIGURES

Miss and Woman

This is the tallest type, well-proportioned. It is also the most common, offering the largest choice of styles. High-style, special-design patterns are always made in Misses sizes.

Bust	78	80	83	86	92	96	100	cm.
Waist	56	58	61	65	69	74	79	cm.
Hip	83	85	88	91	97	100	102	cm.
Back Waist Length	39	40	41	41	42	43	43	cm.
Misses Size	**6**	**8**	**10**	**12**	**14**	**16**	**18**	

Bust	102	112	117	122	127	132	137	cm.
Waist	86	92	96	103	109	116	122	cm.
Hip	112	117	122	127	132	137	142	cm.
Back Waist Length	44	44	44	45	45	45	46	cm.
Woman's Size	**38**	**40**	**42**	**44**	**46**	**48**	**50**	

Junior

Shorter than the Miss—hence shorter-waisted—but well-proportioned, with a high-placed bust. Junior styles tend to the youthful, without being juvenile, and can usually be worn by all ages.

Bust	76	79	81	85	89	94	cm.
Waist	55	57	60	62	66	71	cm.
Hip	81	84	86	90	94	99	cm.
Back Waist Length	38	39	39	40	41	41	cm.
Junior Size	**5**	**7**	**9**	**11**	**13**	**15**	

Half-Size

The fraction added to the size indicates narrower shoulders and greater middle-fullness in proportion to height. Styles in the Half-Sizes tend to be on the conservative side.

Bust	84	89	94	99	104	109	114	119	cm.
Waist	66	71	76	81	86	92	99	105	cm.
Hip	89	94	99	104	109	116	122	128	cm.
Back Waist Length	38	39	39	40	40	41	41	41	cm.
Half-Size	**$10\frac{1}{2}$**	**$12\frac{1}{2}$**	**$14\frac{1}{2}$**	**$16\frac{1}{2}$**	**$18\frac{1}{2}$**	**$20\frac{1}{2}$**	**$22\frac{1}{2}$**	**$24\frac{1}{2}$**	

Junior Petite

Designed for the well-proportioned diminutive figure. Waist is small.

Bust	76	79	81	84	86	89	cm.
Waist	56	57	60	62	65	67	cm.
Hip	80	81	84	86	89	92	cm.
Back Waist Length	36	36	37	38	38	39	cm.
Jr. Petite Size	**3JP**	**5JP**	**7JP**	**9JP**	**11JP**	**13JP**	

DEVELOPING FIGURES

Young Junior/Teen

A size range designed for the shorter pre-teen and teen figure with bust not fully developed.

Bust..............	71	74	78	81	85	89	cm.
Waist.............	56	58	61	64	66	69	cm.
Hip..............	79	81	85	89	92	96	cm.
Back Waist Length...	24	36	37	38	39	40	cm.
Young **Junior/Teen Size.....**	**5/6**	**7/8** **9/10**		**11/12** **13/14**	**15/16**		

Chubby

Designed for a figure not yet developed and with more girth all around than most girls the same age.

Breast..............	76	80	84	88	cm.
Waist..............	71	74	76	79	cm.
Hip................	84	88	92	95	cm.
Back Waist Length...	31	32	34	36	cm.
Approx. Heights.....	132	142	149	155	cm.
Chubby Size........	**8½c**	**10½c**	**12½c**	**14½c**	

Girl

Designed for the flat, immature figure.

Breast................	66	69	72	76	81	cm.
Waist................	58	60	62	65	67	cm.
Hip..................	69	71	76	81	86	cm.
Back Waist Length......	27	31	32	24	36	cm.
Approx. Heights........	127	132	142	149	155	cm.
Girl Size..............	**7**	**8**	**10**	**12**	**14**	

EXAMPLE: Let's see how a 'Mary Mythical' goes about finding her figure type and size. Mary has taken her measurements. (See chart on page 121.)

Next, she turns to the **Charts of Types and Sizes** and reads the introductory paragraph. Whatever Mary's age may be, she happens to know that she does not have a child's figure, and so disregards the whole 'Developing' group. Her longer back waist measurement eliminates Junior Petite. As for Half-size, while she is a bit wider in the beam than she likes, and only short-average in height, she does not have the bust-waist-hip fullness and comparatively narrow shoulders that are characteristic of this figure-type. This leaves Miss and Junior, whose styles she likes best anyway. On the two charts she now checks, her measurements fall like this:

Bust.............	78	80	83	86	92	96	100	cm.
Waist...........	56	58	61	65	69	74	79	cm.
Hip.............	83	85	88	91	97	100	102	cm.
Back Waist Length	39	40	41	41	42	43	43	cm.
Misses Size......	**6**	**8**	**10**	**12**	**14**	**16**	**18**	

Bust..............	76	79	81	85	89	94	cm.
Waist.............	55	57	60	62	66	71	cm.
Hip...............	81	84	86	90	94	99	cm.
Back Waist Length...	38	39	39	40	41	41	cm.
Junior Size........	**5**	**7**	**9**	**11**	**13**	**15**	

On the Misses chart, the Back Waist Length is entirely out of line, which means that the up-and-down points (points of bust, elbow, etc.) will fall in the wrong places. On the Junior chart this measurement is almost perfect, while the important bust measurement is right, too. It is no trick to add 13 mm. to the waist and 38 mm. to the hips. Mary's pattern will be a Junior 11.

CHECKING YOUR PATTERN FOR FIT

Even if your body measurements and those on the pattern envelope match perfectly, this does not, unfortunately, guarantee that the pattern will be a perfect fit otherwise (though there is a good chance of its being so). We are sorry to say that you cannot even depend on a difference in a basic measurement (such as Mary Mythical's 50 mm. in the hips) being the correct one on which to base an alteration—there is that matter of **ease,** on which pattern companies not only vary with each other, but in which they may make changes according to the style.

The only way to be safe with a pattern is to compare *all* its relevant measurements with either:

. . . the same measurements taken from a well-fitting garment of the same design, at exactly the same points, or

. . . your own complete measurements, plus ease wherever called for.

To Make Your Personal Measurements Chart, have someone help you with the measuring. Measure over well-fitting undergarments. Tie a narrow ribbon, tape, or string snugly around your waist to mark exact location of waistline.

Use a full sheet of ruled paper. Mark it off in seven columns (see sample chart on p. 121). In the first column, list the eleven points to measure, as given below. In the second column, enter the measurements, taken as instructed:

1. **Bust**—(measured firmly around fullest part).
2. **Waist**—(at ribbon around waist).
3. **Hips**—(around fullest part, 228 mm. below waist for Misses, Women and Junior; 178 mm. below waist for Half-Sizes, Junior Petite and Young Junior/Teen).
4. **Back Waist Length**—(from prominent vertebra at back of neck to waistline ribbon).
5. **Front Waist Length**—(from middle of shoulder over point of bust to waistline ribbon).
6. **Point of Bust**—(from middle of shoulder to point of bust only; note when taking measurement No. 5).

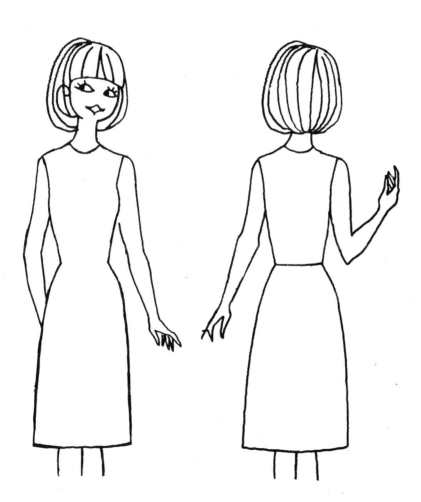

7. **Back Width**—(across back, 102 mm. down from neck bone, between body folds formed by arms hanging straight).

8. **Sleeve Length**—(from edge of shoulder, where sleeve would be set in, over bended elbow to desired length).

9. **Point of Elbow**—(above measurement to point of elbow only).

10. **Upper Arm**—(around arm, 25 mm. below armpit; if one arm is larger, use larger measurement).

11. **Skirt Length**—(measure centre front of a garment of correct length, from bottom edge of waistband to hem of skirt).

The third and fourth columns are for 'Ease' and 'Total'. Under 'Ease', enter the following amounts on the proper line (these are *average* ease allowances, which you can make larger or smaller depending on whether you want your garment loose or snug). The other measurements do not need ease—just make a dash in the column instead.

1. **Bust**—76 mm. to 102 mm. for fitted bodice
127 mm. to 152 mm. for loose top or jacket
3. **Hips**—50 mm. to 64 mm. for straight skirt
5. **Front Waist Length**—about 6 mm.
7. **Back Width**—13 mm. to 25 mm.
10. **Upper Arm**—25 mm. to 50 mm. for fitted sleeve

NOTE: Do not confuse *body ease*, above, with *design ease* (blousy top, full skirt, etc.). The latter is a matter of design, not fit. Fortunately, such loosely-fitted garment-parts practically never need an alteration. Add up body measurement and ease and enter the total in the 'Total' column. Where there is no ease, enter the body measurement.

You now have a basic measurements chart for your figure, which will change only with your weight (or posture). The exception is the skirt length, which is subject only to fashion. Date the chart—you will want to check your measurements against it from time to time.

The Pattern Pieces you will use for your garment must now be selected, with the help of your primer. Smooth out the creases with a warm, dry iron. With pencil and yardstick, extend both ends of grain lines the entire length of pattern.

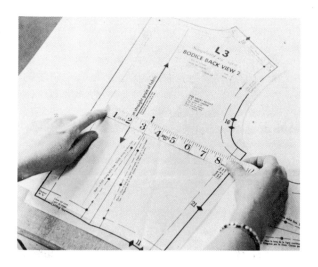

Measuring Your Pattern must be done with care, of course, but it is not difficult if you go about it right.

. . . Work with pattern piece flat on table.

. . . When bodice front has both waist and side darts, draw a line through centre of each dart to just beyond point; where the two lines meet will be point of bust.

. . . When bodice front has only one dart, point of bust will be about 13 mm. beyond point of dart.

. . . Take all measurements *without* seam allowances.

. . . When only half a pattern is given (main body pieces), be sure to double measurement before writing it down.

In the fifth column on your chart, enter measurements taken from your pattern as follows:

1. **Bust**—(centre front and centre back to side seamlines, about 50 mm. below armhole or at point-of-bust level. Double this measurement.).

2. **Waist**—(copy from pattern envelope—disregard for loose-waisted garment).

3. **Hip**—(centre front and centre back to side seamlines, at same distance from waist as body measurement was taken. Double this measurement. Disregard for full or flaring skirt.).

4. **Back, Neck to Waist**—(copy from pattern envelope).

5. **Front, Shoulder to Waist**—(middle of shoulder to point of bust and down to waistline).

6. **Point of Bust**—(middle of shoulder to point of bust).

7. **Back Width**—(across back, 76 mm. below the shoulder edge at armhole seamline).

8. **Sleeve Length**—(centre top to wrist edge).

9. **Point of Elbow**—(centre top to middle dart or centre of ease area in seamline).

10. **Upper Arm**—(across sleeve from seamline to seamline, 25 mm. below top of underarm seam—disregard for full sleeve).

11. **Skirt Length**—(at front, from waist to hemline—

measure off the hem allowance indicated on your pattern, and mark).

Now compare these figures with the ones in column 4 ('Total') and enter the difference, if any, in column 6, as shown in the chart below. For the alteration needed, study the **Pattern Alterations** that follow on the next page.

Below is part of Mary Mythical's chart. It indicates what alterations she will make.

MARY MYTHICAL'S CHART

	BODY MEAS.	EASE	TOTAL	PATTERN MEAS.	DIFFERENCE	ALTERATION
1. Bust	85 cm	76–102 mm	93 – 95 cm	95 cm	None	None
2. Waist	64 cm	—	64 cm	62 cm	12 mm needed	Add to seam
3. Hip	94 cm	51–64 mm	99–100 cm	95 cm	50 mm needed	Add to side seam
4. Back waist length	40 cm	—	40 cm	40 cm	3 mm needed	None Difference negligible

PATTERN ALTERATIONS

The alterations that follow are the ones indicated by the comparison of measurements just made. If you are difficult to fit in ready-made clothes, you may need alterations that we do not have space for here, and it may be very much to your advantage to make a **Muslin Basic,** as described on p. 132, to establish once and for all where—aside from the above measurements—your pattern needs adjustment. Two possible defects that do not show up until the garment, or the Muslin Basic, is tried on, are a neckline or a sleeveless armhole either too wide or too snug. We give the alteration, however, on p. 131, for use on your

next pattern, or correction of the present one after trying on the Muslin Basic.

All alterations given here are made on a Basic Pattern —i.e., one with fitted bodice, straight skirt, and long, fitted sleeves.

The principle of good pattern alteration is to change the measurements indicated without changing the pattern's essential outline.

Alterations in length and width are made in two locations:

[a] Along cutting lines, when taking off or adding on can be done without disturbing the lines; i.e.,

. . . in **length,** at hem of a plain skirt, a short sleeve, etc. (see skirt alteration on p. 125).

. . . in **width,** when a very small change in each of a number of seams (and darts) will total up to whatever is necessary (see Hip and Waist alterations, p. 127).

[b] Through body of pattern, by folding to reduce size or cutting-and-spreading to increase. This method preserves the shape of the outer pattern, the place of darts, etc., and is described under **Three Basic How-To's,** following.

For Easy and Accurate Altering . . .

. . . make alterations with pattern piece spread flat on table,

. . . for some increases in size, you will need tissue paper,

. . . secure alterations with pins, cellophane tape, or baste-stitching on sewing machine,

. . . try to combine alterations (one operation often takes care of two; see **Shortening and Lengthening of Bodice and Sleeve),**

. . . most patterns have a printed line showing where a skirt, bodice, or sleeve can best be lengthened or shortened (alteration line). If there is no such line, draw one in with pencil and ruler, if needed. Directions for specific alterations on the next pages will show you where to place alteration line.

Remember that after an alteration . . .

. . . pattern must still *lie flat,*

. . . matching seamlines must *still match,*

. . . printed or perforated lines (seam, grain, etc.) broken by alteration must be redrawn as they were before, the straight lines with a ruler, the curved lines by hand (see p. 123).

Three Basic How-To's

How to fold a pattern to reduce size

Measuring from alteration line, mark amount to be taken out. Draw second line as shown (1), either parallel with first, or on a slant (9, p. 124), as necessary.

Fold pattern on first line and bring fold to second line. Smooth out pattern carefully (2). Secure fold.

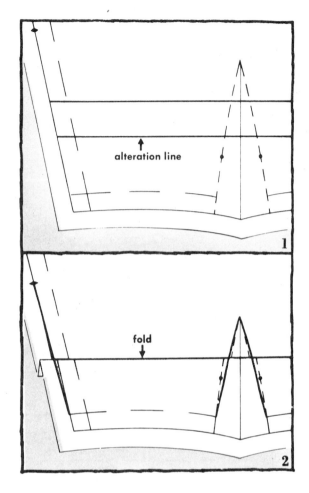

With ruler, redraw all lines crossing fold to connect smoothly and maintain pattern shape. With a slanted fold (9, p. 124), this means that, beyond fold, lines must be redrawn as a continuation of the original line, and that side edges will be trimmed on one side and added to on the other.

How to spread a pattern to increase size

Cut pattern piece along alteration line.

Secure cut edge of main section to a piece of tissue paper (3). With pencil and ruler, extend all straight lines across tissue (grain line, centre line, centre of dart).

Measure on tissue amount to be added. To mark amount, draw a line either parallel with cut edge or on a slant (11, p. 124), as necessary.

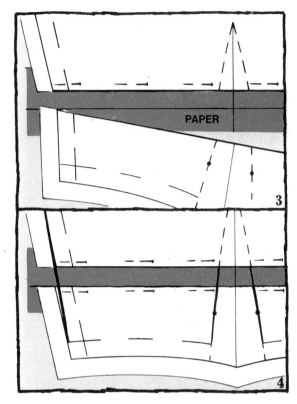

Secure remaining pattern section to tissue, with cut edge on marked line (4), matching at vertical lines drawn in.

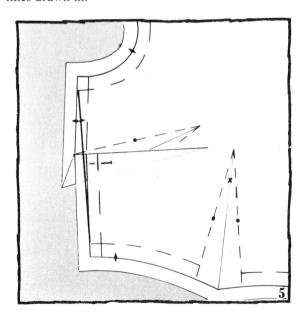

Redraw all lines to connect smoothly and maintain pattern shape. If inset tapers, this means that, on the smaller pattern section, lines must be redrawn as a continuation of the original line, before section was cut off, and that side edges will be trimmed on one side and added to on the other (11, p. 124).

How to make a new cutting line after dart alteration

If a dart coming from a seam has been altered in size or direction, cutting line must be redrawn. Pin altered dart together (5) and fold (down at side, toward centre at waist). Redraw and cut cutting line across fold (5), with ruler for a straight seam, freehand for a curved seam (waistline). Remove pins (6).

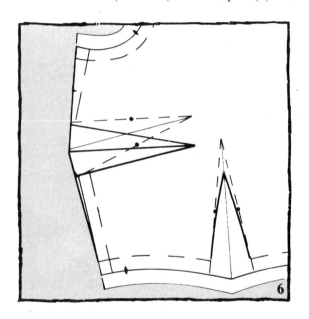

SHORTENING AND LENGTHENING

Bodice (Measurements 4 and 5)

If there is no printed alteration line, draw one 50 mm. to 76 mm. above waistline, at right angles to centre front and/or back (7, 8).

NOTE: When making an alteration in length on bodice front, take into account any alteration needed in Measurement 6.

An alteration line placed *above* the bust dart will take care of at least part of the alteration in length (all of it,

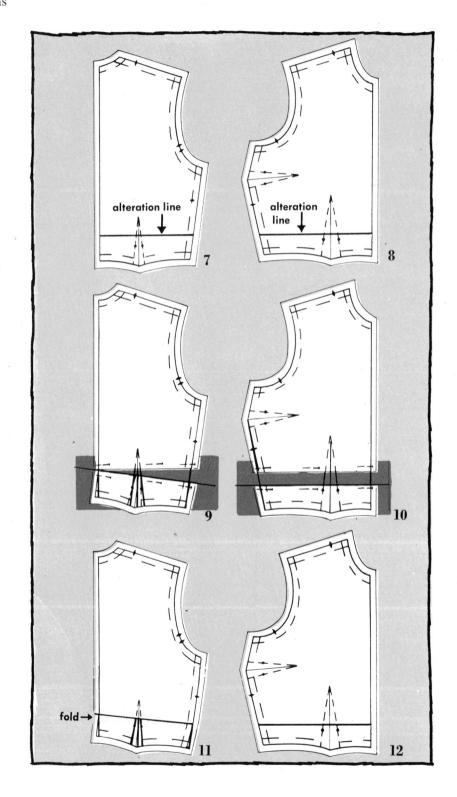

if alterations needed for Measurement 5 and Measurement 6 are the same).

See Method II under **Bust Darts,** on p. 126.

Follow **How-To** instructions on pp. 122–123. Matching seamlines will automatically continue to match if alteration is the same for Measurement 4 and Measurement 5 (back and front), and fold or spread will go straight across back and front.

If, however, the alteration is made only on front or only on back, or in both but in different amounts, the fold or the tissue inset, as the case may be, must taper or widen at the seams (9–10, 11–12), depending on

which is needed, if you are to keep seam edges matching.

Follow **How-To's** for straightening lines.

Skirt (Measurement 11)

A skirt is usually shortened or lengthened at hemline (13). If there is a pleat, however, draw an alteration line above pleat as shown (14), and follow **How-To** instructions on pp. 122–123.

Sleeve (Measurement 8)

On a long sleeve, if there are no printed alteration lines, draw lines about 127 mm. below underarm and 127 mm. above bottom edge, as shown (15).

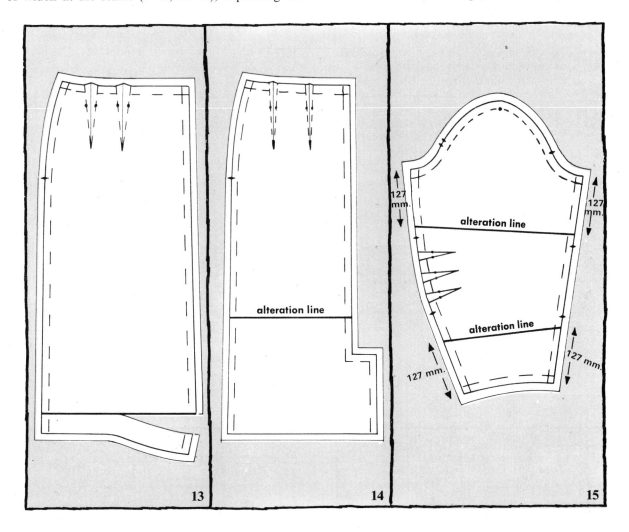

NOTE: See **Sleeve Darts** on p. 127, and check Measurement 9. Any alteration in position of sleeve darts may be taken care of while altering length of sleeve.

Using one or both alteration lines, as necessary, follow the **How-To** instructions which you will find on pp. 122–123.

On a straight, short sleeve, make alteration at the bottom edge.

LOWERING AND RAISING DARTS

Darts correctly placed are essential to the fit of a garment.

Bust Darts (Measurement 6)

For a smooth fit, underarm dart should point directly toward point of bust. Moving an underarm dart is a simple alteration which can be done by either of the two methods that follow if bodice length needs no change; or by Method II if it is done in combination with an alteration in bodice length.

METHOD I. If dart is *horizontal* (16), point can be raised as much as 25 mm., but cannot be lowered; if dart is *slanted upward* (17), it can be lowered 25 mm. but can't be raised. Mark new point of dart; using ruler, connect point with the two base points at seamline, as shown. Correct cutting line as directed in last

How-To on p. 122. Raise or lower point of waist dart (if any) the same amount.

METHOD II. May be used in combination with shortening or lengthening bodice front (see that heading), in which case the lower alteration line would be either omitted or the amount taken out or added would be changed as needed. As described here, the method preserves original bodice length.

Draw two alteration lines: one 50 mm. to 76 mm. above waistline, the other above bust dart—both at

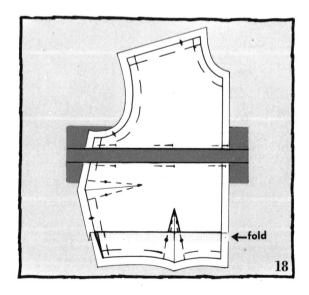

right angles to centre front. See **How-To** instructions on pp. 122–123.

To lower dart, cut pattern on upper alteration line and spread to amount needed; fold pattern on lower alteration line, taking in the same amount (18).

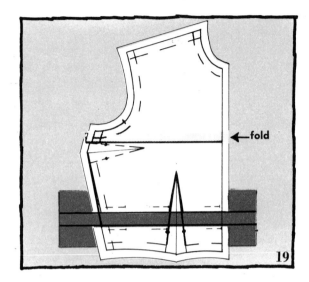

To raise dart, fold pattern on upper alteration line, taking in amount needed; cut on lower alteration line and spread to the same amount (19).

On waist dart, if any, draw new lines from point to two base points.

Sleeve Darts (Measurement 9)

See **Shortening and Lengthening Sleeve** (Measurement 8). Middle dart, or mid-point between notches, should be directly at bend of elbow (Measurement 9).

REDUCING AND INCREASING WIDTH

Hip (Measurement 3)

A hip alteration must be carried all the way to the hem.

. . . For an alteration of 50 mm. or less:
Add or take off at side seams. *One-quarter* the amount of alteration (13 mm. for 50 mm.) added to or taken off each edge will add up to total. Measure down from waistline to point of hip measurement. Mark alteration at that point; then, using yardstick, redraw line down

to hem, parallel to old line. Above altered point, draw a line tapering to waistline, as shown (20).
. . . For an increase of more than 50 mm.:
Add 50 mm. as above. Then, with yardstick, draw an alteration line through dart to hem, on back and front sections (if there are two darts, go through dart nearest side seam). Spread each piece one-quarter the total amount needed. Adjust waistline by taking deeper darts.

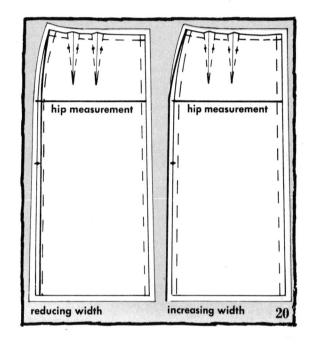

Waist (Measurement 2)

A waist alteration must be made on both bodice and skirt.

. . . For an alteration of 50 mm. or less:
Add or take off at side seams. *One-quarter* the amount (13 mm. for 50 mm.) added to or taken off each edge will add up to total. Then draw new cutting lines: on skirt, taper to join existing cutting line at hip; on bodice, pin up bust darts, if any, and use ruler to draw new cutting line from underarm to waist.
. . . For an alteration of more than 50 mm.:
Alter side seams as above to take out or add 50 mm. Divide *remaining* amount by number of waist darts. Then draw new stitching lines for darts: *inside* existing dart for an increase in size (21), *outside* existing

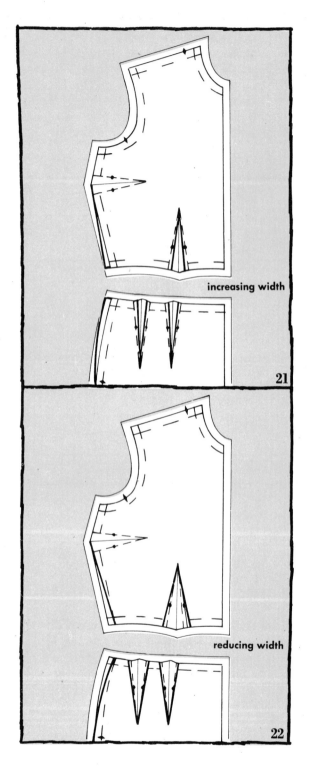

increasing width

21

reducing width

22

dart (22) for a decrease (a change of 3 mm. at each stitching line—i.e., 6 mm. added to each dart—will make a change of 25 mm. on a garment with 4 darts).

Bust (Measurements 1 and 7)

A bust alteration is generally divided equally between front and back of bodice. If you are either full-busted or flat-chested, alteration may need to be made entirely on the front. If your back is very broad or very narrow (Measurement 7), it may need to be made entirely on the back. Or it may be divided unequally between front and back.

NOTE for both **Front** and **Back**: After completing alteration below . . .

Restore original waist measurement by measuring the amount that pattern has been overlapped or spread at waistline level; then add or trim away an equal amount at side seam and draw new cutting line with ruler.

Redraw waistline to conform with original line, shortening pattern when there was a decrease in width, lengthening for an increase.

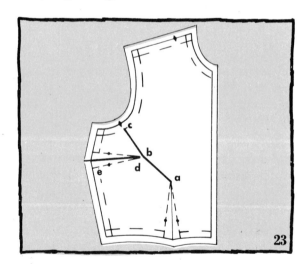

23

Front—Using ruler, draw lines as shown (23) . . .
. . . from point of waistline dart [a], to 3 mm. from point of underarm dart [b], then to armhole seamline near notch [c],
. . . through centre of underarm dart, if not printed on pattern [d-e].

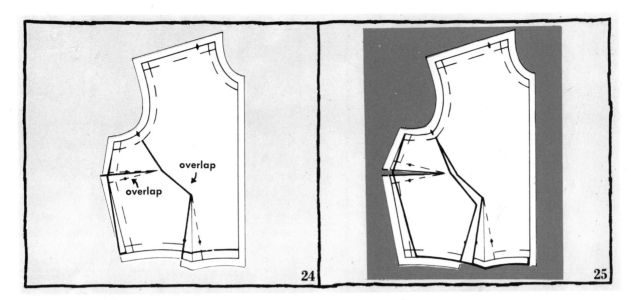

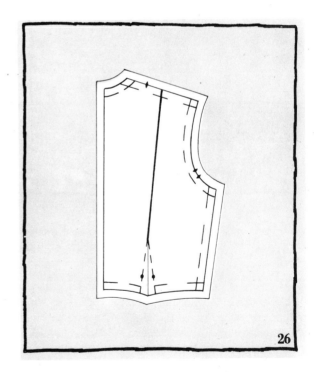

Cut up along outer line of waistline dart (nearer side seam) and along drawn line to points a-b-c. Do not cut beyond armhole seamline.

... *To reduce size,* measure one half of total front alteration out from cut, just above point b; lap edge with waistline dart on it over as far as mark, smooth out pattern carefully, and secure overlap at this point. Cut through centre of underarm dart (d-e). Shift bottom section of pattern so that bust dart and waist are altered about the same amount. Secure overlaps (24). Restore original waist measurement and waistline. Waistline dart remains original size while bust dart is decreased.

... *To increase size,* slip tissue paper under pattern. Spread out cut, measuring on tissue, just above point b, one half the total alteration for front. Secure cut edges to tissue at this point. Cut through centre of underarm dart (d-e). Shift bottom section of pattern so that bust dart and waist are altered about the same amount (25). Secure all cut edges to tissue. Restore original waist measurement and waistline. Waistline dart remains original size while bust dart is increased.

Back—Using ruler, draw a line from point of dart to centre of shoulder (26). Cut up along outer line of waistline dart (nearer side seam) and along drawn line to shoulder seamline. Make sure that you do not cut beyond seamline.

Amount of alteration is measured at a level 25 mm. below top of underarm seam.

... *To reduce size,* measure one half of total back alteration out from cut; mark. Lap dart edge over as far as mark; smooth out pattern carefully and

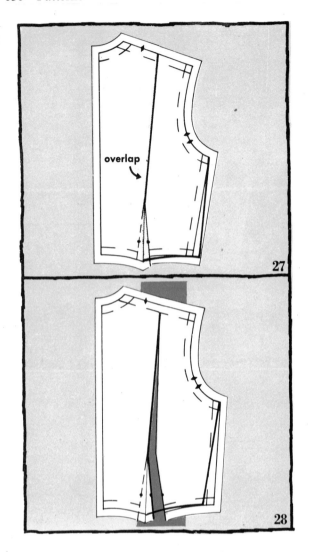

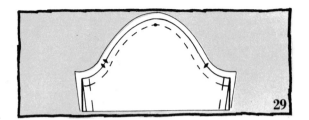

taking in seam after trying on garment. A short sleeve can usually be widened or narrowed at the underarm seam, as shown (29).

Upper part of a long or three-quarter sleeve can be widened as follows. Since it leaves armhole untouched, not more than 25 mm. should be added by this method.

Using yardstick, draw a line parallel with grain line from centre of sleeve cap to centre of wrist; and a line across as shown, 25 mm. below top of underarm seam (30). Cut along both lines, stopping and starting *inside* seamlines (do not cut into seam allowance).

secure overlap (27). Restore original waist measurement and waistline. Waistline dart remains original size.

. . . *To increase size,* slip tissue paper under pattern. Spread pattern to one half of total back alteration and secure cut edges to tissue (28). Restore original waist measurement and waistline. Waistline dart remains original size.

Sleeve (Measurement 10)

A sleeve sometimes needs widening, practically never narrowing. Tightening the lower part can be done by

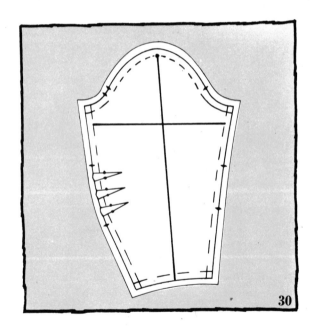

Slip tissue paper under pattern. Spread the lengthwise cut the necessary amount, meanwhile letting crosswise edges overlap to keep pattern flat. Secure all cut edges. Draw new grain line through centre of tissue insert. Redraw cutting line at wrist (31).

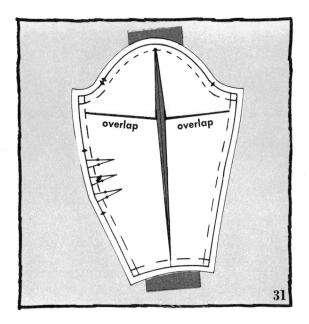

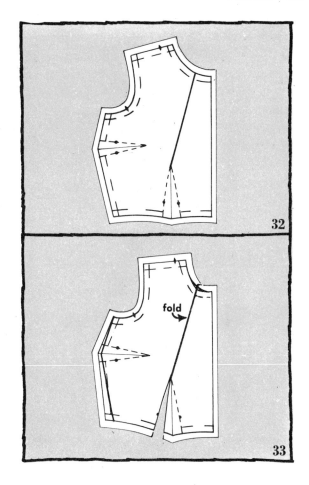

MISCELLANEOUS

As mentioned earlier, the fact that a neckline or an armhole in a sleeveless garment is either too wide or too snug cannot be established through measurements. You may know from your ready-to-wear that your clothes tend to have these defects. In anything home-sewn, they will not show up until you try on the garment (or Muslin Basic). Once you know the alteration is needed, however, it can be made in the pattern.

Gaping Neckline

Determine amount to be taken out by pinning a tuck at centre front and/or centre back. Alteration on pattern will be half this amount.

Using ruler, draw a line from point of waistline dart to neckline, about 50 mm. from centre (32). At neckline, measure and mark amount to be taken out.

Cut along outer line (nearer side seam) of waistline dart, to point of dart *only*. Fold pattern on pencil line, bringing fold to alteration mark at neckline and tapering to nothing at point of dart. Secure fold. Pattern will have spread on cut line; slip a piece of tissue paper under gap in pattern; secure cut edges to tissue.

To restore original waist measurement, measure in from cutting line at side seam an amount equal to pattern spread. Draw new cutting line (33). Waistline dart remains original size.

Reshape neckline curve, adding tissue if necessary. Alter facing to fit new neckline.

High Neckline or Sleeveless Armhole
Too Snug or Too Wide

A neckline close to the neck or an armhole in a sleeveless garment may not fit properly because they are either too snug or too loose. In such a case the pattern is altered by re-drawing the cutting line, placing it higher (34) or lower (35) as the case may be.

Any alterations made on the bodice must naturally

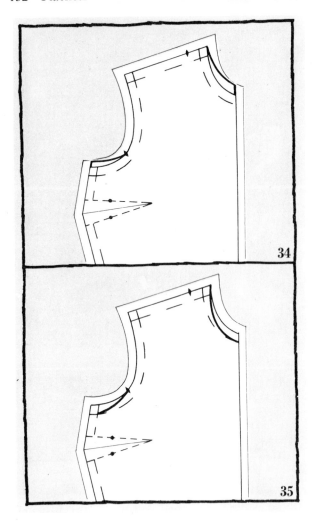

be repeated on the facings and on the collar, if there is one.

MAKING A MUSLIN BASIC

A Muslin Basic is a partly-finished trial garment, made out of preshrunk, firmly-woven cotton (unbleached muslin or an old sheet), for the purpose of taking any uncertainty out of size and fit. To be really 'basic,' it should be made from the Basic Pattern (from which actual garments can be made in several variations) to establish all your measurements, the alterations you may need and so on, for future reference. You may, however, wish to make 'a muslin'

before cutting out any dress, especially if the cut is tricky and/or the fabric expensive.

Do not, just because this is a muslin, omit any of the preparations—this, in fact, is where you will try them out. Select your pattern as directed in the preceding pages, check it for fit, and carefully make the alterations indicated.

See CUTTING, pp. 47-48. After cutting out muslin, transfer markings from pattern to muslin as directed in MARKING, p. 113. In addition, mark all seamlines, so that any alterations made on muslin will be easier to transfer to pattern.

No edges (neck, hem) will be finished. To check fit of neckline or a sleeveless armhole later, make a line of stitching directly on seamline, and clip around through seam allowance to stitching.

For construction, use long stitch to facilitate opening seams (it may be necessary), and follow pattern primer. Leave edges, zip-fastener opening, etc., unfinished (when trying on, pin up opening).

Try on muslin (have someone help you). See if pattern alterations have come out right. *Do not overfit!* But if additional alterations are needed, do not hesitate to mark and slash into the muslin to remove or add fullness where needed, as indicated in the foregoing **Pattern Alterations.**

When you are satisfied with the fit of the muslin, transfer any alterations you have made on it to the paper pattern, and make a note of them on your personal measurement chart. Unless your figure changes, you will now know exactly what alterations to make on your patterns.

Plackets

A placket is a partial opening (i.e., closed at one or both ends) that allows a garment to be put on and taken off. It is most often in a seam, but may be cut as a slash in the fabric. For zip-fastener plackets, see ZIP-FASTENERS. Other plackets may be finished with a strip of fabric or a facing. See the following.

PLACKET WITH CONTINUOUS OPENING

This may be in a seam, as when it forms the lower part (skirt portion) of a child's dress placket; or in a slash, as in long shirtsleeves.

Placket in a Seam

At bottom of opening (end of stitched seam), clip through seam allowance to seamline (1).

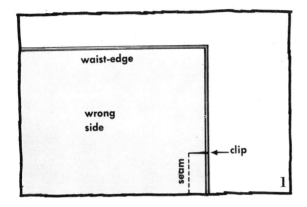

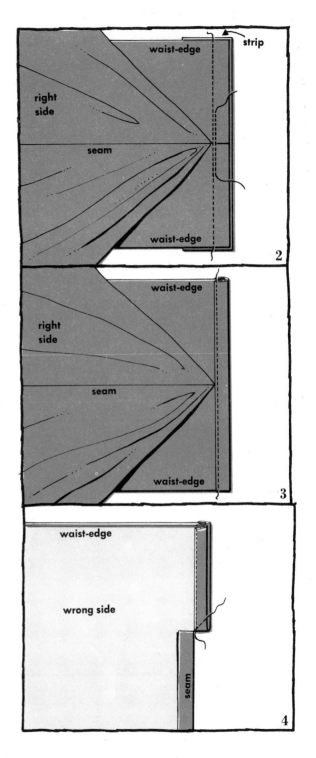

For lap, cut a strip of fabric, either on straight grain or on bias, 48 mm. wide and twice as long as opening.

Spreading out opening as shown (2) and matching edges evenly, pin wrong side of opening edges in a straight line over right side of strip. Stitch, with ordinary seam allowance. Where seam allowance is clipped, reinforce by doubling stitching for about 50 mm., as shown. Trim seam allowance to 6 mm.

Press strip and seam away from garment. Turn in free edge of strip 6 mm; press. Folding strip in half lengthwise, topstitch free edge over first stitching (3).

From inside, fold lap (4); stitch diagonally across fold as shown.

Fold one side of lap (left edge on a centre back opening) along seamline and press (5).

Placket in a Slash—NOTE: *Do not* slash until you have reinforced point with stitching.

If stitching line is not indicated on pattern, use ruler to draw lines as shown (6), from end of slash line to 6 mm. on either side of line at fabric edge.

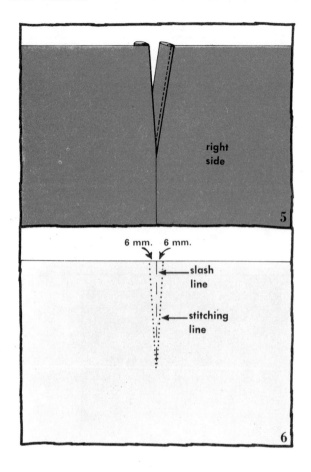

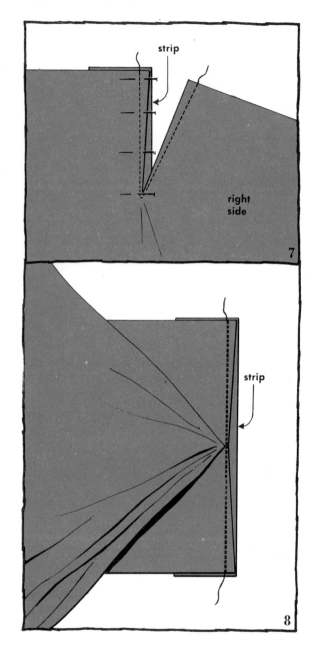

Using small machine stitch for reinforcement, stitch on marked line, taking two stitches across point. Cut on slash line, being careful not to clip stitching at point.

For lap, cut a strip of fabric, either on straight grain or on bias, 38 mm. wide and twice as long as slash line.

Pin wrong side of one edge of slash over right side of strip, keeping stitched line on slash 6 mm. from edge of strip (7).

Still using small stitch, stitch just outside existing stitched line, going toward point. At point, *leave needle down* in fabric. Bring other edge of slash forward and match end to end of strip, so that stitched line is lined up as before. Continue stitching to end of slash (8).

For finishing, see 3, 4, 5, in **Placket in a Seam,** p. 133.

FACED PLACKET IN A SLASH

Used at necklines that may be intended for zip-fastener closure, or for a button or hook at top. Also on long shirtsleeves.

NOTE: *Do not* slash until after facing is applied.

If stitching line is not indicated on facing pattern, use a ruler to draw lines as shown (6): from end of slash line to 6 mm. on either side of line at fabric edge.

Pin facing (free edges finished, as shown) to garment, right side to right side. Using a small stitch on marked line, going toward point. At point, leave

needle down in fabric, pivot, take two stitches across, pivot again, and stitch down other edge (9).

Cut on slash line through both thicknesses, being careful not to clip stitching at point (9). Turn facing to inside; press.

Finish placket with zip-fastener, or a hook, button, or snap at top. Unless a zip-fastener is used, reinforce bottom of opening with a bar tack on wrong side (10).

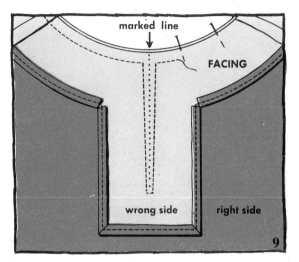

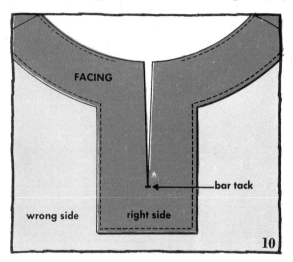

Pleats

Pleats are folds in fabric providing controlled fullness. They may be placed in a garment singly or in a series.

For a single pleat in a dress or skirt, you need only follow the directions of your pattern instruction sheet. What we give you here is general information on pleats, and the principles of all-round pleating in skirts; all are meant to supplement, not replace, the directions in your instruction sheet. We also give you directions for a Dior Pleat, which has several advantages over an ordinary one. For useful pointers on finishing a pleat, see HEMS, p. 99.

KINDS OF PLEATS

NOTE: The first three pleats (Knife, Box, Inverted) described at right can be either pressed all the way

down, stitched down part of the way, or left unpressed; they may also be edge-stitched along one or both folds. Pressed pleats can be done commercially.

Knife or Side Pleats (1) have folds all turned in one direction. Folds start across back from left to right, automatically becoming right to left across front, with last pleat covering placket.

Box Pleats (2) consist of two equal folds turned away from each other, with under-folds meeting in centre underneath.

Inverted Pleats (3) consist of two equal folds turned toward each other and meeting.

As you can see, Box and Inverted Pleats are two sides

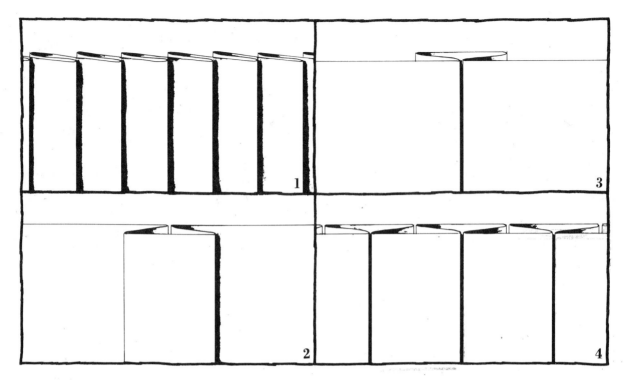

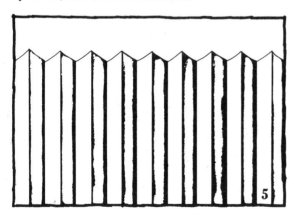

of the same pleat; hence, they look alike on both sides when made in a series (4).

Accordion Pleats (5) are narrow pleats opening out to resemble the folds in an accordion. They can only be made commercially, are always pressed all the way down, and are never stitched.

FABRIC IN RELATION TO PLEATS

Synthetic fabrics (except rayon) and blends usually hold a well-pressed-in crease perfectly, even through washing. Wools and heavy silks hold a crease well. Cotton, lightweight silk, and rayon do not as a rule hold a crease too well; but they do so better if they are treated for wash-and-wear. Pleats in such fabrics can be edge-stitched for sharpness.

SKIRT WITH PLEATS (PRESSED, UNPRESSED OR STITCHED) MADE FROM PATTERN

Pattern for a straight pleated skirt is bought by hip measurement, since pleats should hang straight from hips. Waistline may be adjusted if necessary.

Alteration in width, if any, will be made while forming pleats. See p. 137.

Cutting is done on single thickness of fabric, with pattern placed right side up on right side of fabric.

Marking is done on right side of fabric, since pleats are formed on right side. Pattern gives two lines for each pleat: one on which fold is made, another to which fold is brought. One of these lines may be solid and the other broken, or they may be otherwise differentiated—pattern or instruction sheet will indicate which is which. Before unpinning pattern to cut next section(s), mark position of all pleats with a type of broken basting called simplified Tailor Tacking, as follows:

Indicate the two different fold-marks just described by using two colours of thread, one for each. Use thread length as long as skirt (forget the 305 mm. rule for once). Take a small stitch through pattern and fabric at beginning of fold-line, leaving a 25 mm. thread-end. Take a small stitch about every 76 mm. all the way down line. When all lines are basted, snip thread between stitches (6), and carefully remove pattern. Repeat on next skirt section(s).

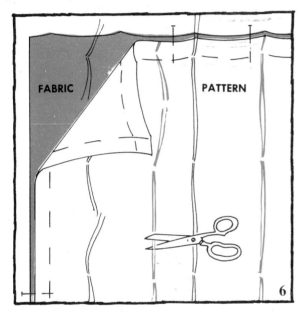

Follow your instruction sheet for seaming, etc. If your pleats are to be pressed, you will note that the skirt is hemmed before pleats are put in. For a smooth hem where there is a seam at the underfold of a pleat, see **Hem in Pleats,** p. 99. Determine length carefully, but play safe on the long side, because skirt can be shortened a little at waist later, but not lengthened. With unpressed pleats, hemming is the last step, as usual, and presents no special problem.

Forming Pleats is done on a table, with skirt right side out. Start at placket opening and work round. If an alteration in width is necessary, distribute it through all pleats so their width will remain uniform.

A very small adjustment in each pleat will take care of the 50 mm. (difference between pattern sizes) which would be the maximum alteration. For broader hips or waist, bring fold not quite up to mark; for narrower hips or waist, bring it slightly past mark.

To secure pleats for pressing, use diagonal basting across centre of pleat (7), through all thicknesses. *Do not remove this basting* until skirt is finished.

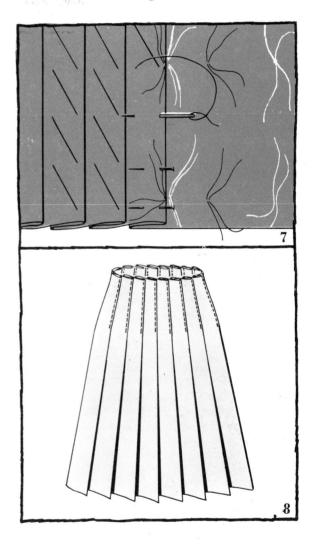

Pressing Pleats is done with steam on both sides, using a press cloth on right side (see PRESSING).

Stitching Pleats, if desired, is done before applying waistband and after placket is finished.

. . . *Stitched-Down Pleats* are stitched between waist and hipline (8). To ensure proper hang, start at hip and stitch toward waist: slide skirt under presser foot with hem away from you; topstitch through all thicknesses, along edge of each pleat. At bottom end of stitching, pull thread-ends through to wrong side of garment and tie.

. . . *Edge-Stitched Pleats* are stitched on one fold or both to keep creases sharp. Such stitching is done mostly on children's and sports clothes. If done on underfold only, it is invisible and can be used on any clothes. To edge-stitch, place edge of fold alone under presser foot and stitch, going from waist to hem (9).

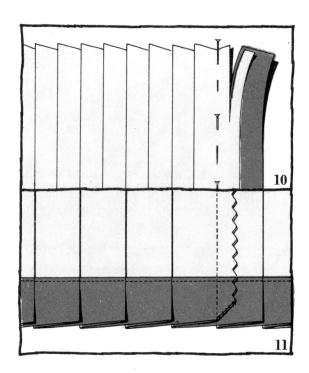

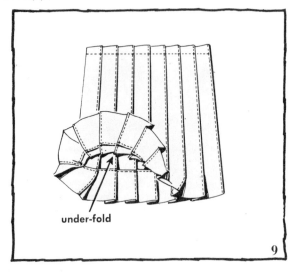

under-fold

9

It is possible to edge-stitch the lower part of a stitched-down pleat. First edge-stitch upper fold of pleat from hipline to hem, then turn skirt round and topstitch through all thicknesses from hipline to waist as described above.

Follow your pattern instruction sheet to apply waistband and finish skirt.

SKIRT WITH COMMERCIAL PLEATING

To find a firm doing commercial pleating, look in a trade directory and in fashion magazines. Check as to which types of pleats they can make. Find out how wide a piece of fabric is needed and how it should be prepared.

Since pleating must be done flat, the usual procedure is to stitch all skirt seams except the one that is to contain placket, and to put in the hem.

To finish skirt when it returns from pleating—Baste pleats in place across hipline and see if measurement conforms with yours. Make sure that remaining seam forms the underfold of a pleat; if necessary, trim fabric to make it so (10). Carefully matching at hem edge, stitch seam *through hem*. Turn in corners of seam at bottom (11), and whipstitch edges together, as shown. Finish placket.

Measure pleated waistline on skirt; taper pleats to fit your waist measurement. When doing this, keep top fold on straight grain, making adjustments underneath. Stay-stitch round waistline. Press.

If desired (except in the case of Accordion Pleats), stitch pleats as described in **Stitching Pleats,** p. 137

Apply waistband.

DIOR PLEAT

We are all familiar with the spectacle of a pleat that has 'tucked out'. Or with a pleat that is bulky to sew

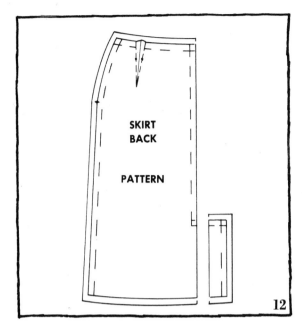

Cutting—*Outer Fabric:* Cut the two back sections from altered pattern. For underlay, cut a rectangle 46 cm. in width and 33 cm. in height.

Lining Fabric: Cut back sections from same pattern, 32 cm. shorter than outer sections.

or wear. These troubles can be avoided by making a pretend pleat—a slit with an underlay, the underlay being attached to the partial lining you will in any case put in the back of your skirt to prevent its 'sitting out'.

To convert a pleat into a Dior pleat, construct skirt back as follows:

Altering Skirt Back Pattern—At centre back, trim away pleat allowance, allow a 38 mm. seam allowance (12).

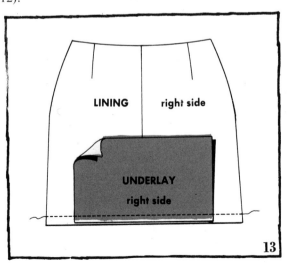

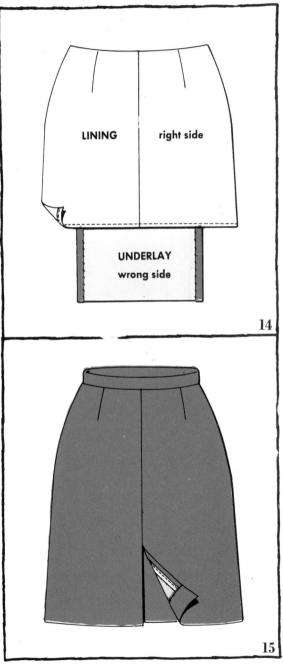

Sewing—*Outer Fabric:* Stitch darts. Stitch centre back seam, starting 25 cm. from bottom (to reinforce this end, first stitch in reverse for about 13 mm.). Join edges of slit by hand- or machine-basting on seamline. Press seam open from top to bottom. Press darts. Finish seam edges.

On rectangle for underlay, make a 25 mm. hem along each 33 cm. edge. Press.

Lining: Stitch darts and centre back seam; press. Pin underlay to lining as shown (13): wrong side of underlay to right side of lining, centres and raw edges matched. Stitch 13 mm. seam, extending stitching across lining edge as shown. Fold seam up on stitched line and topstitch (14).

Joining Outer Fabric and Lining: Match lining and outer sections, wrong sides together; pin. Stay-stitch waist and side edges. From here on, handle this lined section as a single piece.

Complete skirt except for hem. Remove basting at slit. Hem, making underlay 13 mm. shorter than skirt (15).

Pockets

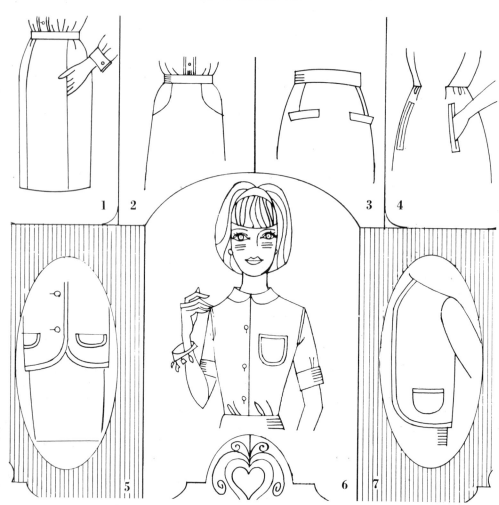

Pockets are part of the design of a garment and may be functional, decorative, or both.

Sometimes the presence of pockets is betrayed only by an edge-seam, as in Pockets in a Seam (1) and Hip Pockets (2). However, Welt Pockets (3), Bound Pockets (4), and Flap Pockets (5) have an outside finish that is a point of interest in the general design.

Patch pockets, placed on the outside and either unlined (6) or lined (7), are made of garment fabric. Inside pockets are made of lining fabric, usually with strips of garment fabric at the opening.

Pockets must be made with precision if they are to enhance, and not spoil, the look of a garment. The extra time this takes is well spent.

A FEW POINTERS

The pattern instruction sheet will tell you how to make your pockets. A few additional pointers, however, may help you to achieve the precision you want.
. . . Position markings for all pockets except 1 and 2 must be transferred to right side of garment with a line of basting or tailor tacking.

. . . Interfacing the opening edges of pockets is generally a good idea; whether or not it is a necessity will depend on the texture and body of your fabric.

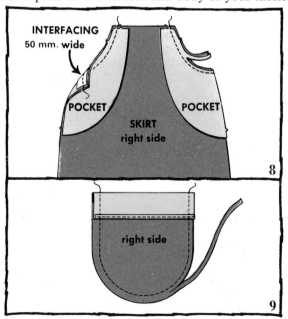

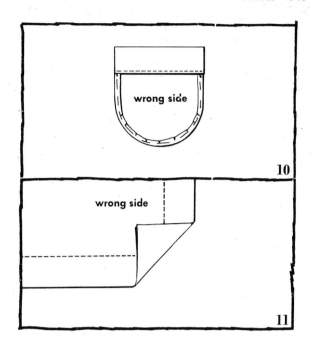

Pocket in a Seam and Hip Pocket (1, 2)—For sharp edge-seams, follow **Processing the Seam,** p. 76 under FACINGS. Interface, trim, grade, clip, and understitch as directed (8). NOTE: If you have a pocket in a side seam with a zip-fastener, make your life easier by moving zip-fastener to centre back, if possible.

Welt Pocket, Bound Pocket, Flap Pocket (3, 4, 5)— The openings of these pockets are constructed on the same principle as a patch buttonhole. It will help you to refer to the BUTTONHOLES chapter.

Patch Pockets (6, 7)—The procedures that follow ensure neat curves and corners.

Unlined patch pocket

Turn raw top edge of pocket section 6 mm. to wrong side and stitch. Fold hem to *right* side, on fold line indicated on pattern. Stitch along seamline around remaining edges, as shown. Trim seam to 10 mm., and trim corners at top fold (9). Turn hem to wrong side.

. . . On a rounded pocket, clip through seam allowance at curves. Turn to wrong side on stitched line, baste and press (10).

. . . On square pocket, fold corners to wrong side (11); press. Turn seam allowance on stitched line;

mitre corners by folding as shown (12); baste and press the pocket.

Baste pocket to garment; topstitch. To reinforce top corners, you can either . . .
. . . Stitch a triangle (13).
. . . Make close zigzag stitch, about 3 mm. wide, for 13 mm. (14).
. . . Backstitch for about 13 mm. (15).

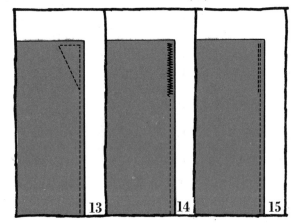

Lined patch pocket (if you desire a lining not indicated in pattern).

Cut lining from pocket pattern with top edge of pattern folded on fold line. Press top edge of lining 19 mm. to wrong side. Pin to pocket, right sides together, side and bottom edges even (16).

Fold top edge of pocket over lining on fold line indicated on pattern; pin. Stitch on seamline around raw edges, as shown. Trim and grade seams; trim corners at top (17). If pocket is rounded, clip through seam allowance at curves; on square pocket, trim corners.

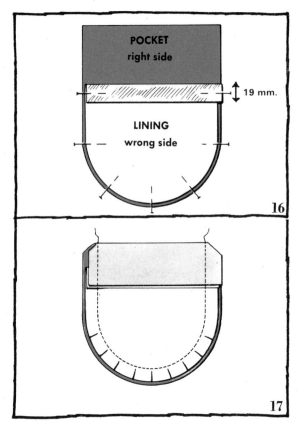

Turn pocket right side out, carefully pushing out corners and seams. Press carefully.

Slipstitch lining to hem (18).

Baste pocket to garment. Either slipstitch in place, or topstitch, following directions for unlined pocket.

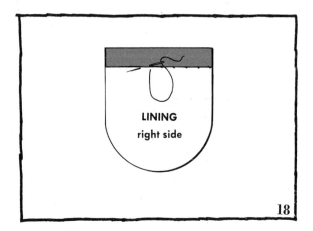

Pressing

Stitch-and-Press—the practice of pressing a stitched seam before it is crossed by another, and all details as they are finished—is perhaps *the* Golden Rule of Good Dressmaking, the process you cannot afford to neglect if you want professional-looking work. Besides, the fine aspect of the work as you go along gives you continual satisfaction, and the final pressing—otherwise a very complicated procedure—is reduced to almost nothing.

See EQUIPMENT for what you need.

PRESSING PRINCIPLES

Pressing is part of sewing—hence directions for pressing specific sewing details will be found in their covering chapters (SEAMS, EASING, BUTTONHOLES, etc.). Following are the general rules:

Have iron and ironing board set up and ready before you start on any sewing project. You will need them to smooth out your pattern, and perhaps press out creases in fabric before cutting (see PATTERNS, CUTTING, etc.), and continually thereafter.

Do not confuse pressing with ironing, the hearty, bearing-down and stroking operation that follows laundering. In pressing, you lower the iron, in most cases lightly, lift and lower it again a little farther on; or you use a light, sliding motion without ever letting the full weight of the iron rest on fabric (this might leave an impression, or, if done on right side, cause a shine). In seams, you work only with tip of iron (1). On most fabrics, pressing action comes from a combination of steam and partial weight of iron.

All construction pressing (pressing of construction stitching) is done initially on wrong side. Pressing done on right side, or final pressing, is kept at a minimum.

Stitch-and-press does not mean that you have to press each seam, dart, etc., immediately after it is stitched. Just make sure it is pressed before either end is caught in another seam. You can usually press several seams at one time.

Never press over pins—they will scratch your iron and may make an indelible impression on your fabric.

Remove basting whenever possible before pressing. Always remove it before final pressing, because even the thread may leave a mark.

Most irons show clearly what heat setting to use with what fabric (fibre content)—linen taking the highest, synthetics the lowest. With all the new blends and finishes, however, play safe by trying the iron on a scrap of fabric before touching it to the garment itself. Whether or not to use steam will depend on fibre and weave (see following).

If fabric is of a type that will mark through to outside, place a strip of brown paper between an edge (seam allowance or other) and garment fabric before you press (2).

In any pressing done on outside, a shine is likely to occur on *any* fabric at details with bulkier parts, such as zip-fastener placket, facing, pocket, etc. To

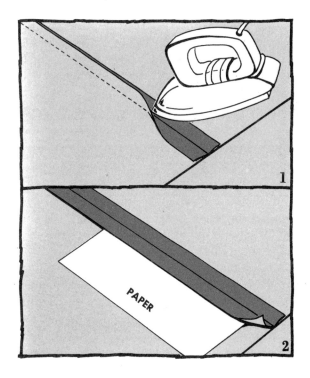

avoid this, use a dry press cloth with a steam iron. With a dry iron, use a press cloth dampened like this: wet half of it, wring out, fold damp half over dry, and place on garment with dry side down.

As you have pressed at each stage, the garment will require only a general all-over press.

PRESSING THE STANDARD FABRICS

For special-handling fabrics (Wash-and-Wear, Knits, Bonded and Stretch Fabrics, Pile Fabrics, Fake Fur, Sheers, Lace, Vinyl), see pp. 66–73 in FABRICS.

Cotton presents no problem. Except when it is of dark colour (when it may tend to shine), it can be pressed on either side, either with a steam iron, or with a dry iron after being directly dampened with a sponge.

Linen is as easy to press as cotton, but is more apt to shine if pressed on right side. With dark colours, use a press cloth.

Wool requires considerable steam in pressing. It responds excellently to the steam iron, or to a dry iron with a press cloth, used half-damp, half-dry as described at left. It lends itself to shrinking and shaping by means of steam (see EASING). If used on right side, press cloth should preferably be of wool, especially with dark fabric. NOTE: With wool crepe, use very little steam, or it will shrink, even if pre-shrunk. Never let iron rest on crepe, as it will leave an imprint.

Silk is handled according to its weight. Heavy and medium-weight silk is handled like wool. Sheer silk, such as chiffon, is pressed entirely dry. The note for wool crepe also applies to silk crepe.

Rayon requires a moderately warm iron. Press on wrong side.

Seams and Seam Finishes

A seam is the line of stitching, usually done by machine, that holds two pieces of a garment together. It may be decorative as well as functional, and outlined by added topstitching, or by cording or piping inserted between the two pieces of fabric (see BIAS, p. 28). The great majority of seams, however, are plain.

Seams can be made in different ways and with different finishes, depending on fabric, design, and purpose of garment. On wash-and-wear fabric, be careful about using seams with outside stitching, as they may pucker.

The seam allowance is the fabric between seamline and raw edge; after a seam is made, seam allowances are on wrong side of garment. Standard seam allowance in commercial patterns is 16 mm., sometimes trimmed afterwards, for one reason or another, to a narrower width.

To maintain the size and lines of a garment, it is very important to keep seam allowance even and at given width. Some machines have guidelines etched on the throat plate, along which you guide the raw edge of the fabric as you stitch. Seam guide attachments are also available. Otherwise, you can make your own guide, or gauge, with a strip of adhesive tape. Tape 13 mm. wide will give you graded guidelines for seam widths from 6 mm. to 19 mm. Cut a piece 76 mm. long. Place on machine exactly 6 mm. from needle, parallel with presser foot. Measure and draw lines on it 3 mm. apart, as shown (1).

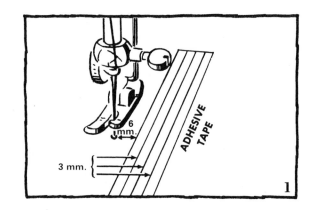

Stitch length in seams will depend on fabric, type of garment, etc. (see charts on pp. 151–164 in THREAD AND NEEDLES). For general use, 12 to 25 mm. is a good stitch length. A seam on the true bias, however, needs to be reinforced by a shorter stitch.

PLAIN SEAM

This is the simplest and most commonly-used seam. All other seams begin with a plain seam.

Place the two pieces of fabric together, wrong sides out, edges even (2).

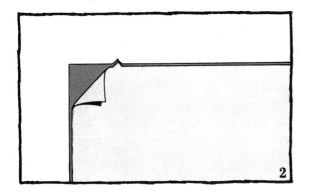

Stitch on seamline.

First press line of stitching without opening seam (3), then press seam open with point of iron only, applying slight pressure (4). Then lightly press open

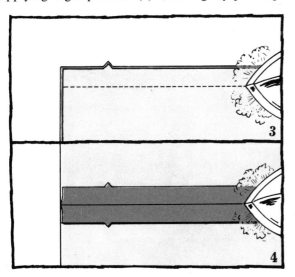

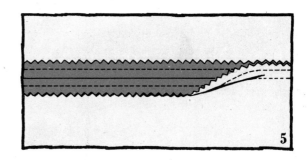

seam. Even if a seam is to be pressed to one side, press it open first—the seamline will be much smoother.

SEAM FINISHES

For neatness, and to prevent ravelling, a plain seam is finished unless garment is lined. Use the finish suited to your fabric. With firmly woven fabric, the seam allowance can be left as it is.

Most fabrics: Trim seam allowance with pinking shears, or stitch-and-pink (5).

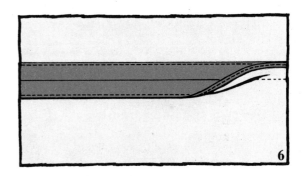

Lightweight fabric: Turn edges of seam allowance under about 3 mm. and stitch (6). Used in unlined jackets.

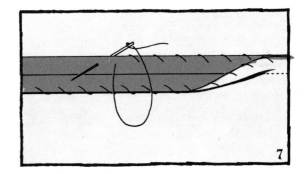

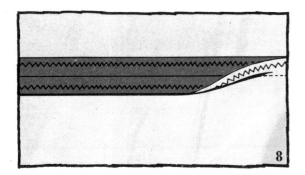

Ravelly fabric: Overcast seam allowances by hand. Hold work with edge you are working on up. You can go either from right to left or from left to right. Take stitches (3 mm. to 6 mm. deep and 6 mm. apart) over edge as shown (7), putting needle through from wrong side to right side of fabric. Or finish edges with zigzag stitch on sewing machine (8).

Sheer fabric or lace: Do not press seam open. With seam allowances together, make a second line of stitching in seam allowance 3mm. from stitched seamline. Trim close to second line (9). Press to one side.

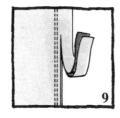

Heavier fabrics in unlined jacket or coat: Enclose edge of each seam allowance in Seam Binding. Fold binding so that one edge is slightly above the other. Insert seam edge between edges of binding and topstitch (10).

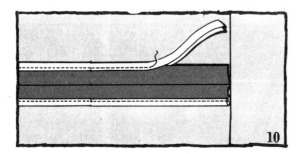

TOPSTITCHED SEAM

A decorative seam, used mostly on sports clothes.

After pressing a plain seam open, turn work to right side and topstitch on either side of seamline, being very careful to have both sides equal (11). Width of stitching varies according to thickness of fabric and preference.

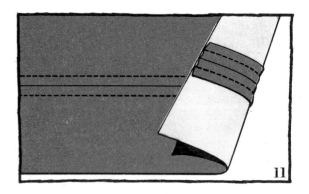

FLAT FELLED SEAM

(also called Felled Seam or Run and Fell Seam)

A strong, neat seam, good on garments that are laundered often. It can be made on inside or on outside of garment. The fell (stitched-down overlap)

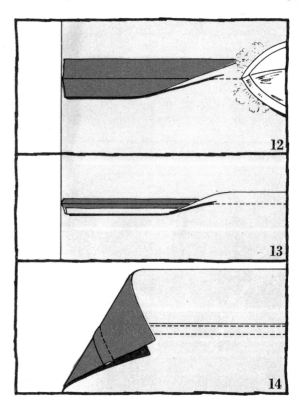

appearing on the outside is a feature of sports clothes, pyjamas, etc. You can fell an armhole seam only if top of sleeve is almost straight, as in a shirtsleeve, with a very shallow cap and no ease.

Make a plain seam, as on p. 145 (right sides out, if you want an outside fell).

After pressing seam open, press it again with both seam allowances turned in one direction (12).

Trim away under seam allowance to about 3 mm. (13). Fold in top seam allowance to half its width (with some fabrics, you may wish to hand-baste or press this before stitching). Edge-stitch fold (fell) to garment (14).

WELT SEAM

A variation of the Felled Seam, used on heavier fabrics, for strength and for the decorative addition

of the line of stitching. It is topstitched from outside, after seam is made on inside.

Make a plain seam. After pressing seam open, press it again with both seam allowances turned in one direction.

Trim away under seam allowance to about 6 mm. On outside, topstitch along side of seam with allowances underneath (15).

FRENCH SEAM

Another very neat seam, used on fine fabrics, where a raw edge would show through. The first line of stitching is done with right sides out.

To make a French seam:

With fabric right sides out, stitch a plain seam 13 mm. from raw edges. Trim seam allowances to 3 mm. (16).

Press seam allowances to one side. Fold work on stitched line, wrong sides out. Stitch again (17), 6 mm. from fold.

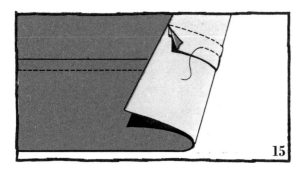

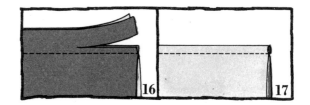

Sleeves

Sleeves and the way they are set in—high or low on the shoulder, widening or narrowing the shoulder-line, emphasizing or playing down parts of the silhouette—are one of the focal points in the changes of fashion (sometimes even by their absence). While they may be of every length and width, and vary greatly as to shape, sleeves fall into just three basic categories:

The set-in sleeve, cut separately from garment body and seamed into an armhole. This sleeve may have a smooth cap, a darted cap, or a full, gathered cap.

The raglan sleeve, cut separately from garment body, but continuing to neckline over shoulder and seamed to a modified armhole extending from underarm to neck.

The kimono sleeve, cut in one with garment body; it sometimes has an underarm gusset.

The lower edge of any sleeve is finished by a cuff, a hem, a facing, etc., as indicated in pattern. For additional help see those chapter headings.

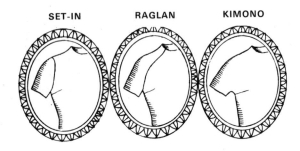

SET-IN　　　RAGLAN　　　KIMONO

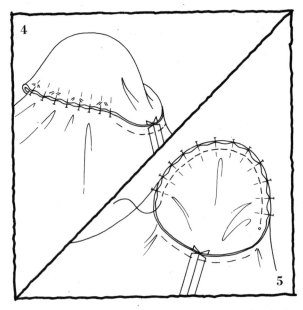

SETTING IN SLEEVES

With garment right side outwards and the made-up sleeve right side outwards, *and working from the right side*, place sleeve seam to bodice seam and pin.

Pin the underarm section of the sleeve and baste (1) and (2).

Turn bodice inside out and pull sleeve head through armhole. Pin sleeve head point to shoulder seam (3).

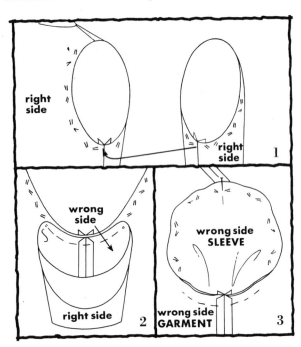

Fold turnings back so that sleeve is on top. Pin sleeve head by placing pins across the fitting line, distributing ease evenly (although there is always a little more at the front) (4).

The seam allowances will flute but there should be

no folds of fabric under the pins. Careful manipulating is necessary to prevent the ease in the sleeve head from forming pleats (5).

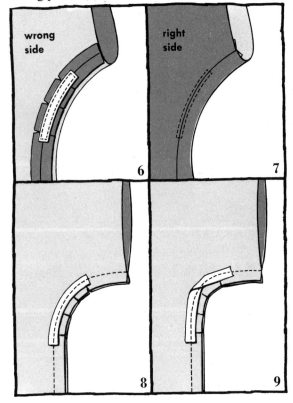

Baste across the centre of the pins exactly on the fitting line.

Use very small stitches. Fit the garment.

Stitch sleeves in either by using double thread and working a back stitch (best as the work can be held over the hand) or machine very slowly and carefully around the armhole. Always stitch from the sleeve side.

Remove bastings. All turnings are pressed towards the sleeve as they provide support in the sleeve head.

THE RAGLAN SLEEVE

Raglan sleeves are cut in two sections shaped by a shoulder seam, or in one section shaped by a large curved dart tapering from neck over top of arm. Mark and stitch this dart carefully (see DARTS). When seaming sleeve to garment body, be careful not to stretch seam.

THE KIMONO SLEEVE

Kimono sleeves are usually shaped by a shoulder seam, and may or may not have a gusset at underarm (for handling gusset, see GUSSETS). When pattern calls for no gusset, reinforce underarm seam by one of the following two methods:

METHOD I—Shorten stitch at curve of underarm. Then clip seam allowance and press seam open. Baste a piece of seam binding 76 mm. to 102 mm. long over opened seam (or pin, putting pins through *from right side*); stitch on right side of garment 3 mm. from each side of seam (6, 7).

METHOD II—Before stitching underarm seam, pin a piece of seam binding 76 mm. to 102 mm. long over seamline (8); if there is a sharp curve, fold tape as shown (9). Stitch seam with shortened stitch. Clip seam allowance *without clipping tape*. Press seam open.

Thread and Needles

Thread and needle, without which no sewing could be done, are practically a unit. Not only is one useless without the other, but, to do a proper job, they must be suited to each other. And, above all, to the fabric you want them to stitch.

THREAD

LIGHTWEIGHT FABRICS

Use Coats Drima or Coats Super Sheen No. 50 for lightweight fabrics such as organdie or lawn.

MEDIUMWEIGHT-HEAVY FABRICS

For mediumweight-heavy cottons, poplins and woollens, Coats Drima, Coats Satinised No. 40 and Coats Chain Cotton No. 40 will give the best results.

HOUSEHOLD LINENS AND PLASTIC MATERIALS

When household linens and towels have to be stitched, use Coats Drima, or Coats Chain Cotton No. 40.

SYNTHETIC FABRICS

Coats Drima is a fine yet extremely strong multi-purpose thread which is especially suitable for stitching synthetic fabrics.

OTHER THREADS

Clark's Anchor Button Thread is a strong thread specially processed for hard wear and it is particularly suitable for tailored buttonholes and for sewing on buttons. It is available in all the shades used in tailoring and also in certain bright colours.

For basting, Gun Basting Cotton is the best and most economical thread to use. It is wound on reels of 914 metre lengths.

One other thread for use on sewing machines must be mentioned here. It is the thread which will allow an outlet for all artistic ideas and yearnings. It is Anchor Machine Embroidery Thread and it is used for every kind of decorative machine stitching—embroidery on household linen, monograms on personal linen, personal motifs on lingerie.

There are many colours and shades of Anchor Machine Embroidery Thread available. It is made in two sizes, No. 30 and No. 50. The latter is the finer thread and is recommended for use on fine fabrics. And remember, No. 50 Anchor Machine Embroidery Thread is the thread to be used when darning household linens.

NEEDLES

Needles are made in different types, to suit the type of work they are used for; and in different sizes, so they may draw thread of different sizes easily through fabrics of different weights.

Sewing Machine Needles—The make and model of your sewing machine will determine the type of needle you buy. Some needles, such as Milward, will fit several popular makes of sewing machines (see package). Size of needle is determined by weight of fabric to be sewn (see charts, pp. 151–164). Size numbers vary with brands—to be safe, ask for fine, medium, coarse, etc. (see chart). Buy quality needles —poorly-made needles may have rough spots that will cause thread to break.

Hand-Sewing Needles—Buy good quality needles— an inferior needle may have a blunt point or a rough eye which may fray the thread. Milward needles come in ten sizes, from No. 1, very coarse, to No. 10, very fine. *Sharps* are needles of medium length, most commonly used. Other sewing needles differ from them only in length: *Betweens,* shorter, good for fine stitching on heavy fabric; *Milliners,* longer, best for millinery and basting. Packaged assortments of needles, size 3 to 9 and 5 to 10, are practical. *Calyx Eyed Sharps,* in assorted sizes, are open at the top for easy threading.

Milward Embroidery Needles are often preferred for sewing because of their long eye, which makes for easy threading. Otherwise they are like Sharps. They are also called Crewel Needles.

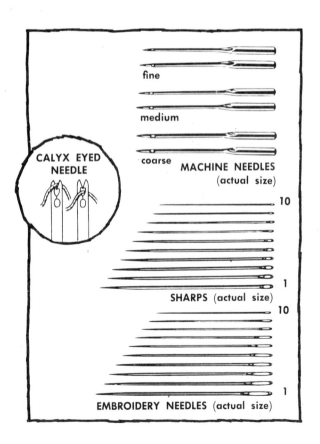

CALYX EYED NEEDLE

fine

medium

coarse **MACHINE NEEDLES** (actual size)

10

1

SHARPS (actual size)

10

1

EMBROIDERY NEEDLES (actual size)

FABRIC AND THREAD CHARTS

To obtain the best stitching results on your sewing machine, it is important that choice of thread, needle size, stitch length and tension are in relation to the choice of fabric.

In the machine needle numbering sections:

> B—British Needle sizing
> C—Continental Needle sizing

Note that the tensions given are only a commencing guide and may vary slightly according to the weight of the selected fabric. The machines quoted are:

> Singer
> Necchi 544
> Pfaff Automatic 360
> Elna Supermatic
> Bernina Record 730

MACHINE BUTTONHOLES

Satisfactory buttonholes may be made with the Swing Needle Machine. Each machine gives its own method in the sewing machine manual. If a fine buttonhole is desired, use Anchor Machine Embroidery Thread No. 50 for light fabrics and No. 30 for heavier fabrics. If a heavier buttonhole is required for a mediumweight fabric use the thread which has been used to stitch the garment.

Buttonholing can also be done perfectly by a zigzag attachment on certain straight stitching machines. In this instance, the thread recommended is Anchor Machine Embroidery No. 50.

SINGER			STRAIGHT STITCHING—NATURAL FABRICS			
	Fabric	Thread	Machine Needle No. B	Hand Needle No.	No. of Stitches to 25 mm.	*Upper Thread Tension
Fine Fabrics	Net	Coats Drima	9 or 11	8 or 9	8–10	4–6
	Organdie	or	9 or 11	8 or 9	8–10	4–6
	Chiffon	Coats Super	9 or 11	8 or 9	8–10	4–6
	Lace	Sheen No. 50	9 or 11	8 or 9	8–10	4–6
	Silk		9 or 11	8 or 9	8–10	4–6
	Lawn		9 or 11	8 or 9	8–10	4–6
	Crepe		9 or 11	8 or 9	8–10	4–6
	Tulle		9 or 11	8 or 9	8–10	4–6
	Voile		9 or 11	8 or 9	8–10	4–6
Fine-Medium Fabrics	Cotton	Coats Drima	11 or 14	7 or 8	10–12	4–6
	Poplin	or	11 or 14	7 or 8	10–12	4–6
	Taffeta	Coats Super	11 or 14	7 or 8	10–12	4–6
	Linen	Sheen No. 50	11 or 14	7 or 8	10–12	4–6
	Satin		11 or 14	7 or 8	10–12	4–6
Medium-Heavy Fabrics	Brocade	Coats Drima	14	7 or 8	12	4–6
	Dress Wool	or	14	7 or 8	12	4–6
	Jersey	Coats Satinised	14	7 or 8	12–14	4–6
	Corduroy	No. 40 or	14 or 16	7 or 8	12	4–6
	Velvet	Coats Chain	14 or 16	7 or 8	12	4–6
	Terry Cloth	Cotton No. 40	14 or 16	7 or 8	12	4–6
	Flannel		14 or 16	7 or 8	12	4–6
	Denim		14 or 16	7 or 8	12	4–6
	Repp		14 or 16	7 or 8	12	4–6

*Lower Thread Tension—Medium

SINGER — STRAIGHT STITCHING—SYNTHETIC FABRICS

Nylon, Terylene, Tricel, Acetate, Viscose Rayon, Dicel, Courtelle, Crimplene, Acrilan, Orlon

	Fabric	Thread	Machine Needle No. B	Hand Needle No.	No. of Stitches to 25 mm.	*Upper Thread Tension
Fine Fabrics	Net	Coats Drima	9 or 11	8	8–10	4–6
	Chiffon		9 or 11	8	8–10	4–6
	Locknit		9 or 11	8	8–10	4–6
	Seersucker		9 or 11	8	8–10	4–6
	Lawn		9 or 11	8	8–10	4–6
	Surah		9 or 11	8	8–10	4–6
	Taffeta		9 or 11	8	8–10	4–6
	Voile		9 or 11	8	8–10	4–6
Fine-Medium Fabrics	Pique	Coats Drima	11 or 14	7 or 8	10–12	4–6
	Matelasse		11 or 14	7 or 8	10–12	4–6
	Brocade		11 or 14	7 or 8	10–12	4–6
	Nylon		11 or 14	7 or 8	10–12	4–6
Medium Fabrics	Linen	Coats Drima	14	7	12–14	4–6
	Jersey		14	7	12–14	4–6
	Satin		14	7	12–14	4–6
	Silk Slub		14	7	12–14	4–6
	Tweed		14	7	12	4–6
	Suiting		14	7	12	4–6
	Velvet		14	7	12	4–6
	Fleece		14 or 16	6 or 7	10	4–6

SINGER — BUTTONHOLES

	Fabric	Thread	Machine Needle No. B (1)	Machine Needle No. B (2)	Stitch Length	Stitch Width (1)	Stitch Width (2)	*Upper Thread Tension
Fine Fabrics	Organdie	1 Coats Drima	9	9	Fine	3 & 5	2½ & 4	2–3
	Chiffon	or	9	9	,,	3 & 5	2½ & 4	2–3
	Lace	Coats Super Sheen	9	9	,,	3 & 5	2½ & 4	2–3
	Silk	No. 50	9	9	,,	3 & 5	2½ & 4	2–3
	Lawn	2 Clark's Anchor	11	11	,,	3 & 5	2½ & 4	2–3
	Crepe	Machine Emby No. 50	11	11	,,	3 & 5	2½ & 4	2–3
Fine-Medium Fabrics	Cotton	1 Coats Drima	11 or 14	11 or 14	Fine	3 & 5	2½ & 4	2–3
	Poplin	or	11 or 14	11 or 14	,,	3 & 5	2½ & 4	2–3
	Taffeta	Coats Super Sheen	11 or 14	11 or 14	,,	3 & 5	2½ & 4	2–3
	Linen	No. 50 or	11 or 14	11 or 14	,,	3 & 5	2½ & 4	2–3
	Satin	2 Clark's Anchor Machine Emby No. 50	11 or 14	11 or 14	,,	3 & 5	2½ & 4	2–3
Medium-Heavy Fabrics	Brocade	1 Coats Drima	14	14	Fine	3 & 5	2½ & 4	2–3
	Dress Wool	or	14	14	,,	3 & 5	2½ & 4	2–3
	Jersey	Coats Satinised	14	14	,,	3 & 5	2½ & 4	2–3
	Corduroy	No. 40	14 or 16	14	,,	3 & 5	2½ & 4	2–3
	Flannel	Coats Chain	14 or 16	14	,,	3 & 5	2½ & 4	2–3
	Denim	Cotton No. 40	14 or 16	14	,,	3 & 5	2½ & 4	2–3
	Tweed	2 Clark's Anchor Machine Emby No. 30	14 or 16	14	,,	3 & 5	2½ & 4	2–3
Synthetic Fabrics	Nylon 'Terylene'	1 Coats Drima or 2 Clark's Anchor Machine Emby No. 50	11	9	Fine	3 & 5	2½ & 4	2–3

*Lower Thread Tension—Medium

SINGER		DECORATIVE STITCHING—MACHINE EMBROIDERY			
	Fabric	Thread	Machine Needle No. B	Stitch Length	*Upper Thread Tension
Fine Fabrics	1 Ply Organdie	Clark's Anchor Machine Emby No. 50	9	Fine	2–3
	1 Ply Chiffon		9	,,	2–3
	1 Ply Silk		9	,,	2–3
	1 Ply Lawn		11	,,	2–3
	1 Ply Cotton		11	,,	2–3
	1 Ply Crepe		11	,,	2–3
Medium Fabrics	1 Ply Cotton	Clark's Anchor Machine Emby No. 30	14	Fine	2–3
	1 Ply Poplin		14	,,	2–3
	1 Ply Linen		14	,,	2–3
	1 Ply Gingham		14	,,	2–3
Synthetic Fabrics	1 Ply Nylon	Clark's Anchor Machine Emby No. 50	9	Fine	2–3

*Lower Thread Tension—Medium

SINGER		DARNING			
	Fabric	Thread	Machine Needle No. B	Stitch Length	*Upper Thread Tension
Fine Fabrics	1 Ply Lawn	Clark's Anchor Machine Emby No. 50	9	Fine	2–4
Medium Fabrics	1 Ply Cotton	Clark's Anchor Machine Emby No. 50	11	Fine	2–4
	1 Ply Linen		11	,,	2–4

*Lower Thread Tension—Medium

NECCHI		STRAIGHT STITCHING—NATURAL FABRICS				
	Fabric	Thread	Machine Needle No. B	C	Hand Needle No.	No. of Stitches to 25 mm. and Stitch Length No.
Fine Fabrics	Net	Coats Drima	10 or 12	70 or 80	8 or 9	8–10 ($3\frac{1}{4}$–3)
	Organdie	or	10 or 12	70 or 80	8 or 9	8–10 ($3\frac{1}{4}$–3)
	Chiffon	Coats Super Sheen	10 or 12	70 or 80	8 or 9	8–10 ($3\frac{1}{4}$–3)
	Lace	No. 50	10 or 12	70 or 80	8 or 9	8–10 ($3\frac{1}{4}$–3)
	Silk		10 or 12	70 or 80	8 or 9	8–10 ($3\frac{1}{4}$–3)
	Lawn		10 or 12	70 or 80	8 or 9	8–10 ($3\frac{1}{4}$–3)
	Crepe		10 or 12	70 or 80	8 or 9	8–10 ($3\frac{1}{4}$–3)
	Tulle		10 or 12	70 or 80	8 or 9	8–10 ($3\frac{1}{4}$–3)
	Voile		10 or 12	70 or 80	8 or 9	8–10 ($3\frac{1}{4}$–3)
Fine-Medium Fabrics	Cotton	Coats Drima	12 or 14	80 or 90	7 or 8	10–12 (3–$2\frac{3}{4}$)
	Poplin	or	12 or 14	80 or 90	7 or 8	10–12 (3–$2\frac{3}{4}$)
	Taffeta	Coats Super Sheen	12 or 14	80 or 90	7 or 8	10–12 (3–$2\frac{3}{4}$)
	Linen	No. 50	12 or 14	80 or 90	7 or 8	10–12 (3–$2\frac{3}{4}$)
	Satin		12 or 14	80 or 90	7 or 8	10–12 (3–$2\frac{3}{4}$)
Medium-Heavy Fabrics	Brocade	Coats Drima	14	90	7 or 8	12 ($2\frac{3}{4}$)
	Dress Wool	or	14	90	7 or 8	12 ($2\frac{3}{4}$)
	Jersey	Coats Satinised	14	90	7 or 8	12–14 ($2\frac{3}{4}$–$2\frac{1}{2}$)
	Corduroy	No. 40	14 or 16	90 or 100	7 or 8	12 ($2\frac{3}{4}$)
	Velvet	or	14 or 16	90 or 100	7 or 8	12 ($2\frac{3}{4}$)
	Terry Cloth	Coats Chain Cotton	14 or 16	90 or 100	7 or 8	12 ($2\frac{3}{4}$)
	Flannel	No. 40	14 or 16	90 or 100	7 or 8	12 ($2\frac{3}{4}$)
	Denim		14 or 16	90 or 100	7 or 8	12 ($2\frac{3}{4}$)
	Repp		14 or 16	90 or 100	7 or 8	12 ($2\frac{3}{4}$)

NECCHI		STRAIGHT STITCHING—SYNTHETIC FABRICS				
		Nylon, Terylene, Tricel, Acetate, Viscose Rayon, Dicel, Courtelle, Crimplene, Acrilan, Orlon				
	Fabric	Thread	Machine Needle No. B	C	Hand Needle No.	No. of Stitches to 25 mm. and Stitch Length No.
Fine Fabrics	Net	Coats Drima	10 or 12	70 or 80	8	8–10 ($3\frac{1}{4}$–3)
	Chiffon		10 or 12	70 or 80	8	8–10 ($3\frac{1}{4}$–3)
	Locknit		10 or 12	70 or 80	8	8–10 ($3\frac{1}{4}$–3)
	Seersucker		10 or 12	70 or 80	8	8–10 ($3\frac{1}{4}$–3)
	Lawn		10 or 12	70 or 80	8	8–10 ($3\frac{1}{4}$–3)
	Surah		10 or 12	70 or 80	8	8–10 ($3\frac{1}{4}$–3)
	Taffeta		10 or 12	70 or 80	8	8–10 ($3\frac{1}{4}$–3)
	Voile		10 or 12	70 or 80	8	8–10 ($3\frac{1}{4}$–3)
Fine-Medium Fabrics	Pique	Coats Drima	12 or 14	80 or 90	7 or 8	10–12 (3–$2\frac{3}{4}$)
	Matelasse		12 or 14	80 or 90	7 or 8	10–12 (3–$2\frac{3}{4}$)
	Brocade		12 or 14	80 or 90	7 or 8	10–12 (3–$2\frac{3}{4}$)
	Nylon		12 or 14	80 or 90	7 or 8	10–12 (3–$2\frac{3}{4}$)
Medium Fabrics	Linen	Coats Drima	14	90	7	12–14 ($2\frac{3}{4}$–$2\frac{1}{2}$)
	Jersey		14	90	7	12–14 ($2\frac{3}{4}$–$2\frac{1}{2}$)
	Satin		14	90	7	12–14 ($2\frac{3}{4}$–$2\frac{1}{2}$)
	Silk Slub		14	90	7	12–14 ($2\frac{3}{4}$–$2\frac{1}{2}$)
	Tweed		14	90	7	12 ($2\frac{3}{4}$)
	Suiting		14	90	7	12 ($2\frac{3}{4}$)
	Velvet		14	90	7	12 ($2\frac{3}{4}$)
	Fleece		14 or 16	90 or 100	6 or 7	10 ($3\frac{3}{4}$)

NECCHI		BUTTONHOLES					
	Fabric	Thread	Machine Needle No.				Stitch Length
			B 1	C 1	B 2	C 2	
Fine Fabrics	Organdie Chiffon Lace Silk Lawn Crepe	1 Coats Drima or Coats Super Sheen No. 50 2 Clark's Anchor Machine Emby No. 50	10 10 10 10 12 12	70 70 70 70 80 80	10 10 10 10 12 12	70 70 70 70 80 80	Fine ,, ,, ,, ,, ,,
Fine-Medium Fabrics	Cotton Poplin Taffeta Linen Satin	1 Coats Drima or Coats Super Sheen No. 50 or 2 Clark's Anchor Machine Emby No. 50	12 or 14 12 or 14 12 or 14 12 or 14 12 or 14	80 or 90 80 or 90 80 or 90 80 or 90 80 or 90	12 12 12 12 12	80 80 80 80 80	Fine ,, ,, ,, ,,
Medium-Heavy Fabrics	Brocade Dress Wool Jersey Corduroy Flannel Denim Tweed	1 Coats Drima or Coats Satinised No. 40 or Coats Chain Cotton No. 40 or 2 Clark's Anchor Machine Emby No. 30	14 14 14 14 or 16 14 or 16 14 or 16 14 or 16	90 90 90 90 or 100 90 or 100 90 or 100 90 or 100	12 12 12 14 14 14 14	80 80 80 90 90 90 90	Fine ,, ,, ,, ,, ,, ,,
Synthetic Fabrics	Nylon and 'Terylene'	1 Coats Drima or 2 Clark's Anchor Machine Emby No. 50	12	80	10	70	Fine

NECCHI	DECORATIVE STITCHING—MACHINE EMBROIDERY			
	Fabric	Thread	Machine Needle No.	
			B	C
Fine Fabrics	1 Ply Organdie 1 Ply Chiffon 1 Ply Silk 1 Ply Lawn 1 Ply Cotton 1 Ply Crepe	Clark's Anchor Machine Emby No. 50	10 10 10 10 10 10	70 70 70 70 70 70
Medium Fabrics	1 Ply Cotton 1 Ply Poplin 1 Ply Linen 1 Ply Gingham	Clark's Anchor Machine Emby No. 30	12 12 12 12	80 80 80 80
Synthetic Fabrics	1 Ply Nylon	Clark's Anchor Machine Emby No. 50	10	70

NECCHI	DARNING			
	Fabric	Thread	Machine Needle No. B	C
Fine Fabrics	1 Ply Lawn	Clark's Anchor Machine Emby No. 50	10	70
Medium Fabrics	1 Ply Cotton 1 Ply Linen	Clark's Anchor Machine Emby No. 50	12 12	80 80

PFAFF	STRAIGHT STITCHING—NATURAL FABRICS						
	Fabric	Thread	Machine Needle No. C	Hand Needle No.	No. of Stitches to 25 mm. and Stitch Length No.	*Upper Thread Tension (1)	(2)
Fine Fabrics	Net	1 Coats Drima	70 or 80	8 or 9	8–10 ($3-2\frac{3}{4}$)	4	4
	Organdie	or	70 or 80	8 or 9	8–10 ($3-2\frac{3}{4}$)	4	4
	Chiffon	2 Coats Super Sheen	70 or 80	8 or 9	8–10 ($3-2\frac{3}{4}$)	4	$3\frac{1}{2}$
	Lace	No. 50	70 or 80	8 or 9	8–10 ($3-2\frac{3}{4}$)	4	3
	Silk		70 or 80	8 or 9	8–10 ($3-2\frac{3}{4}$)	4	3
	Lawn		70 or 80	8 or 9	8–10 ($3-2\frac{3}{4}$)	4	3
	Crepe		70 or 80	8 or 9	8–10 ($3-2\frac{3}{4}$)	4	3
	Tulle		70 or 80	8 or 9	8–10 ($3-2\frac{3}{4}$)	4	3
	Voile		70 or 80	8 or 9	8–10 ($3-2\frac{3}{4}$)	4	4
Fine-Medium Fabrics	Cotton	1 Coats Drima	80 or 90	7 or 8	10–12 ($2\frac{3}{4}-2\frac{1}{2}$)	4	4
	Poplin	or	80 or 90	7 or 8	10–12 ($2\frac{3}{4}-2\frac{1}{2}$)	4	4
	Taffeta	2 Coats Super Sheen	80 or 90	7 or 8	10–12 ($2\frac{3}{4}-2\frac{1}{2}$)	$3\frac{3}{4}$	4
	Linen	No. 50	80 or 90	7 or 8	10–12 ($2\frac{3}{4}-2\frac{1}{2}$)	4	3
	Satin		80 or 90	7 or 8	10–12 ($2\frac{3}{4}-2\frac{1}{2}$)	4	4
Medium-Heavy Fabrics	Brocade	1 Coats Drima	90	7 or 8	12 ($2\frac{1}{2}$)	4	4
	Dress Wool	or	90	7 or 8	12 ($2\frac{1}{2}$)	4	4
	Jersey	2 Coats Satinised	90	7 or 8	12–14 ($2\frac{1}{2}-2\frac{1}{4}$)	4	$3\frac{1}{2}$
	Corduroy	No. 40	90 or 100	7 or 8	12 ($2\frac{1}{2}$)	4	$3\frac{3}{4}$
	Velvet	or	90 or 100	7 or 8	12 ($2\frac{1}{2}$)	4	4
	Terry Cloth	Coats Chain Cotton	90 or 100	7 or 8	12 ($2\frac{1}{2}$)	4	4
	Flannel	No. 40	90 or 100	7 or 8	12 ($2\frac{1}{2}$)	4	4
	Denim		90 or 100	7 or 8	12 ($2\frac{1}{2}$)	4	4
	Repp		90 or 100	7 or 8	12 ($2\frac{1}{2}$)	$4\frac{1}{4}$	$4\frac{1}{4}$

*Lower Thread Tension—Medium

PFAFF		STRAIGHT STITCHING—SYNTHETIC FABRICS				
		Nylon, Terylene, Tricel, Acetate, Viscose Rayon, Dicel, Courtelle, Crimplene, Acrilan, Orlon				
	Fabric	**Thread**	**Machine Needle No. C**	**Hand Needle No.**	**No of Stitches to 25 mm. and Stitch Length No.**	***Upper Thread Tension**
Fine Fabrics	Net	Coats Drima	70 or 80	8	$8-10$ $(3-2\frac{3}{4})$	3
	Chiffon		70 or 80	8	$8-10$ $(3-2\frac{3}{4})$	3
	Locknit		70 or 80	8	$8-10$ $(3-2\frac{3}{4})$	3
	Seersucker		70 or 80	8	$8-10$ $(3-2\frac{3}{4})$	3
	Lawn		70 or 80	8	$8-10$ $(3-2\frac{3}{4})$	3
	Surah		70 or 80	8	$8-10$ $(3-2\frac{3}{4})$	3
	Taffeta		70 or 80	8	$8-10$ $(3-2\frac{3}{4})$	3
	Voile		70 or 80	8	$8-10$ $(3-2\frac{3}{4})$	3
Fine- Medium Fabrics	Pique	Coats Drima	80 or 90	7 or 8	$10-12$ $(2\frac{3}{4}-2\frac{1}{2})$	3
	Matelasse		80 or 90	7 or 8	$10-12$ $(2\frac{3}{4}-2\frac{1}{2})$	3
	Brocade		80 or 90	7 or 8	$10-12$ $(2\frac{3}{4}-2\frac{1}{2})$	3
	Nylon		80 or 90	7 or 8	$10-12$ $(2\frac{3}{4}-2\frac{1}{2})$	3
Medium Fabrics	Linen	Coats Drima	90	7	$12-14$ $(2\frac{1}{2}-2\frac{1}{4})$	4
	Jersey		90	7	$12-14$ $(2\frac{1}{2}-2\frac{1}{4})$	4
	Satin		90	7	$12-14$ $(2\frac{1}{2}-2\frac{1}{4})$	4
	Silk Slub		90	7	$12-14$ $(2\frac{1}{2}-2\frac{1}{4})$	4
	Tweed		90	7	12 $(2\frac{1}{2})$	4
	Suiting		90	7	12 $(2\frac{1}{2})$	4
	Velvet		90	7	12 $(2\frac{1}{2})$	$4\frac{1}{4}$
	Fleece		90 or 100	6 or 7	10 (3)	$4\frac{1}{4}$

*Lower Thread Tension—Medium

PFAFF — BUTTONHOLES

	Fabric	Thread	Machine Needle No. C (1)	C (2)	Stitch Length (1)	(2)	*Upper Thread Tension (1)	(2)
Fine Fabrics	Organdie Chiffon Lace Silk Lawn Crepe	1 Coats Drima or Coats Super Sheen No. 50 or 2 Clark's Anchor Machine Emby No. 50	70 70 70 70 80 80	70 70 70 70 80 80	0·4 0·4 0·4 0·4 0·4 0·4	0·3 0·3 0·3 0·3 0·3 0·3	$1\frac{1}{4}$ $1\frac{1}{4}$ $1\frac{1}{4}$ $1\frac{1}{4}$ $1\frac{1}{4}$ $1\frac{1}{4}$	$1\frac{1}{2}$ $1\frac{1}{2}$ $1\frac{1}{2}$ $1\frac{1}{2}$ $1\frac{1}{2}$ $1\frac{1}{2}$
Fine-Medium Fabrics	Cotton Poplin Taffeta Linen Satin	1 Coats Drima or Coats Super Sheen No. 50 or 2 Clark's Anchor Machine Emby No. 50	80 or 90 80 or 90 80 or 90 80 or 90 80 or 90	80 or 90 80 or 90 80 or 90 80 or 90 80 or 90	0·5 0·5 0·5 0·5 0·5	0·4 0·5 0·5 0·5 0·5	$1\frac{1}{4}$ $1\frac{1}{4}$ $1\frac{1}{4}$ $1\frac{1}{4}$ $1\frac{1}{4}$	$1\frac{3}{4}$ $1\frac{1}{4}$ $1\frac{1}{2}$ $1\frac{1}{2}$ $1\frac{1}{2}$
Medium-Heavy Fabrics	Brocade Dress Wool Jersey Corduroy Flannel Denim Tweed	1 Coats Drima or Coats Satinised No. 40 or Coats Chain Cotton No. 40 or 2 Clark's Anchor Machine Emby No. 30	90 90 90 90 or 100 90 or 100 90 or 100 90 or 100	90 90 90 90 90 90 90	0·5 0·5 0·5 0·5 0·5 0·5 0·5	0·5 0·5 0·5 0·5 0·5 0·5 0·5	$1\frac{1}{4}$ $1\frac{1}{4}$ $1\frac{1}{4}$ $1\frac{1}{4}$ $1\frac{1}{4}$ $1\frac{1}{4}$ $1\frac{1}{4}$	$1\frac{1}{2}$ $1\frac{1}{2}$ $1\frac{1}{2}$ 2 2 2 2
Synthetic Fabrics	Nylon and 'Terylene'	1 Coats Drima or 2 Clark's Anchor Machine Emby No. 50	80	70	0·4	0·3	$1\frac{1}{4}$	$1\frac{1}{2}$

PFAFF — DECORATIVE STITCHING—MACHINE EMBROIDERY

	Fabric	Thread	Machine Needle No. C	*Upper Thread Tension
Fine Fabrics	1 Ply Organdie 1 Ply Chiffon 1 Ply Silk 1 Ply Lawn 1 Ply Cotton 1 Ply Crepe	Clark's Anchor Machine Emby No. 50	60 60 60 70 70 70	$1\frac{3}{4}$ $1\frac{1}{4}$ $1\frac{1}{4}$ 1 1 $1\frac{1}{2}$
Medium Fabrics	1 Ply Cotton 1 Ply Poplin 1 Ply Linen 1 Ply Gingham	Clark's Anchor Machine Emby No. 30	80 80 80 80	$1\frac{1}{4}$ $1\frac{1}{4}$ $1\frac{1}{4}$ $1\frac{1}{4}$
Synthetic Fabrics	1 Ply Nylon	Clark's Anchor Machine Emby No. 50	60	1

*Lower Thread Tension—Medium

PFAFF		DARNING		
	Fabric	Thread	Machine Needle No. C	*Upper Thread Tension
Fine Fabrics	1 Ply Lawn	Clark's Anchor Machine Emby No. 50	70	2
Medium Fabrics	1 Ply Cotton 1 Ply Linen	Clark's Anchor Machine Emby No. 50	80 80	2 2

*Lower Thread Tension—Medium

ELNA		STRAIGHT STITCHING—NATURAL FABRICS									
	Fabric	Thread	Machine Needle No.		Hand Needle No.	No. of Stitches to 25 mm. and Stitch Length No.	Upper Thread Tension		Lower Thread Tension	
			B	C			(1)	(2)	(1)	(2)
Fine Fabrics	Net	1 Coats Drima	10 or 12	70 or 80	8 or 9	8–10 ($3\frac{1}{2}$–3)	4	3	1	1
	Organdie	or	10 or 12	70 or 80	8 or 9	8–10 ($3\frac{1}{2}$–3)	4	3	1	1
	Chiffon	2 Coats Super	10 or 12	70 or 80	8 or 9	8–10 ($3\frac{1}{2}$–3)	4	3	1	1
	Lace	Sheen No. 50	10 or 12	70 or 80	8 or 9	8–10 ($3\frac{1}{2}$–3)	4	$3\frac{1}{4}$	1	1
	Silk		10 or 12	70 or 80	8 or 9	8–10 ($3\frac{1}{2}$–3)	4	3	1	1
	Lawn		10 or 12	70 or 80	8 or 9	8–10 ($3\frac{1}{2}$–3)	4	3	1	1
	Crepe		10 or 12	70 or 80	8 or 9	8–10 ($3\frac{1}{2}$–3)	$4\frac{1}{2}$	$3\frac{1}{4}$	1	1
	Tulle		10 or 12	70 or 80	8 or 9	8–10 ($3\frac{1}{2}$–3)	4	3	1	1
	Voile		10 or 12	70 or 80	8 or 9	8–10 ($3\frac{1}{2}$–3)	4	3	1	1
Fine- Medium Fabrics	Cotton	1 Coats Drima	12 or 14	80 or 90	7 or 8	10–12 (3–$2\frac{1}{2}$)	$4\frac{1}{2}$	5	$1\frac{1}{4}$	1
	Poplin	or	12 or 14	80 or 90	7 or 8	10–12 (3–$2\frac{1}{2}$)	5	5	$1\frac{1}{4}$	1
	Taffeta	2 Coats Super	12 or 14	80 or 90	7 or 8	10–12 (3–$2\frac{1}{2}$)	$4\frac{1}{2}$	5	$1\frac{1}{4}$	1
	Linen	Sheen No. 50	12 or 14	80 or 90	7 or 8	10–12 (3–$2\frac{1}{2}$)	5	5	$1\frac{1}{4}$	1
	Satin		12 or 14	80 or 90	7 or 8	10–12 (3–$2\frac{1}{2}$)	5	5	$1\frac{1}{4}$	1
Medium - Heavy Fabrics	Brocade	1 Coats Drima	14	90	7 or 8	12 ($2\frac{1}{2}$)	5	5	$1\frac{1}{4}$	1
	Dress Wool	or	14	90	7 or 8	12 ($2\frac{1}{2}$)	5	5	$1\frac{1}{4}$	1
	Jersey	2 Coats	14	90	7 or 8	12–14 ($2\frac{1}{2}$–$2\frac{1}{4}$)	5	5	$1\frac{1}{4}$	1
	Corduroy	Satinised	14 or 16	90 or 100	7 or 8	12 ($2\frac{1}{2}$)	5	5	$1\frac{1}{4}$	1
	Velvet	No. 40	14 or 16	90 or 100	7 or 8	12 ($2\frac{1}{2}$)	5	5	$1\frac{1}{4}$	1
	Terry Cloth	or	14 or 16	90 or 100	7 or 8	12 ($2\frac{1}{2}$)	5	5	$1\frac{1}{4}$	1
	Flannel	Coats Chain	14 or 16	90 or 100	7 or 8	12 ($2\frac{1}{2}$)	5	5	$1\frac{1}{4}$	1
	Denim	Cotton No. 40	14 or 16	90 or 100	7 or 8	12 ($2\frac{1}{2}$)	5	5	$1\frac{1}{4}$	1
	Repp		14 or 16	90 or 100	7 or 8	12 ($2\frac{1}{2}$)	5	5	$1\frac{1}{4}$	1

ELNA — STRAIGHT STITCHING—SYNTHETIC FABRICS

Nylon, Terylene, Tricel, Acetate, Viscose Rayon, Dicel, Courtelle, Crimplene, Acrilan, Orlon

	Fabric	Thread	Machine Needle No.		Hand Needle No.	No. of Stitches to 25 mm. and Stitch Length No.	Upper Thread Tension	Lower Thread Tension
			B	C				
Fine Fabrics	Net	Coats Drima	10 or 12	70 or 80	8	8–10 (3½–3)	4½	1
	Chiffon		10 or 12	70 or 80	8	8–10 (3½–3)	5	1
	Locknit		10 or 12	70 or 80	8	8–10 (3½–3)	4	1¼
	Seersucker		10 or 12	70 or 80	8	8–10 (3½–3)	4½	1
	Lawn		10 or 12	70 or 80	8	8–10 (3½–3)	4½	1
	Surah		10 or 12	70 or 80	8	8–10 (3½–3)	5	1
	Taffeta		10 or 12	70 or 80	8	8–10 (3½–3)	5	1¼
	Voile		10 or 12	70 or 80	8	8–10 (3½–3)	4	1
Fine-Medium Fabrics	Pique	Coats Drima	12 or 14	80 or 90	7 or 8	10–12 (3–2½)	5	1¼
	Matelasse		12 or 14	80 or 90	7 or 8	10–12 (3–2½)	5	1¼
	Brocade		12 or 14	80 or 90	7 or 8	10–12 (3–2½)	5	1
	Nylon		12 or 14	80 or 90	7 or 8	10–12 (3–2½)	5	1
Medium Fabrics	Linen	Coats Drima	14	90	7	12–14 (2½–2)	5½	1
	Jersey		14	90	7	12–14 (2½–2)	5	1
	Satin		14	90	7	12–14 (2½–2)	4½	1
	Silk Slub		14	90	7	12–14 (2½–2)	4½	1
	Tweed		14	90	7	12 (2½)	5½	1¼
	Suiting		14	90	7	12 (2½)	5½	1¼
	Velvet		14	90	7	12 (2½)	5½	1¼
	Fleece		14 or 16	90 or 100	6 or 7	10 (3¼)	5	1¼

ELNA — ORDINARY BUTTONHOLES

	Fabric	Thread	Machine Needle No.		Stitch Length	Upper Thread Tension	Lower Thread Tension
			B	C			
Fine Fabrics	Organdie	Coats Drima or Coats Super Sheen No. 50	10	70	Fine	1¼	¾
	Chiffon		10	70	,,	1¼	¾
	Lace		10	70	,,	1¼	¾
	Silk		10	70	,,	1¼	¾
	Lawn		12	80	,,	1¼	¾
	Crepe		12	80	,,	1¼	¾
Fine-Medium Fabrics	Cotton	Coats Drima or Coats Super Sheen No. 50	12 or 14	80 or 90	Fine	2	1
	Poplin		12 or 14	80 or 90	,,	2	1
	Taffeta		12 or 14	80 or 90	,,	2	1
	Linen		12 or 14	80 or 90	,,	2	1
	Satin		12 or 14	80 or 90	,,	2	1
Medium-Heavy Fabrics	Brocade	Coats Drima or Coats Satinised No. 40 or Coats Chain Cotton No. 40	14	90	Fine	2	1
	Dress Wool		14	90	,,	2	1
	Jersey		14	90	,,	2	1
	Corduroy		14 or 16	90 or 100	,,	2	1
	Flannel		14 or 16	90 or 100	,,	2	1
	Denim		14 or 16	90 or 100	,,	2	1
	Tweed		14 or 16	90 or 100	,,	2	1
Synthetic Fabrics	Nylon and 'Terylene'	Coats Drima	12	80	Fine	1¼	¾

ELNA			AUTOMATIC BUTTONHOLES		Upper Thread Tension	Lower Thread Tension
	Fabric	Thread	Machine Needle No.			
			B	C		
Fine Fabrics	Organdie Voile Chiffon Lace Silk Lawn Fine Cotton Crepe	Clark's Anchor Machine Emby No. 50	10 10 10 10 10 12 12 12	70 70 70 70 70 80 80 80	$1\frac{1}{2}$ $1\frac{1}{2}$ $1\frac{1}{2}$ $1\frac{1}{2}$ $1\frac{1}{2}$ $1\frac{1}{2}$ $1\frac{1}{2}$ $1\frac{1}{2}$	$\frac{3}{4}$ $\frac{3}{4}$ $\frac{3}{4}$ $\frac{3}{4}$ $\frac{3}{4}$ $\frac{3}{4}$ $\frac{3}{4}$ $\frac{3}{4}$
Medium Fabrics	Cotton Poplin Linen Gingham Pique Dress Wool Fine Suiting Fine Corduroy	Clark's Anchor Machine Emby No. 50	14 14 14 14 14 14 14 or 16 14 or 16	90 90 90 90 90 90 90 or 100 90 or 100	$2\frac{3}{4}$ $2\frac{3}{4}$ $2\frac{3}{4}$ $2\frac{3}{4}$ $2\frac{3}{4}$ $2\frac{3}{4}$ $2\frac{3}{4}$ $2\frac{3}{4}$	1 1 1 1 1 1 1 1
Heavy Fabrics	Denim Tweed	Clark's Anchor Machine Emby No. 30	16 or 18 16 or 18	100 or 110 100 or 110	3 3	1 1
Synthetic Fabrics	Nylon and 'Terylene'	Clark's Anchor Machine Emby No. 50	10	70	$1\frac{1}{2}$	$\frac{3}{4}$

ELNA			DECORATIVE STITCHING—MACHINE EMBROIDERY		Upper Thread Tension	Lower Thread Tension
	Fabric	Thread	Machine Needle No.			
			B	C		
Fine Fabrics	1 Ply Organdie 1 Ply Chiffon 1 Ply Silk 1 Ply Lawn 1 Ply Cotton 1 Ply Crepe	Clark's Anchor Machine Emby No. 50	8 8 8 10 10 10	60 60 60 70 70 70	$1\frac{1}{2}$ $1\frac{1}{2}$ $1\frac{1}{2}$ $1\frac{1}{2}$ $1\frac{1}{2}$ $1\frac{1}{2}$	$\frac{3}{4}$ $\frac{3}{4}$ $\frac{3}{4}$ $\frac{3}{4}$ $\frac{3}{4}$ $\frac{3}{4}$
Medium Fabrics	1 Ply Cotton 1 Ply Poplin 1 Ply Linen 1 Ply Gingham	Clark's Anchor Machine Emby No. 30	12 12 12 12	80 80 80 80	2 2 2 2	$\frac{3}{4}$ $\frac{3}{4}$ $\frac{3}{4}$ $\frac{3}{4}$
Synthetic Fabrics	1 Ply Nylon	Clark's Anchor Machine Emby No. 50	8	60	1	$\frac{1}{2}$

ELNA			DARNING			
	Fabric	Thread	Machine Needle No.		Upper Thread Tension	Lower Thread Tension
			B	C		
Fine Fabrics	1 Ply Lawn	Clark's Anchor Machine Emby No. 50	10	70	1	$\frac{1}{2}$
Medium Fabrics	1 Ply Cotton 1 Ply Linen	Clark's Anchor Machine Emby No. 50	12 12	80 80	2 2	$\frac{1}{2}$ $\frac{1}{2}$

BERNINA			STRAIGHT STITCHING—NATURAL FABRICS		
	Fabric	Thread	Machine Needle No. C	Hand Needle No.	No. of Stitches to 25 mm. and Stitch Length No.
Fine Fabrics	Net	Coats Drima	70 or 80	8 or 9	8–10 $(3–2\frac{1}{2})$
	Organdie	or	70 or 80	8 or 9	8–10 $(3–2\frac{1}{2})$
	Chiffon	Coats Super	70 or 80	8 or 9	8–10 $(3–2\frac{1}{2})$
	Lace	Sheen No. 50	70 or 80	8 or 9	8–10 $(3–2\frac{1}{2})$
	Silk		70 or 80	8 or 9	8–10 $(3–2\frac{1}{2})$
	Lawn		70 or 80	8 or 9	8–10 $(3–2\frac{1}{2})$
	Crepe		70 or 80	8 or 9	8–10 $(3–2\frac{1}{2})$
	Tulle		70 or 80	8 or 9	8–10 $(3–2\frac{1}{2})$
	Voile		70 or 80	8 or 9	8–10 $(3–2\frac{1}{2})$
Fine-Medium Fabrics	Cotton	Coats Drima	80 or 90	7 or 8	10–12 $(2\frac{1}{2}–2\frac{1}{4})$
	Poplin	or	80 or 90	7 or 8	10–12 $(2\frac{1}{2}–2\frac{1}{4})$
	Taffeta	Coats Super	80 or 90	7 or 8	10–12 $(2\frac{1}{2}–2\frac{1}{4})$
	Linen	Sheen No. 50	80 or 90	7 or 8	10–12 $(2\frac{1}{2}–2\frac{1}{4})$
	Satin		80 or 90	7 or 8	10–12 $(2\frac{1}{2}–2\frac{1}{4})$
Medium-Heavy Fabrics	Brocade	Coats Drima	90	7 or 8	12 $(2\frac{1}{4})$
	Dress Wool	or	90	7 or 8	12 $(2\frac{1}{4})$
	Jersey	Coats Satinised	90	7 or 8	12–14 $(2\frac{1}{4}–2)$
	Corduroy	No. 40	90 or 100	7 or 8	12 $(2\frac{1}{4})$
	Velvet	or	90 or 100	7 or 8	12 $(2\frac{1}{4})$
	Terry Cloth	Coats Chain	90 or 100	7 or 8	12 $(2\frac{1}{4})$
	Flannel	Cotton No. 40	90 or 100	7 or 8	12 $(2\frac{1}{4})$
	Denim		90 or 100	7 or 8	12 $(2\frac{1}{4})$
	Repp		90 or 100	7 or 8	12 $(2\frac{1}{4})$

BERNINA	STRAIGHT STITCHING—SYNTHETIC FABRICS				
	Nylon, Terylene, Tricel, Acetate, Viscose Rayon, Dicel, Courtelle, Crimplene, Acrilan, Orlon				
	Fabric	Thread	Machine Needle No. C	Hand Needle No.	No. of Stitches to 25 mm. and Stitch Length No.
Fine Fabrics	Net	Coats Drima	70 or 80	8	8–10 $(3–2\frac{1}{2})$
	Chiffon		70 or 80	8	8–10 $(3–2\frac{1}{2})$
	Locknit		70 or 80	8	8–10 $(3–2\frac{1}{2})$
	Seersucker		70 or 80	8	8–10 $(3–2\frac{1}{2})$
	Lawn		70 or 80	8	8–10 $(3–2\frac{1}{2})$
	Surah		70 or 80	8	8–10 $(3–2\frac{1}{2})$
	Taffeta		70 or 80	8	8–10 $(3–2\frac{1}{2})$
	Voile		70 or 80	8	8–10 $(3–2\frac{1}{2})$
Fine-Medium Fabrics	Pique	Coats Drima	80 or 90	7 or 8	10–12 $(2\frac{1}{2}–2\frac{1}{4})$
	Matelasse		80 or 90	7 or 8	10–12 $(2\frac{1}{2}–2\frac{1}{4})$
	Brocade		80 or 90	7 or 8	10–12 $(2\frac{1}{2}–2\frac{1}{4})$
	Nylon		80 or 90	7 or 8	10–12 $(2\frac{1}{2}–2\frac{1}{4})$
Medium Fabrics	Linen	Coats Drima	90	7	12–14 $(2\frac{1}{4}–2)$
	Jersey		90	7	12–14 $(2\frac{1}{4}–2)$
	Satin		90	7	12–14 $(2\frac{1}{4}–2)$
	Silk Slub		90	7	12–14 $(2\frac{1}{4}–2)$
	Tweed		90	7	12 $(2\frac{1}{4})$
	Suiting		90	7	12 $(2\frac{1}{4})$
	Velvet		90	7	12 $(2\frac{1}{4})$
	Fleece		90 or 100	6 or 7	10 $(3\frac{1}{2})$

BERNINA	ORDINARY BUTTONHOLES			
	Fabric	Thread	Machine Needle No. C	Stitch Length
Fine Fabrics	Organdie	Coats Drima	80	$\frac{1}{4}–\frac{1}{2}$
	Chiffon	or	80	$\frac{1}{4}–\frac{1}{2}$
	Lace	Coats Super Sheen No. 50	80	$\frac{1}{4}–\frac{1}{2}$
	Silk		80	$\frac{1}{4}–\frac{1}{2}$
	Lawn		80	$\frac{1}{4}–\frac{1}{2}$
	Crepe		80	$\frac{1}{4}–\frac{1}{2}$
Fine-Medium Fabrics	Cotton	Coats Drima	80 or 90	$\frac{1}{4}–\frac{1}{2}$
	Poplin	or	80 or 90	$\frac{1}{4}–\frac{1}{2}$
	Taffeta	Coats Super Sheen No. 50	80 or 90	$\frac{1}{4}–\frac{1}{2}$
	Linen		80 or 90	$\frac{1}{4}–\frac{1}{2}$
	Satin		80 or 90	$\frac{1}{4}–\frac{1}{2}$
Medium-Heavy Fabrics	Brocade	Coats Drima	90	$\frac{1}{4}–\frac{1}{2}$
	Dress Wool	or	90	$\frac{1}{4}–\frac{1}{2}$
	Jersey	Coats Satinised No. 40	90	$\frac{1}{4}–\frac{1}{2}$
	Corduroy	or	90 or 100	$\frac{1}{4}–\frac{1}{2}$
	Flannel	Coats Chain Cotton No. 40	90 or 100	$\frac{1}{4}–\frac{1}{2}$
	Denim		90 or 100	$\frac{1}{4}–\frac{1}{2}$
	Tweed		90 or 100	$\frac{1}{4}–\frac{1}{2}$
Synthetic Fabrics	Nylon and 'Terylene'	Coats Drima	70	$\frac{1}{4}–\frac{1}{2}$

BERNINA	AUTOMATIC BUTTONHOLES		
	Fabric	**Thread**	**Machine Needle No. C**
Fine Fabrics	Organdie Voile Chiffon Lace Silk Lawn Fine Cotton Crepe	Clark's Anchor Machine Emby No. 50	70 70 70 70 70 80 80 80
Fine-Medium Fabrics	Cotton Poplin Linen Gingham Pique	Clark's Anchor Machine Emby No. 50	80 or 90 80 or 90 80 or 90 80 or 90 80 or 90
Medium-Heavy Fabrics	Dress Wool Fine Suiting Fine Corduroy Denim Tweed	Clark's Anchor Machine Emby No. 30	90 90 or 100 90 or 100 90 or 100 90 or 100
Synthetic Fabrics	Nylon and 'Terylene'	Clark's Anchor Machine Emby No. 50	70

BERNINA	DECORATIVE STITCHING—MACHINE EMBROIDERY		
	Fabric	**Thread**	**Machine Needle No. C**
Fine Fabrics	1 Ply Organdie 1 Ply Chiffon 1 Ply Silk 1 Ply Lawn 1 Ply Cotton 1 Ply Crepe	Clark's Anchor Machine Emby No. 50	70 70 70 70 70 70
Fine-Medium Fabrics	1 Ply Cotton 1 Ply Poplin 1 Ply Linen 1 Ply Gingham	Clark's Anchor Machine Emby No. 30	80 80 80 80
Synthetic Fabric	1 Ply Nylon	Clark's Anchor Machine Emby No. 50	70

BERNINA	DARNING		
	Fabric	**Thread**	**Machine Needle No. C**
Fine Fabrics	1 Ply Lawn	Clark's Anchor Machine Emby No. 50	70
Fine-Medium Fabrics	1 Ply Cotton 1 Ply Linen	Clark's Anchor Machine Emby No. 50	80 80

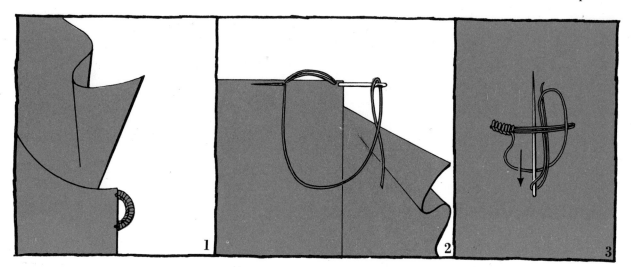

Thread Loops

Thread loops consist of a core of a few threads covered with blanket stitch. Used in slightly different form for various purposes, they vary, especially in the degree in which they 'loop'. The Bar Tack and the French Tack (p. 166) are not really loops at all, but are made the same way.

Blanket Stitch on a loop differs from blanket stitch in embroidery in that needle is used eye-first, as shown above (3). When length of central threads is entirely covered with blanket stitch, worked close together but not too tight, fasten thread securely (on wrong side when possible) and cut off.

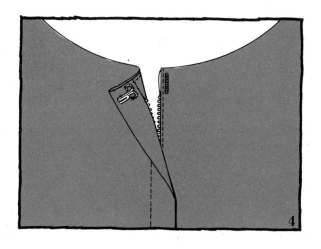

Button Loop

An inconspicuous loop usually placed at the neck corner of an opening (1), often for use with a small button concealed under a collar.

Use thread single; bring out at one end of loop-position in a manner that will conceal knot. Across loop-position, take three or four stitches (2), loose enough to form loop of desired size. Then cover with blanket stitch (3).

Thread Eye

Used in place of a metal eye in a hook-and-eye closure (4). About 6 mm. long.

Follow instructions for Button Loop, but draw thread up so 'eye' is straight.

Belt Carrier

Used on side seams of dresses to keep belt in place (5).

Mark position (width of belt, one half above and one half below centre of belt line). Cut 122 cm. of thread matched to fabric; use doubled, with ends knotted together. At bottom mark of position, put needle and thread through from inside of garment to outside. Take a small horizontal stitch at top mark (6) and draw thread up, leaving necessary slackness in loop.

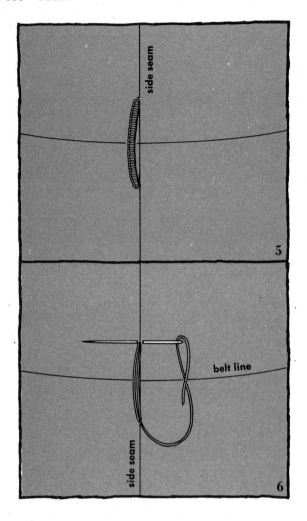

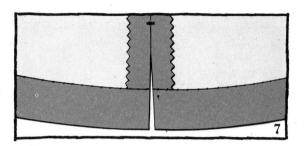

as end of a slit at hem or neck. Hardly more than 3 mm. long (7).

Follow instructions for Button Loop, but draw thread up completely, leaving no slackness.

French Tack

Used to hold two parts of a garment, such as lining and outer part of a coat, loosely together at hem, usually at side seams (8).

Bring needle out in one of the two garment parts, then take a small stitch in the other, holding the two apart the desired amount (probably 25 mm. or so). Take three or four stitches back and forth in the same manner, then anchor thread with another small stitch. Cover with blanket stitch (3).

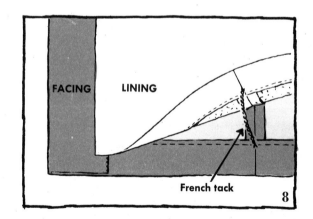

Repeat down and up three or four times, as shown. Take an extra stitch to fasten thread; cover with blanket stitch (3).

Bar Tack

An inconspicuous reinforcement, generally placed on wrong side of garment, at points of strain such

Tucks

A tuck is a fold of fabric, usually not very deep, that is stitched along all or part of its length. A tuck stitched in its entire length serves as decoration only.

A tuck stitched only to a certain point furnishes full-ness and contributes to fit, and may or may not be decorative as well (e.g., the Pin Tucks as shown serve

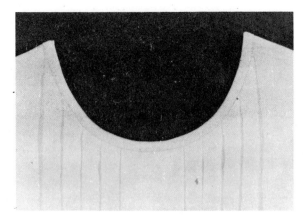

both design and fit, while the Dart Tucks are for fit only).

Where there is a series of decorative tucks (as in some blouses) stitched in their entire length, the tucks are usually made before pattern is cut out. As a general rule, stitching on decorative tucks is done on the outside and is very visible—almost a part of the design. It can be done by machine with carefully selected thread and a small stitch. It can also be done by hand, with a small running stitch. If

you are fond of tucks, you would do well to learn to use the 'tucker' sewing machine attachment, which will help to make equally-spaced tucks (see your sewing machine manual).

When making tucks, transfer tuck markings carefully from pattern to fabric. In some fabrics a thread can be drawn if tucks are on straight grain. Crease or press on marked line and stitch at distance from fold indicated; use a gauge (self-made or otherwise) to keep depth even (1).

Pin Tucks are very narrow tucks stitched close to fold. They are often stitched on wrong side of garment (2).

Dart Tucks serve the purpose of darts, but without coming to a point, and release fullness at one or both ends (3, 4).

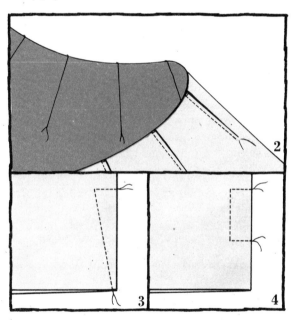

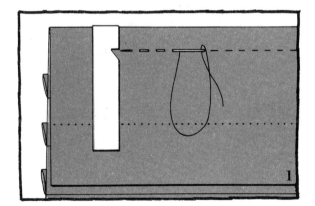

Waistbands

A waistband, the doubled, straight-grain strip of fabric, stitched to the top of a skirt or slacks to make it fit the waist, may be as narrow as 16 mm. or as wide as 50 mm. Its ends overlap in the usual direction for

female clothes: right over left on a front or side closure, left over right on a back closure. The top end, which has the buttonhole or the hooks, is made even with opening edge (sometimes it is extended

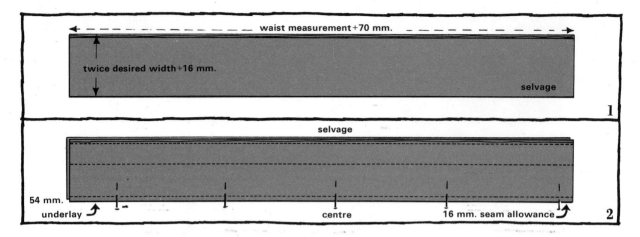

just enough to have the end rounded or pointed). The other end, which has the button or the hook-eyes, extends about 38 mm. underneath.

The raw top edge of the skirt or slacks (unless skirt is gathered) is usually 13 mm. to 25 mm. wider than the finished waistline (waist measurement), and is eased to the waistband.

Patterns generally include a piece for the waistband and instructions for its application. You may, however, wish to vary the width and the method according to your preference and your fabric. The methods of application that follow have been found most practical from every standpoint.

The narrowest waistband width (16 mm.) is automatically reinforced by the width of the seam allowances. To keep a wider band from rolling, it must be reinforced either with interfacing or with waistband stiffening.

Ordinary Waistband—suitable for any fabric. A waistband should, if possible, be cut on the lengthwise grain, preferably on a selvage. Length: waist measurement plus 70 mm. Width: on a selvage, twice desired width plus 16 mm. (1). If there is no selvage, add 6 mm. to this width, turn under and topstitch. Use this edge as 'selvage edge'.

Cut interfacing (if any) to match above strip. Stitch to wrong side of strip along both long edges. Measuring across width from selvage (or finished) edge, mark width of finished waistband less 3 mm. At this point, make a line of stitching along length of band to hold interfacing in place, as shown (2).

Measure and pin-mark raw edge as shown (2): 54 mm. at underlying end, 16 mm. at overlap; divide space between into four equal parts. Divide raw edge of garment into four equal parts, starting at the zip-fastener opening (3).

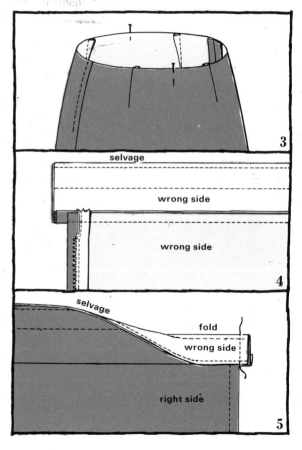

Pin garment edge to raw edge of waistband, right sides together, matching at pin marks, edges even. Baste, easing garment edge. Stitch. Press waistband and seam up (4).

Fold waistband in half wrong side out. If you plan to hand-sew loose edge down, match edge to seamline; if you plan to machine-stitch, bring edge 3 mm. below seamline. Pin ends; stitch across 16 mm. from edges (5). Trim and grade the two end-seams. Turn waistband right side out and press.

To attach loose edge, either (a) slipstitch to seamline; or (b) baste in place with edge 3 mm. below stitched line, then machine-stitch from the *outside*, either on waistband close to seamline (topstitching), or in seamline (invisible stitching).

Press. Sew on hooks and eyes, or make worked buttonhole and sew on button.

Waistband Backed with Waistband Stiffening—For bulky or pile fabrics, leather and suede. Use stiffening 16 mm. to 25 mm. wide and 70 mm. longer than waist measurement. Cut waistband of fabric to same length as stiffening and 22 mm. wider. Lap one edge of stiffening 6 mm. over one edge of waistband (right side) and topstitch (6). Then follow directions in third paragraph under Ordinary Waistband.

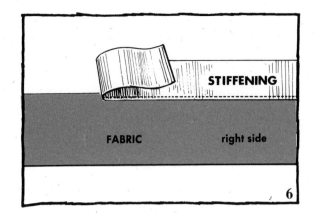

Self-Interfaced Waistband—For light- to medium-weight, firmly-woven washable fabrics only. Eliminates need for separate interfacing.

Cut waistband to waist measurement plus 70 mm., and four times desired finished width plus 32 mm. for seam allowance.

Fold waistband in half lengthwise and stitch raw edges together. Measuring across width from folded edge, mark width of finished waistband less 3 mm. At this point make a line of stitching along length of band to hold the two layers together. From here on follow directions in third paragraph under **Ordinary Waistband.**

Zip-fasteners

Zip-fasteners are another of those things that scare a home-sewer. Yet inserting a zip-fastener takes no particular skill or practice. There's a trick to it, of course, but it is by no means a difficult trick once you know what the motions are (i.e., once you have *followed* the directions). What's more, the job is done in a few minutes.

The motions are simple—if the instructions seem lengthy, it is because we do not want to leave you with questions on your mind. Do not try to understand the procedure by reading the directions all at once. For an ordinary (non-separating) zip-fastener, first read and follow through on **Prepara-** tion—Half the Job, on p. 171. Then turn to the page that applies to your placket and type of application (concealed or semi-concealed). Follow the directions *one step at a time*, consulting the related illustration. The zip-fastener will be in before you know it.

There are two ways of inserting a zip-fastener:

. . . **The Concealed Application** (1), in which one edge of opening forms a lap that completely conceals the zip-fastener. It has only one line of visible stitching, and is neat and smart. It is suitable in any garment, provided fabric (not too bulky) and design lend themselves to it.

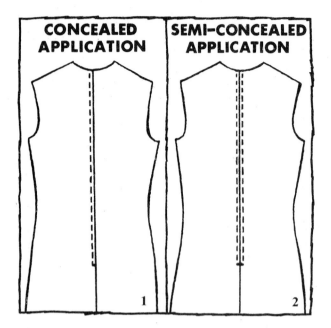

... **The Semi-concealed Application** (2), in which the two edges of opening meet over the zip-fastener which is centred underneath. It has two lines of visible stitching. It is suitable in any garment, but is particularly good for bulky fabrics.

ABOUT THE ZIP-FASTENERS THEMSELVES

Zip-fasteners consist of either synthetic coils or metal teeth (referred to as a chain when closed), fastened to tapes, and locked together by means of a slider. It is essential to use good quality zip-fasteners and we recommend Lightning which are available for every type of opening.

Care of Zip-fasteners

When pressing a synthetic zip-fastener, never allow your iron to come into contact with the coils. Whenever possible, keep zip-fastener closed when pressing. If zip-fastener must be open, cover coils well with a press cloth.

When putting on or taking off a garment, open zip-fastener all the way. This prevents straining and possible breakage.

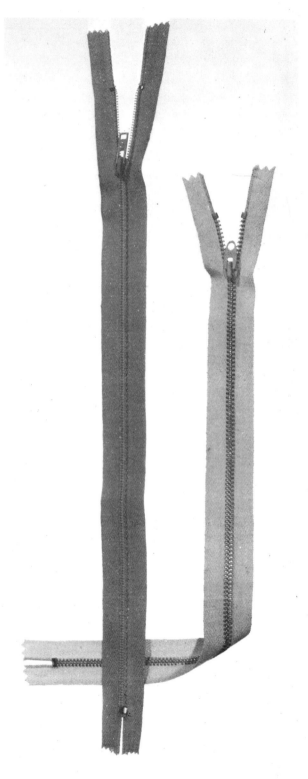

Be sure to close zip-fastener for washing or dry-cleaning a garment. This prevents possible distortion which may result in a malfunctioning of the zip-fastener.

When closing a separating zip-fastener, be sure to have the slider all the way down and to insert the pin *through* the slider and firmly *down* into the 'box' (3).

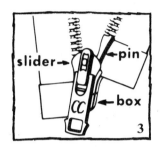

If zip-fastener has become stiff after washing or dry-cleaning, run a piece of candlewax, beeswax, or pencil lead over teeth.

Never cut the tape ends, sew them neatly to the seam allowance or mitre at the top edge if they are beyond the fitting line.

Length of Zip-fastener

The length of a zip-fastener, whether mentioned in the directions in this book or on a pattern envelope, *never* includes the tape-ends. Measurement is from lower edge of bottom stop to top of slider. Suitable zip-fastener length for a garment is always given on the pattern envelope. If—for wearing convenience or because of your figure proportions—you should prefer a different length, adjust length of opening as instructed at right.

PREPARATION—HALF THE JOB

With an ordinary zip-fastener, the preparation is the same for a **Concealed Application** or for a **Semi-Concealed Application.**

A zip-fastener foot must be on hand before starting—without one you cannot stitch close enough to coil or teeth. A plain zip-fastener foot does the job but a hinged foot is easier to manage. Changing to zip-fastener foot, when directions call for it, doesn't take a

minute by the clock. Be careful to have needle exactly centred in notch of foot.

When stitching the seam containing zip-fastener placket, stop at marks (usually notches) that indicate opening, but do not tie off threads.

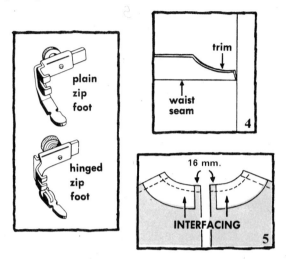

Length of opening is adjusted, if necessary, when you are ready to insert zip-fastener. A little extra space is needed if zip-fastener is to close properly.

To select the correct length of fastener for the garment measure the opening accurately. Check the length of the opening, particularly on skirts, shorts and slacks; if it is too short, the fastener will be subjected to strain at the closed end and will eventually break. At the same time it must be remembered that the zip slider is still above the bottom stop when fully opened. Therefore, your zip opening will be 13 mm. less in length, i.e. an 203 mm. fastener provides a 190 mm. opening.

Any interfacing that may extend to a zip-fastener placket (as at a neck and waist) must be trimmed as shown (4, 5), i.e., you cut away the width of seam allowance along placket edge.

In any application, seam allowance must never be less than 16 mm. wide—a narrower allowance will escape stitching of overlap. If allowance is too narrow, widen it by stitching a piece of seam binding over raw edge of the allowance that is to form the lap (6).

Never stretch zip-fastener during application.

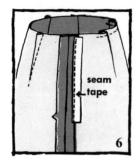

ZIP-FASTENER APPLICATION

Three methods of applying zips are listed below.

A] Semi-concealed

The semi-concealed method of application is simpler to construct than the concealed method. The following instructions are for a skirt placket opening.

(i) Stitch the seam leaving the opening free, and finish the stitching securely. Press the seam allowance of the seam and the opening flat. Baste along the folded edges of the opening.

(ii) Place the fastener in position, under the opening, with the right side of the fastener to the wrong side of the garment, the bottom stop just visible on the right side and the top of the slider on the fitting line.

(iii) Place one folded edge of fabric on top of the teeth, just a fraction over the centre. Pin and baste this

edge in position to the fastener tape. Repeat with the other folded edge so that it also lies on top of the teeth, just a fraction over the centre.

(iv) Stitch round the fastener, approximately 6 mm. from the folded edge. The stitching line at the bottom may be horizontal or pointed (diagram 1).

(v) Catch the lower tape ends lightly to the seam allowance on the wrong side.

If this method of application is used on the side opening of a dress, stitch round the fastener (diagram 2), having each end either horizontal or pointed. Catch the ends of the tapes to the seam allowance.

B] Concealed Method of Application

The following instructions are for a skirt placket opening. In this case, stitch from the bottom stop upwards on both sides, so that there will be no extra fullness at the lower end of the opening.

(i) Stitch the seam leaving the opening free and finish the stitching securely. Press the seam allowance of the seam and the opening flat. Baste along the folded edge of the opening on the front section of the garment. Extend the other folded edge (back edge) 3 mm. beyond the fitting line (diagram 3). Baste.

(ii) Place the fastener in position under the opening, with the right side of the fastener to the wrong side of the garment.

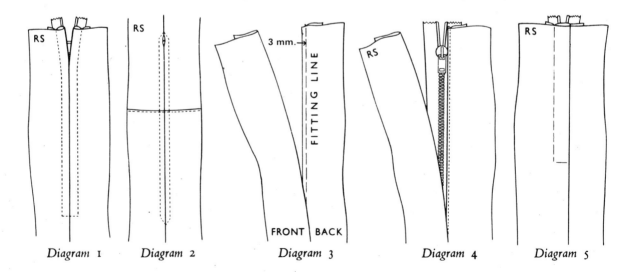

Diagram 1   Diagram 2   Diagram 3   Diagram 4   Diagram 5

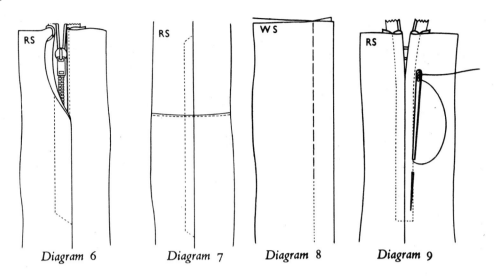

| Diagram 6 | Diagram 7 | Diagram 8 | Diagram 9 |

(iii) With the bottom stop just visible on the right side and the top of the slider on the fitting line, place the back edge of opening at least 2 mm. in from the teeth, ensuring that the slider can still pass freely up and down. Baste this edge to the fastener tape. Stitch (diagram 4).

(iv) Pin the front fitting line to the back fitting line.

(v) Baste in position to the tape, down the length of the opening and across the lower end of the fastener (diagram 5).

(vi) Stitch approximately 10 mm. from the fitting line. At the bottom the stitching line may be horizontal or pointed (diagram 6).

(vii) Catch the tape ends to the seam allowance on the wrong side. If this method of application is used on the side opening of a dress, stitch the fastener with either horizontal or pointed ends (diagram 7). Catch the ends of the tapes to the seam allowance.

Methods A and B may also be done by hand, with small back stitches replacing the machine stitching.

C] Hand Inserted

This is a particularly suitable method for the inexperienced needlewoman. The following instructions are for a neck opening.

(i) Stitch the seam, leaving the opening free, and finish

the stitching securely. Press the seam allowance of the seam and the opening flat. Baste the opening together on seam line (diagram 8).

(ii) Stitch 6 mm. on each side of the seam line the length of the fastener. The stitching line at the lower end may be horizontal or pointed.

(iii) Place the right side of the zip face downwards on top of the wrong side of the opening and baste the zip tape to the seam allowance.

(iv) Catch fastener in position from the right side with single back stitches on top of the stitching line (diagram 9).

Application of Shield

In order to prevent underwear being caught in the fastener teeth, especially with slacks, shorts and tight-fitting garments, the use of a backing piece or shield is recommended. Follow the instructions given in the 'Lightning' zip-fastener packet.

FINISHING A NECK FACING IN A CONCEALED APPLICATION

USUAL FINISH

Facing is applied either before or after zip-fastener.

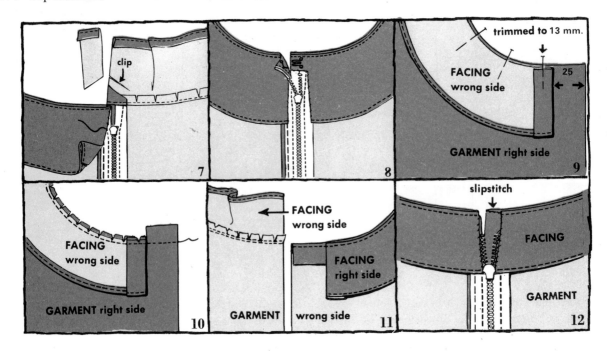

Trim, clip, turn in and sew down raw edges as shown (7). Add hook and eye at top (8).

SPECIAL FINISH

Facing must be applied before zip-fastener.

This facing finish is excellent for any neckline, with or without collar, regardless of fabric. Bulk is minimal and handling easy; finished corners lie flat and smooth. It is equally good at other zip-fastener openings, wherever there is a facing. It requires only that, *regardless of pattern primer instructions,* facing be applied before zip-fastener, as directed here.

As you pin facing in place, turn back 25 mm. of facing at the left-hand side. Trim this folded end to 13 mm. (9).

Stitch facing to garment. Trim, grade, and clip seam, *except* for the 25 mm. of unfaced neck seam allowance (10). Understitch facing.

Turn folded end of facing and the 25 mm. of unfaced seam allowance to inside of garment (11).

After zip-fastener is in, placket pressed, and machine-basting removed, fold facing to inside with remaining facing-end turned under, and press. Slip-stitch all folded edges down (12). Sew on hook and eye.

IN CASE OF ZIP-FASTENER STRAIN IN A DRESS—Waistline Stay

A snug fit at the waist, in a dress, can put quite a strain on the zip-fastener. This can be eased by a sturdy waistline stay.

Use 13 mm. seam binding or 16 mm. grosgrain ribbon; or cut a 25 mm. strip along the selvage of your dress fabric and press it folded through centre so that selvage edge extends just beyond raw edge. Cut stay 25 mm. longer than body waist measurement.

Turn ends of strip 13 mm. under. Sew on a hook and eye, placed so that ends of strip meet. With dress wrong side out, place stay around waist, hooking ends at zip-fastener, as shown. Pin stay to waist seam allowance on either side of zip-fastener, with garment *looser than* stay at this point—this is essential if strain on zip-fastener is to be removed. Pin rest of stay to seam allowance, easing seam to stay as needed.

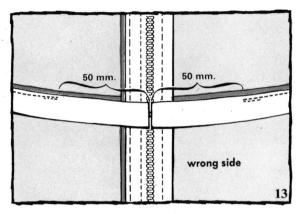

Starting and stopping 50 mm. from either side of hook and eye, as shown (13), stitch stay to seam allowance, either by machine or by hand.

On a dress without a waist seam (princess style), tack stay to seam and darts.

REPLACING A ZIP-FASTENER IN A SKIRT, DRESS OR NECK PLACKET

To replace a zip-fastener in a skirt, dress or neck placket, first examine your garment to see how zip-fastener was put in, then remove old zip-fastener. Since you must follow the lines of old folds and stitching, you may have to adapt directions to variations in construction.

In a dress placket, no extra ripping is necessary; in a skirt or neck placket, remove enough stitching on waistband or neck facing so that the parts of garment attached to zip-fastener can be opened out. Press out folds of seam allowances.

Application—Follow instructions for **Concealed Application,** or **Semi-concealed Application.**

INDEX